THE BLAZE OF OBSCURITY

CLIVE JAMES is the author of more than thirty books. As well as his four previous volumes of autobiography, *Unreliable Memoirs*, *Falling Towards England*, *May Week Was In June*, and *North Face of Soho*, he has published collections of literary and television criticism, essays, travel writing, verse and novels. As a television performer he has appeared regularly for both the BBC and ITV, most notably as writer and presenter of the 'Postcard' series of travel documentaries. He helped to found the independent television company Watchmaker and the Internet enterprise Welcome Stranger, one branch of which is now operating as the world's first serious multimedia personal website, www.clivejames.com. In 1992 he was made a Member of the Order of Australia and in 2003 he was awarded the Philip Hodgins memorial medal for literature.

ALSO BY CLIVE JAMES

AUTOBIOGRAPHY

Unreliable Memoirs   Falling Towards England
May Week Was In June   Always Unreliable
North Face of Soho

FICTION

Brilliant Creatures   The Remake
Brrm! Brrm!   The Silver Castle

VERSE

Peregrine Prykke's Pilgrimage Through the London Literary World
Other Passports: Poems 1958–1985
The Book of My Enemy: Collected Verse 1958–2003
Angels Over Elsinore: Collected Verse 2003–2008
Opal Sunset: Selected Poems 1958–2008

CRITICISM

The Metropolitan Critic (new edition, 1994)
Visions Before Midnight   The Crystal Bucket
First Reactions (US)   From the Land of Shadows
Glued to the Box   Snakecharmers in Texas
The Dreaming Swimmer   Fame in the Twentieth Century
On Television   Even As We Speak
Reliable Essays   As of This Writing (US)
The Meaning of Recognition   Cultural Amnesia
The Revolt of the Pendulum

TRAVEL

Flying Visit

CLIVE JAMES

The Blaze of Obscurity

PICADOR

First published 2009 by Picador

First published in paperback 2009 by Picador

This edition published 2010 by Picador
an imprint of Pan Macmillan, a division of Macmillan Publishers Limited
Pan Macmillan, 20 New Wharf Road, London N1 9RR
Basingstoke and Oxford
Associated companies throughout the world
www.panmacmillan.com

ISBN 978-0-330-45737-8

1 3 5 7 9 8 6 4 2

A CIP catalogue record for this book is available from
the British Library.

Typeset by SetSystems Ltd, Saffron Walden, Essex
Printed in the UK by CPI Mackays, Chatham ME5 8TD

Visit www.picador.com to read more about all our books
and to buy them. You will also find features, author interviews and
news of any author events, and you can sign up for e-newsletters
so that you're always first to hear about our new releases.

To the memory of

Richard Drewett

All my clever dealings, he said to himself, have not made me happy. I remain a broken, restless man.

– Stefan Zweig, *Ungeduld des Herzens*

Fool, of thyself speak well.

– *Richard II*, V, 5

Contents

Introduction

With this fifth volume of my memoirs I begin the story of what happened to me when I left Fleet Street in 1982 and went into television as the main way of earning my bread. The effect on my literary reputation was immediate. It was thoroughly compromised, and even now, after a quarter of a century, it has only just begun to recover. After the calamitous reception of my *Charles Charming* show in the West End – the disaster is only partly evoked in the final chapters of my previous volume, because so many of the details remain too humiliating to write down – I regained the will to live by painting bicycles for my children. This creative upsurge extended itself to the construction of a novel, *Brilliant Creatures*. Overly decorated with flash, filigree and would-be-satirical pseudo-scholarship, the book nevertheless achieved the approval of the public. It even hung up there near the top of the bestseller list for a little while, like a parachute flare with delusions of stardom. I had to admit that the change of title might have helped. My original title had been *Tactical Voting in the Eurovision Song Contest*.

The book even got some favourable reviews, but the unfavourable ones were a clear indication of which way the wind would blow. My Sunday night television show about television – an early instance of the medium consuming itself – was pulling about ten million viewers, and my hostile literary critics drew the conclusion that to them seemed necessary. Nobody getting so famous for being so frivolous could possibly be serious. I wasn't *that* famous – Britain, after all, was no longer the whole world – but it was true that I had got into a different area of experience.

It must have seemed obvious, therefore, that I had yielded up my claims to the area in which I had begun. Useless to protest that I thought all the different media were the one field. For one thing, I had not yet thought it. But I had always felt it, and indeed my *Observer* television column, which had been the real backbone of my career as a writer, was based on just that feeling.

Much later on, the next generation of savage young critics would embarrassingly confer on me the title of Premature Postmodernist, a title that they meant as praise, even when they bestowed it with the back of the hand. But in the early eighties and for some time forward, the savage young critics that I had to deal with were of my own generation, steadily getting less young and therefore even more critical of any of their number who showed signs of selling out. Though it was no fun to be told that I had sacrificed my gravitas on the altar of popular success, I tried not to let it bother me. The kind of television entertainment that I wanted to do could not be done without seriousness for bedrock, and I had large plans for pursuing my literary career in any spare time that I might happen to get. There was also a potential plus. Writing during my weeks off – they soon turned out to be days off, and then hours – I would have something extra to write about: personal experience of how the big-budget mass entertainment gets done. Going in, I had already guessed that it could never be done in solitude. Thus I would be safe from the ivory tower, an ambience to which I was suited by a reclusive, nose-picking nature, but in which my writing was always fated not to flourish. Left to myself, I would have no direct experience to report on except my own interior workings, which consisted of not much more than a couple of cog wheels, a few rusty springs and some loose screws. In broadcasting, a more richly populated territory beckoned. Really there was no choice, and not just because the work would be well rewarded. The dough was a factor, but not decisive. What mattered was the adventure.

To go on being a writer in solitude would have felt like defeat, because it would have too well served a sense of superiority that I knew to be fatal. Having dedicated my television column to the principle that mass entertainment would be a bad thing only if such a thing as a mass existed, I was now in a position to prove that I could get into mass entertainment myself, and play a full part as one of those countless individual people. They might well be viewed by political theorists as an abstract conglomerate, but they would never do any viewing themselves except one at a time. To hold their attention, you had to be one of them. It was equality; the new equality; the only real equality that there had ever been. When Tocqueville, visiting America in the early nineteenth century, said that the new democracy was imaginary, he didn't mean that it was illusory: he meant that for the first time in history the haves and the have-nots could share the same condition, even if only in their minds. Since then, the imaginary democracy had spread to the whole Western world, and in Britain it was a continuing tendency that not even Mrs Thatcher could put into reverse. How could she? She was a product of it. Though I was still trying to get all this straight in my head as a prelude to getting it down on paper, here is the story of how I made a beginning on the second stage of my long voyage, to a destination which would yield nothing more than a view of the world, though nothing less either. I had my trepidations on setting out, but I was confident enough, although even I wondered if I were wise to navigate by limelight.

In the long run, the limelight gave me a whole new subject: the celebrity culture. During my television career I was able to take my first crack at analysing it, with an ambitious but sadly doomed series called *Fame in the Twentieth Century*, and after I retired at the turn of the millennium I had time to explore it in greater depth as part of the basket-work of themes that formed my books *The Meaning of Recognition* and *Cultural Amnesia*. But neither early nor late would I have been able to write with any force on the subject if I had not known something about what it was like to inhabit the strange world where everybody knows your face while you hardly ever know theirs. Since there are no deep instincts for coping with it, this condition is fundamentally unsettling, as I shall try to describe. Scrambled brains heat your forehead. In *Cat Ballou*, somebody says to the permanently hungover gunfighter played by Lee Marvin: 'Your eyes are so *red*.' Marvin replies: 'You ought to see them from my side.' Marvin got a Best Actor Oscar for saying that, but there should have been a trophy for the writer, because it was a profound insight.

There is no substitute for actually visiting the foreign country. In the course of twenty years I visited dozens of foreign countries, but the most foreign was, and was increasingly, the realm of celebrity. I discovered it to be a floating world all by itself, like the Yoshiwara district of old Tokyo, or Swift's Laputa. One of its driving forces was the desire to create envy, and the subservient readiness to be envious. I can give myself credit for staying out of all that from the jump. I never lived high, and even today I have few toys apart from my website www.clivejames.com, which I can recommend as an example of how an otherwise ungovernable ego can possibly be put to lasting use.

In the real, non-virtual world, of course, the ego is subject to the rules of time: hence the hair-transplants and the facelifts, which admit the inevitable by the blatancy with which they deny it. I never did any of that stuff either, but I certainly had the urge to save something from the wreck. These later books of memoirs arise from that same impulse, and I suppose the earlier ones did too. I just didn't know it yet. Not knowing things yet, and finding them out after reflecting on experience, has been the continuing story of my life, and will probably go on being so right to the end, or as near to the end as I can get with my memory still in some kind of working order. In my last volume, which will probably be the one after this, I will undoubtedly be tempted to try summing up a lifetime of reflections on my own existence. Socrates, after all, said that the unexamined life was not worth living. He might have added, however, that continual self-examination would leave us no time to live. The moribund, who don't get out much, have the privilege of preparing each of their few remaining actions with due thought. In the period I recount here, I was as busy as a fundamentally slothful man can ever be, and scarcely thought at all. Readers who find it a strange spectacle ought to see it from my side.

1. OUT OF THE FRYING PAN

As you grow older, you are forcibly reminded of your essential personality more and more often, and especially when you are lost in reverie. When I am living alone with my work at my flat in London, I breakfast off a pot of coffee and two slices of unadorned toast. The aim is to control my weight, and it works: my weight remains controlled at about fifty pounds above the level that my doctor recommends as the maximum for continued life. But even though the plan goes reasonably well on the whole, it goes wrong enough in detail to remind me that there is a defective mind doing the planning. Somewhere between every fourth and fifth breakfast, on average, I leave the toast toasting in the toaster while I go to my desk in the next room for a quick fiddle with that paragraph that got stuck in a tangle at three o'clock in the morning. After a few hours' sleep my mind is now clear enough to make further fiddling look beneficial. How about making a regular sentence out of that bit in brackets? And then what about putting this bit before that bit instead of after . . .

I am still fiddling when I notice that there is something strange about the air around me. It has turned bluish grey, as if it had been piped in from the Battle of Jutland. Back in the kitchen, I lever two jet-black slices of carbon out of the toaster while noticing that my whole apartment is full of a strangely delicate pastel mist, like a film set dressed by Ridley Scott in his *Blade Runner* period. Still in my ratty dressing gown, I start a process of opening windows and waving the smoke through them with a wet tea towel. With any luck the place will look less like the aftermath of a powder-cloud avalanche by the time my assistant Cecile Menon shows up and realizes all over again that she has been hired to help a man beyond help. You will ask why I don't buy an automatic toaster, and the answer is that I have, several times, but they all broke. I have a cupboard full of their corpses, each preserved in case the plug should come in handy. Here is yet more proof that I remain, as I approach the last lap of my life, someone who, left to himself, would die of exposure even on a warm day. On the tropical island with everything, I would choke on a coconut. There was once a terrible song that started 'People who need people'. Barbra Streisand used to sing it. As far as I remember, the next line wasn't 'Are to be avoided'. It should have been. In the concourse of the great railway stations you can pick us out by the way we stand in front of the automatic ticket machines and look around for advice. All too often we take it from each other, with predictable results.

Even as a freelance journalist I had depended on editorial supervision, lest my unrestrained enthusiasm lead me into the law courts and the publication I was attached to into bankruptcy. For my last year at the *Observer* I had the excellent John Lucas available to oversee my latest thousand-word effort on a Friday morning. Indeed he wasn't just available, he was unavoidable: Terence Kilmartin, the revered arts editor who figured so prominently as my reliable mentor in the previous volume of these unreliable memoirs, insisted that my copy was always to be combed for time-bombs as well as booby traps. Terry's caution might have been inspired by pressure from the management floor, where it had not been forgotten that I had cost the paper £10,000 by using a single wrong word about a TV director. Such is the long shadow of a British libel case that I can't say what that wrong word was even now.

Now, in 1982, I was saying goodbye to Fleet Street and going into television full time. In Fleet Street I had been a freelance, all right, but there was always backup within reach, only a few desks away. In television, the backup is right there in the room with you. As I completed the transfer of my main effort from the old

Observer building at the north end of Blackfriars Bridge to LWT's stubby skyscraper across the river on the South Bank, I entered the experience of the previously freebooting Rudolph Rasendyll when he was sworn in to fulfil the duties of King of Ruritania, while the real king, his look-alike, began a new career as the Prisoner of Zenda. Suddenly I was surrounded. I had been absolutely alone when writing in my Barbican flat, and pretty well alone even when writing in the *Observer*'s open-plan office. When writing at home in Cambridge I could lock myself away until some member of my family turned up to ask why a pair of my used socks had been found in the refrigerator. Now I was never alone except in the toilet, where I soon found that locking myself into a cubicle was not much protection from hearing myself talked about by young men standing at the urinals. ('Jesus, he's looking rough.' 'And it's only Monday.') The *Clive James on Television* half-hour show was not only still running, it was about to be up-gunned to the status of a full hour Sunday night prime-time spectacular, starring myself seriously positioned behind a desk instead of perched in a white plastic egg-cup chair.

I rapidly discovered the television rule of thumb by which twice as long on screen computes to four times as long in the office. If you're on screen for an hour a week and writing your own stuff, you can kiss your home life goodbye for four days out of any seven. Richard Drewett, in charge of my support personnel, told me to get used to the idea that it wouldn't be only four days, it would be five: four days to accomplish what we were currently doing, and another day to prepare for what we would do next. The emphasis was on the 'we', not the 'I'. There was a whole open-plan office full of beavering producers, assistant producers and researchers. There was another open-plan office next door full of clerical staff. All these people were dedicated to making me look clever. All of them expected, as part of their reward, that I would be on the case even if I had nothing to contribute except my opinion that we would need to see a shorter version of the Bavarian Folk-dance National Championship finals before we decided whether it would hold the screen. At twenty minutes, there was just no judging, except to say that the sad-looking youth in the felt cap who kept hopping forward with hands on hips was potentially funny. 'Hoi!' his companions cried lustily, and then they cried 'Hoi!' again. But he said nothing. He just hopped. He couldn't hop and 'Hoi!' at the same time. I could always say that he hadn't had time to memorize the script.

Thus I was inducted early into a principle about television that was to affect my life for the next two decades: you have to be there. As Talleyrand once said, he who is absent is wrong. At this point, if I were still writing a television script every week, I would say that I don't mean Charles Maurice de Talleyrand-Périgord, master diplomat: I mean Frank Talleyrand, who shared my desk in class 2B at Kogarah Infants' School, and who was frequently hauled up in front of the class for playing truant. You may recognize the layout of the joke. Yes, I had my standard patterns ready. But they still needed a new variation every time. Though I was proud of every sentence that did the trick, after twenty years of it I was eventually to grow exhausted.

Exhaustion, however, will be a subject for later on. For now, you have to imagine me being relatively young – in my merest early forties – and entirely keen. It was, after all, the madly glamorous medium of television. Intelligent, civilized people were willing to give their lives to it, instead of to some more respectable activity, such as running the country. Richard, for example, could have been an Establishment figure had he so wished. He had the well-schooled background. He had the perfect manners. He was elegant from top to toe. Except, perhaps, for his feet. When he was in the army, an accident to one of them had necessitated an operation, which was botched, and therefore had to be repeated several times over the course of years, with a new bungle each time. The resulting bad foot put paid to his legitimate hopes as a driver of fast cars in competition, although he still owned a stable of them and didn't seem to drive very slowly to anyone in the passenger seat of his road car, a silver 6-Series BMW.

Somehow, while thus crippled, he even managed to set the record in his class in the Shelsley Walsh hill climb, driving a Lotus-Ford V8 that could be heard in the next county. Few people in television knew that he was a driver, and few people in motor-sport knew that he was in television. He could also play several musical instruments to a high standard, but only other musicians knew it.

Richard was one of those few people who can do almost everything, and one of the even fewer who don't tell you. He made a point of not drawing attention to himself, but there could be no doubt that the bad foot might have been designed to frustrate such an aim. The bad foot could not tolerate any downward pressure for more than twenty minutes, so he wore white plimsolls with the top of one of them cut away. Since he was otherwise impeccably dapper from his pale, tightly drawn features on downwards – pain accounted for the pallor – the anomalous footwear was an attention-getter. A gentleman of the old school, he neither apologized nor explained, and, England being England, various bigwigs and mandarins would have deal-ings with him for years on end without ever enquiring as to why a man who could have modelled for Savile Row was wearing joke shoes. The same bigwigs and mandarins, if someone had fallen naked past the window of their top-floor boardroom while they were taking tea together, would have done nothing to change the topic of their conversation. Still the Kid from Kogarah, I blun-dered straight in and asked him for the details. To the extent that he could, he opened up. Underneath, however, he remained uptight. The old country was still the old country and its gentry were still unforthcoming. As an Aussie who forthcame without being asked, I had found that there was a small but interesting percentage of the local upper orders who rather enjoyed being jolted out of their reticence. But reticence was still the rule. This especially applied to the gentry's immediate cousins, the executive upper middle class. Richard was one of these. In an earlier incarnation he would have helped to administer India, taken his holidays at Simla and acquired a bad reputation among his contemporaries for giving the time of day to that fellow Kipling. But here he was, in television. Blighty was continuing to loosen up.

The 1960s, a brief historical period to which the media had almost instantly attributed its own zeitgeist, had been only partly responsible for this transformation. A deep urge to rattle the furniture could be traced all the way back to the fin de siècle, when Lord Alfred Douglas had got off with the leading playwright of the day and, even less forgivably, had contracted a fatal urge to write poetry of his own. Before World War I, the absurdly well-bred young Lady Diana Manners was shooting heroin in quantities that would have impressed Keith Richards, and later on, in her next incarnation as Lady Diana Cooper, she could be seen on stage and in the movies, even if she never did very much beyond looking aristocratic. In the 1920s the poisonously snob-bish young genius Evelyn Waugh, whose dearest wish was to rub waistcoats with the armigerous, did not rule out Fleet Street as a road to his desires. It had never been a clear case of the yobs taking over. There had always been an element of the nobs lusting for the lowlife buzz. But there was a limit to how far they would agree to be ridiculous.

The limit was passed in the rock music of the late 1970s, when even such a wonderfully lyrical band as Led Zeppelin had looked so silly in action that only the blind could stop laughing. Though I had never seen them live, I remembered them well, because late one night I had tuned in to a television pop show in the hope of seeing Pan's People letting their hair down and I had been confronted with Robert Plant instead. He was a bit of a come-down after Dee Dee Wilde. If Dee Dee had been so scantily clad there would have been cause for celebration. But Robert Plant had only a thin chest to bare and seemed, at first, to be doing most of the celebrating all by himself. Brushing his locks impatiently out of his eyes like Janis Joplin in full frenzy, he flounced, stamped and pouted in an ecstasy of self-adoration, for which the bulge in his tight trousers might possibly have been the focus, if a focus can be something so flagrant. He looked as if he was smuggling a gun. Also he was doing an advanced version of that terrible thing where the singer keeps snatching his face away from the microphone after each short phrase, as if in fear of divine punishment for having created so much beauty. Thirty years later he would make one of the most enchanting rock albums ever, but at the time I had no means of knowing that, clairvoyance definitely not being among my gifts. I could tell he had a voice, but I could hardly hear for looking.

I thought that I had never seen anything quite so preposter-ously soaked in the rancid oil of self-regard. But then there came a shot of the audience and it turned out there were thousands of young people present who thought the world of him. My first rational conclusion, after the paroxysm of revulsion, was that the musical component of popular culture was beginning to forget its own history as fast as it was made. Surely such a cruel caricature of Mick Jagger was based on the misapprehension that Mick Jagger had not already been a caricature when he pioneered this mad business of kissing the air as if it were full of imaginary mirrors? Jagger had done a good job of synthesizing the whole poncing, pouting, sexually ambiguous tradition since Piers Gav-eston cocked his bottom for Edward II, but wasn't all that sort of, well, over? Now I realize that the foundations were being laid for what the eighties, the decade on which I was embarked, would call either glam rock or heavy metal or perhaps something else. Something called post-punk was in there too, still finding new forms of nastiness that would push the boundaries beyond those set by the distance to which Johnny Rotten could project a gobbet of phlegm. Glam post-punk heavy metal. Punk metal post-heavy glam. I forget the terminology now, because I hated everything about it that I could not manage to avoid seeing. If my memory serves me at all, the fundamental signs of glam rock were platform boots, lipstick for men and guitars with two tails, like scorpions. Heavy metal was mainly signified by leather pants and a level of noise that left Operation Rolling Thunder sounding like the adagio of the Schubert string quintet in C. The uproar hammered to death any music that might happen to be trapped inside it. To be in on glam rock, heavy metal or any of their noxious hybrids, you had to be interested primarily in money. The toffs, on the whole, had other things in mind.

As an ideal of true creative glamour, television better fitted their specifications. It was bohemian, but not very. The ambitious young among the gentler classes could find a home in it without, as it were, leaving home. From somewhere in that direction, Richard Drewett had arrived early among the camera cables and the lighting gantries. He was looking for something. Already he had found some of it – he produced all the first *Parkinson* programmes – but he remained trapped by his skill at meeting the elevated requirements of BBC2's *Late Night Line-Up*, a respectable minority enterprise that took the arts seriously. Richard was more interested in taking mainstream entertainment seriously, but he needed a front-man. Eventually he decided that I might fill the bill. As I recounted near the end of *North Face of Soho*, we made our first documentary special together, about the Paris fashion shows, while still getting acquainted. His diligence during the editing of the footage had convinced me that he wasn't kidding when he said that I would have to give up my lofty ideas about just pasting a voice-over on the finished product. If I wanted to take a proper part in getting all this stuff into shape, I would first have to climb into it up to my neck. Although the prospect of adding such a commitment to the full week I would have to put into the studio show was worse than daunting, I didn't offer much resistance. After all, it was television, the new rock and roll, the in thing. It wouldn't be like shovelling wet cow dung on a windswept hillside.

2. FERRETS TO THE RESCUE

Is a hillside where the cows are? I still, by reflex action, look around for a spare researcher to send in search of the answer, which in those days you couldn't get by Google. Somebody had to pick up a phone, or even pick up a book. The people who did this were called the ferrets. The term was invented by Richard. Only a very few of the ferrets were ever humourless enough to resent being called that. The rest of them were capable of seeing the respect that their boss held for them under the banter. (Contrary to the received wisdom which holds that men have the sense of humour and women merely play along, it has been my experience that almost all women enjoy banter as long as it respects their dignity, whereas there are men who think you are saying they can't drive.) Most of the ferrets were young, a good half of them were female, and some of those were pretty. I did my best not to notice, aware from the start that nobody had been hired for their looks, only for their ability.

I might say at this point, so as to get my rebuttal in early, that I am very proud of my part in ensuring that the women in our office, over the next twenty years, could always depend on equal treatment. Quite a few of them have high positions in the industry now, and would probably be ready to say, if questioned on the point, that they were never held back. They might also say, alas, that I was heavy-handed with the gallantry and far too free with the waggling eyebrow of admiration. In that respect, I had had a bad education, and was slow to get over it. Marriage had done a good deal to civilize my libidinous urge, but there continued to be a lot more of it that needed convincing.

Surrounded by personable young women working hard on my
behalf, I had trouble wiping the grin off my face, and there were
certainly occasions when beauty turned my head. But it seldom
affected my judgement, and never for long. Richard made sure of
that. He was hard to fault in that matter, and since I wanted his
approval, I tried hard to copy him. But more of that later. The
story will go on. It was one of the stories of our generation
of men, and I often wonder if the next generation ever realized
how lucky it was, whatever its gender, to grow up and work in
an atmosphere where equality was taken for granted, and a man
who allowed lust to warp his sense of justice would be shamed in
his own eyes. I'm talking about Australia and America, of course:
in Britain things remained as bad as ever, although television has
always been a fairer place to work in than Fleet Street, which in
turn is nothing like as bad as the House of Commons, where the
women MPs are still forced to suffer routine abuse from the kind
of men who, even when nominally heterosexual, are at ease only
with each other, and polite to nobody.

Overnight, as our department expanded in anticipation of the
new format, we moved out of the main LWT skyscraper into an
annex called Sea Containers House beside the southern approach
to Blackfriars Bridge. It was here – as Richard was fond of saying
portentously at production meetings, especially if the meeting
was taking place in some glorified corridor decorated with cardboard cut-outs of comedians no longer exactly current – it was
here, in the romantically named Sea Containers House, that we
edited and assembled our first syndicated footage of the Japanese
game show *Endurance*. Our Japanese-speaking stringer in Tokyo
had been watching the show in growing disbelief, and when he
finally ceased spitting noodles he sent us a compilation several
hours long. In those days it was a huge task to send a sample of
a TV show across the world. Today the stringer could have
swiped it straight off air and squirted it halfway around the globe
at the speed of light. In the next generation, when the satellites
up there are touching each other, he will be able to get any

channel in the world at the touch of a button and download the images by saying, 'Shazam!' But we're talking about a time when he had to ask permission, get his physical hands on the actual stuff, wrap it up and pay for the stamps. Just the first step in this sequence, the business of asking permission, took weeks of effort even though he spoke the language. But he never gave up. His determination was a measure of how sure he was that he was on to something rivetingly weird. Our own editors trimmed the several hours of footage back to an hour, so that we could taste it.

It was like tasting an electric light socket. Young Japanese people had volunteered for tests in order to advance towards a grand prize – some kind of holiday – which seemed petty indeed when seen in the light of their sufferings. One of the milder images I made notes on was of young men hanging near-naked upside down over a well-populated snake-pit while their plastic underpants were shovelled full of live cockroaches. Instantly my narrative line started to form on the page. There had been a day when young men like these would have been taking off in planes they barely knew how to fly and heading for a sky full of flak, all in the hope of a different kind of grand prize – the chance to crash into an Allied warship. The producers, on the other hand, would have been preparing some memorable evil for the citizens of Nanking. The yammering front-man would have been an interrogator for the Kempei Tai, or leading a banzai charge on Iwo Jima. Times had changed, and all the most frightening characteristics of an alien culture were in the process of transferring themselves out of the real world and on to television. For anyone such as myself, who had always found the real world unreal in its insanities, here was evidence that television might become a new real world where homicidal tendencies were palliated by the histrionic. The Japanese students confirmed this possibility by plainly enjoying the chance to act out being afraid. There was a lot to be afraid of, by our standards. But they still relished the opportunity to emote. You could tell they were acting because they acted so badly. The one advantage of the Japanese acting style is that you can always tell when someone is acting. The young lady at the front desk of your hotel who apologizes for having given you the wrong key carries on like Toshiro Mifune in *Seven Samurai*.

As the next batch of young student contestants shivered and mugged with feigned fear while the previous batch went through their protracted martyrdom, you were seeing the deadly pseudo-Samurai code of bushido transformed into kabuki. It was kabuki with the accelerator pressed to the floor, but it was recognizably drawn from the same wellspring of inspiration as the average afternoon double bill at the great playhouse in the Ginza district of Tokyo, where the actors, year upon year forever, zealously preserve their ancient tradition of conveying anger by raising their eyebrows, snorting fiercely and stamping out imaginary cigarette butts. This was theatre, and it was formed on the ruins of a sadistic militarist tradition that had richly merited being ruined. As I made my first notes, I was forming something too: the beginnings of a theme that I would pursue for the rest of my career, even into the present day. Civilization doesn't eliminate human impulses: it tames them, through changing their means of expression. That, I decided straight away, would have to be the serious story under the paragraphs that tied the clips together: otherwise the commentary would be doomed never to rise above the level of condescension.

With all of us in the editing room simultaneously lost in thought and yelling with disbelief, we watched through to the end of the reel, after which we decided that there was about five minutes of sure-fire material distributed amongst the chaos. Even then, what we chose had to be further edited so as to make sense as separate clips. It would be a large, long, finicky task to bring a few shaped moments out of the mayhem, but our producers immediately sent the orders to Tokyo to keep the stuff coming. Back in his office, Richard asked how I would handle the commentary. He was understandably worried about the racism angle. I said what I still believe today, that there was no question of racism. It was a question of culture, and what we were seeing was a cultural nightmare being turned into a playground before our eyes. Japan, after all, was a successful nation – rather more successful than Britain, if the truth be told – and to overdo the respect for the supposed unfortunates would be to belittle them. Besides (this was my clincher), if the Japanese themselves thought they were being funny, why couldn't we agree?

So I got the green light. It was a crucial decision on Richard's part, and it sharply demonstrated the weight of the heaviest can any executive producer has to carry, because with this new kind of programme the moral issue would never go away. To condense my account of how we treated a dilemma that would extend into the years to come, let me say now that our biggest problem was Africa. Egypt was tough enough. Egyptian soap operas were so awful that you looked as if you were calling into question the intelligence of an entire population simply by screening them. There was one Egyptian light-entertainment programme based on practical jokes, in which the capering and winking star turn would plant a ticking suitcase in a railway station and they would film the panic when the commuters thought it might be a bomb. At the time this seemed too ridiculous to be harmful, so we screened it. But the real problems started further south. In the sub-Saharan countries, local television featured some wonderfully clumsy commercials. Quiz contestants competed for a packet of biscuits. The current-affairs programmes consisted almost entirely of politicians sitting facing each other in armchairs, doing nothing except getting filmed. We decided that it would look patronizing to screen this stuff, so we didn't. Underdeveloped television was no fun if it came from underdeveloped countries. For as long as I headlined the programme, that was the principle we stuck to. Critics never ceased to sum up my attitude as knowingly parochial, but that was because most critics, like most journalists of any kind, would rather change gender than change a story. To anyone capable of objective judgement, it was obvious that we were bending over backwards to be fair. When in doubt, we left it out, and we didn't need theories of imperialism to tell us to do so: a sense of common humanity was enough to do the trick.

But the constant awareness that we were on the lip of an ethical precipice proved nerve-racking, and eventually racked nerves wear you out more thoroughly than taxed muscles. The constant work of editing for impact was comparatively less tiresome. It had to be done, though, and with unrelenting concentration. You couldn't just shove stuff on the air because it was generally funny. The footage you screened had to be specifically so. A good example was the cinematic oeuvre of the renowned American director Ed Wood, who had spent a dedicated career fighting the closely connected handicaps of insufficient finance and a total absence of gift. We were the first to screen Ed Wood's movies for a television audience, and no other programme but ours ever managed to screen them successfully, because the awkward truth about Wood's justly celebrated lack of talent was that it peaked only intermittently. His masterpiece *Plan 9 from Outer Space* was merely boring if you looked at the whole thing, or even at any long sequence. He had never, in his whole career, got anything right, but the bits that were hilariously wrong were heavily wrapped in mere tedium, and had to be picked out and mounted lovingly for inspection, like treasure from a dump. I liked to think that my intervening commentary gave Ed Wood some of the brio which he had mistakenly assumed was his hallmark.

What was true for Ed Wood was true for almost everything else we screened. Editing is an essentially poetic process akin to compressing carbon until you get diamonds. In our case we were compressing dross to get zircons, but that made the job even more difficult. It was nothing, though, compared to the effort of watching fifty hopeless African current-affairs programmes and deciding you couldn't screen anything. The waste of time was so pure that it ached. With the Japanese game shows, however, we were in heaven, and precisely because all the participants were having such a ball being in hell.

When our first programme to feature excerpts from *Endurance* went to air in the new Sunday night prime-time format, the audience consolidated immediately at ten million plus. In my previous volume of memoirs I recounted how I had a local-area cult hit with my riffs about the South American killer bees in the disastrous disaster movie *The Swarm*, but the Japanese cockroaches were a success of a different order. This time the notoriety was on a national scale – I got an offer of marriage from a man in the Shetlands – and I had very little time to learn how it might be handled. The first thing I learned was that it can't: not beyond a certain point, which is placed very low down on the rising scale to insanity. If everyone in the country recognizes your face, your only hope of normality is to find another country where they don't, but you might be too late. When Elton John first stood on the Great Wall of China, he told the attendant British press pack – trailing him around the earth as if he were a more tractable version of royalty – that it was a relief to be somewhere where a thousand million people didn't know him from Adam. But he was almost certainly bluffing. Poor sap, he had already got to where it felt strange when someone didn't know who he was. I already had a mild sense of that before I left on my next foreign assignment. Kenya was bigger than Britain but blessedly had slightly fewer people in it, and very few of those had seen me explicating on screen the motivation of a bunch of Japanese adolescents as they roasted each other over a bed of embers while their testicles were being colonized by starving maggots.

3. WHITE KNUCKLES OF AFRICA

The Kenya show was to be a documentary special called *Clive James on Safari*. From now on, in this book, I will try to leave my name out of the title of the shows, thus to circumvent the twin fears of wasting space and sounding more than necessarily like a self-glorifying pantaloon. But you can take it for granted that every programme I made for the next couple of decades, whether in the studio or on location, had my name in the title somewhere. Neither I nor my agent ever pressed for this. My agent, Norman North at A. D. Peters, looked very young in those days and remarkably he retains his keen, lean appearance to this day. Some people have access to the fountain of youth. Norman also had access to the fountain of wisdom, and would have scotched the use of my name in the title if he had thought it would be counterproductive. But Richard had no trouble convincing him, and indeed me, that we might as well use what cachet my name had already built up, and try to increase it. 'Never trust anybody with two first names' was a maxim of mine that I tried to make current until I realized it applied to me. (If you start a list in your own mind, don't forget Bruce Willis and Victor Hugo.) But if the public does trust someone's name for something, the name becomes what the PR people call a Brand. The only drawback is that its possessor has to live up to it. My Postcard travel articles for the *Observer* had established a reputation for a certain kind of eager curiosity that started out clueless but came back with what at least sounded like a reasonable set of opinions. This threatened to be harder to achieve on film, where the temptation to clown it up could easily make the cluelessness look like a pose.

Nevertheless, though still devoted to the ideal of evoking a picture with a few words, I was attracted by the prospect of combining a real picture with even fewer. In an *Observer* Postcard about Jerusalem, I had given a faithful report of what it was like for an overweight man to take a running dive into the Dead Sea and find himself lying on top of it, having failed to submerge or even scratch the surface. But at the time I wrote the paragraph I was already thinking that to actually show this happening would have left a chance to say something extra and more interesting at the very moment when the audience was absorbing the mixed signals about the state of my body. I could have been talking about the state of Israel. There would be opportunities to get more said, with a blend of expression like the texture of a song, in which the words and the music reinforce each other. I was thinking this again when we landed in Nairobi and ran full tilt into the comfortable remnants of the old white empire as they clung on to the last of their privileges among the poverty-stricken shambles of the new black state. The slums teemed. Presumably the natives out in the hinterland were leading more dignified lives. Meanwhile the whites in or near town were still taking tea, hitting the bottle and betting on the horses. The British upper crust are never more dauntingly self-assured than when presiding over the wreckage of the superseded order. This lot looked as if they had all once regarded Princess Margaret as a dangerous radical. The worst I can say about my young producer, Helen Fraser, is that she looked as if she would fit right in. When she stepped off the plane, it was as if the Baroness Blixen had returned. Pretty, elegant and well spoken, she immediately had the local beau monde eating out of her finely manicured hand. They loved her.

She found it harder to love them. Partly it was a generation thing: nice girls like her nowadays had real jobs, whereas the old colonial set-up would have condemned them to come out to places like this and help their husbands lord it over the benighted. But largely it was a difference in behavioural evolution: she wasn't

a snob, and this lot were. All the great names of the White
Mischief era still drew their expected plenitude of mutual respect.
The men, especially, seemed to like each other better than ever,
just because their immediate ancestors had led the life in which
there was nothing to do with the day except screw each other's
wives when not hanging around the clubs that had been built to
keep the natives out. Let me hasten to say that there had once
been something to admire about British rule in Kenya, even
though the Mau Mau might not have agreed. Compared to, say,
Belgian rule in the Congo, British rule had been benevolent, and
precisely because the landowners and the administrative class put
more time into living well than into belting the locals. Certainly
there are plenty of locals today who wouldn't mind having their
erstwhile oppressors back on the case, at least to the extent of
running the courts of justice. When I arrived, the white pecking
order was still in full swing even though the system it had once
imposed was long gone. It seemed to occur to few of its drawling members that the privileged life they still possessed was an
historical anomaly, tainted as it was by the misery leaking in from
all around them. Again, the misery could have been worse, but
the slums were hard to ignore even if you drove around them in
a Land Rover. Helen's principal weapon against the plummy
accents was a raised eyebrow. They didn't notice. Tomorrow the
horses would be racing and the gentry looked forward to meeting
us there.

Waiting for that big day, we took the camera to dinner at a
restaurant serving nothing but African game of every type and
stripe. Hugely heaped plates of grilled and roasted meat were
served. Everything was uniformly inedible, and not just because
the original animal had never been designed to be eaten by
humans in the first place. The topkapi, or whatever it was called,
probably tasted like a whoopee cushion no matter what you did
with it, but this bunch couldn't even bring a tender touch to
some form of gazelle that they billed as the most succulent dish
south of the Sahara. You would have been better off chewing

an anorak. The probable cause was that the cooks had no means of preparing anything except to leave it in the fire until its last drop of moisture evaporated. Over more than a quarter of a century of world travel I was eventually to formulate the rule that in any country blessed with an abundance of prime-quality meat roaming around in unprocessed form, nobody knows how to cook it. To make anything taste good, you have to freeze it, load it on to a ship and send it to France. While Helen laughed at my increasingly desperate expression – she had the rare gift of laughing at your face without laughing *in* your face, I was glad to note – our camera caught the scene, which was densely populated by the younger generation of the local whites out for their idea of a dangerously exotic night. Surely the racing horses of tomorrow would be more interesting. At least they would not be cooked.

A day at the races unfolded like a message from God that we had better get out of Nairobi pronto or we would never get to Kenya. Unless you film it from space, a horse race in Africa looks exactly like a horse race at Ascot, especially when the white women present are dressed for the Queen's Garden Party. The white male elders stood around in tight groups, still discussing whether it had really been Jock Delves Broughton who had shot the Earl of Erroll. It was a wonder that they hadn't shot each other, if a day like this had been the principal alternative to peeling the silk knickers off the expatriate vamps.

Next day, before we took off for the wilds, I had another message from on high. Out on my own wandering in the slums, I found a tiny street stall selling exactly one miniature rhinoceros carved out of wood. I presumed from its singularity that it was a rare artefact, and certainly it was accurately carved: nothing about it was not like a rhinoceros except its size. The stall owner, whose refined Nilotic features suggested that he might be a connoisseur dealing only in palace-quality bibelots with which he himself could hardly bear to part, assured me it was 'Rare, very rare.' It would be welcomed in my family home, where my daughters were still young enough to look on miniature animals with favour, and my wife had an eye for sculpture. So I bought the thing from the impassive vendor. He remained impassive at the sheaf of notes I proffered, so I doubled it into a bundle. Eventually he smiled, while shaking his head, presumably taking pity on the condition of a world in which a true work of art could be valued in terms of mere money. Michelangelo probably felt the same when he handed over his finished statue of David.

You can guess what happened next. A hundred yards further on, I wandered into a kind of indoor bazaar – half souk, half swamp – which in turn opened up into a long, low factory. Lining the walls of the factory was shelf upon shelf stacked with thousands of copies of my carved rhinoceros. Shaking and roaring on the floor of the factory, a machine the size of a Fleet Street printing press was turning out carved rhinoceroses which were touched by human hand only when a team of women loaders and stackers lifted them off the belt and found a place for them on the groaning shelves. I thought of running back to the hotel to tell the crew that I had stumbled on a great story about the Kenyan economy, but the deeper message had already hit me. The real rhinoceroses, or rhinoceri, were out there waiting.

Our light aircraft dropped out of the sky in the Mara country, where we were met at the grass-strip airport by Denis Zaphiro, our guide for the safari. Denis, last of the Great White Hunters, was now a Great White Guide, a condition he preferred, because he had never really liked killing animals. He especially hadn't liked the kind of people who do like killing them. I presumed that he had made an exception in the case of Ernest Hemingway, whom he had accompanied on his last safari, the one that had culminated in the plane crash that had finally reduced Papa's lethal urge to a glimmer. Until then, the Great White Writer had put a lot of time, effort and overblown prose into seeking out at least one of every animal that breathed and making sure that its head ended up on a wall of his house in Cuba. That had to have been interesting and I looked forward to getting the story, but meanwhile we were faced with the challenge of getting Denis to act.

When it comes to documentary television, 'challenge' is a bad word, just as 'time was running out' is a bad sentence. ('We had not yet met our challenge and time was running out' is an even worse sentence.) But this really was a challenge, and time really was running out, because soon the sun would be in the wrong part of the sky and we would have to reposition the aircraft in order to do the whole thing again. The thing we had to do seemed simple at first blush. Though Denis was old enough to be my father, he was still in good shape: flat stomach, loping stride, hawk-like features, the works. He even had the mandatory cut-glass voice, ideal for making polite suggestions in either English or Swahili. He was also very clever. In his lightweight khaki safari outfit and bush hat, he looked and sounded better qualified than Stewart Granger playing roughly the same role in *King Solomon's Mines*. But Denis was no actor. Hardly anybody with an authentic personality is, but Denis was an extreme case of not being an actor. His challenge, after I got back alone into the passenger compartment of the aircraft, was to stride towards it while our crew, who had all got out of it, filmed him coming up to me as I stepped down.

He wasn't too bad at the walking bit. He got it right on about the tenth take, after the standard nine different takes of the non-actor's walk. Suddenly rendered self-conscious, the non-actor, when asked to walk for the camera, fatally starts to think about how walking is done, so he has to go through every variation of moving the legs and arms in the wrong combination. Since there are many more than nine combinations, Denis had done that part quite well. But he also had a line to say. 'Well, Clive, you're finally here. Welcome to the real Africa.' He had to do this in a medium close-up while the rifle microphone was aimed from off-camera at his tanned and distinguished face. A rifle microphone will throw anyone who hasn't seen one before, even when he has been carrying a real rifle all his life. 'Well, James, you . . .' Cut.

Helen moved in to explain to Denis how we were taking for granted that he and I had already become acquainted on the telephone, and that he would therefore address me by my first name. Denis apologized profusely, saying that he had already known that but he had forgotten. Take two. 'Well, Clive James, you . . .' Cut. 'Sorry, sorry. But I got the "Clive" in that time. Let's do it again. I'm ready. Sorry.' Denis did it again. 'Well, Clive, we're really in Africa. Welcome to here, finally. Oh God.' The sun was charging across the sky. Time was running out. Soon we would have to reposition the aircraft and not just the camera. But Denis finally met the challenge. He was that kind of guy, and I already knew that I could bet on him not to abandon me when the rhino charged: the real rhino, very large and definitely not carved from wood.

In a convoy of Toyota Land Cruisers, we all drove off to camp, where Denis, out from under the camera's looming threat, proved delightful company. We sat at tables between the tent-line and the campfire while Kungu, Denis's personal driver and servant, got busy proving that there were better ways of preparing a dish of local meat than toasting it with a flamethrower, as they did back in town. Much of Denis's talk on that first evening consisted of instructions about what not to do. Above all, nobody must go out walking alone, even by daylight and for the shortest distance. Denis, by sure instinct, aimed most of these homilies at our cameraman Mike, who looked like the adventurous type. Mike was about my age and equally bald, but there wasn't an ounce of fat on him. Superbly muscled, he was afraid of nothing. Denis politely emphasized that in this part of Africa it was better to be afraid of everything. By implication, there were other parts that were different, but I had no real urge to pack up and go to one of those. This was the place to be. In the flickering half light, the beautiful Helen was doing a convincing Grace Kelly impersonation as she gazed at the masterful Denis. I'm bound to say I was doing the same. Father figures still affect me that way even now.

Next day at breakfast we were informed that a herd of about
a dozen elephant had been through the camp during the night,
so it would be a good day for filming elephant. I liked this use of
'elephant' in the singular: it made you wonder how many of them
there had to be before they got into the plural. The problem of
referring to more than one rhinoceros was thus solved: I had
been in a warehouse stuffed with thousands of miniature wooden
rhinoceros. But I kept all that for later and simply asked the
obvious question. Why hadn't at least one of the many elephant
stepped on a tent? Dennis changed my life on the spot. 'The
elephant thinks that the tent is a solid object.' You have to be
there to find that kind of stuff out. I never forgot what he
said. I never forgot anything he said. Usually we should distrust
any memoir that features a lot of quoted speech, because
nobody's memory is that good. But there are some people to
whom you pay extraordinary attention. When Denis spoke, I was
all ears, like an elephant. Even at the time, however, I was silently
wondering what would have happened if my tent had not been
pointed on top, but flat, like a big box. If one of the elephant
had harboured ambitions of being a circus star, it might have
hopped up.

Within an hour I was finding out how big elephant are.
Kungu trailed the herd and suddenly there they all were, pulling
down small trees and feeding them to their young. Mike and the
crew set up the gear in a tearing hurry, got the wide shots, and
suddenly Mike was off with the camera on his shoulder, heading
for a huge old tusker with one tusk: he was a one-tusk tusker.
The one-tusk tusker seemed to have one task: to vent his anger.
He spread his ears and bellowed. I raced off to include myself in
a possible two-shot while Denis, no doubt feeling his age, raced
after me. Denis was yelling something. I was not as deaf then as
I am now, so I could understand the word he was yelling. The
word was 'no'. 'No, no. Come back! When he spreads his ears
like that it means . . .' But I could already see what it meant. The
one-task, one-tusk tusker was thundering towards us flat out. As

we ran, Denis fell down a hole up to the waist, but luckily the elephant went steaming past him, heading for where I had been the last time he (the elephant, not Denis) had opened his eyes. I was already back in the car. Having run out of puff, the elephant returned from the horizon, gave one last bronchitic bellow and, accompanied by all the other elephant, moved on out of sight. Kungu was shaking his head. Denis showed up limping. He said, 'For fuck's sake don't do anything like that again.' We all registered deep shame, an effect Mike rather spoiled by asking Denis to fall down the hole again for a close-up. But surely we already had the footage that counted: the elephant charges and I run. Couldn't be neater. I could already see it on screen.

Many days later, after the whole safari was over, it turned out that Denis had cracked a rib when he fell down the hole. We had thus come very close to ending the career of the last of the Great White Hunters on our first day out. As yet unaware of the full extent of his injury, Denis typically offered apologies when he should have been demanding them. He made no objection to going on. He even started to get the hang of the acting thing when we did a dung-spotting sequence. With a line of trees in the distance, we walked together on the open ground. Mike circled around us with the camera on his shoulder, getting the angles. Behind Mike walked Nobby the sound man, laden with the huge Nagra tape-recorder which in those days was the last word in technology. Nobby himself, however, was slightly deaf, which you might have thought was a bit of a drawback for a sound man. You, your mother and everyone else except the union shop steward, who was rewarding Nobby for long service by sending him on this luxury expedition, with plenty of overtime and an enhanced life insurance payout if, as seemed quite likely, he was trampled from behind by a buffalo he hadn't heard approaching. Luckily this spoor-sniffing sequence was an easy one for him. He just had to keep rolling and pick up anything Denis and I said about the piles of crap we found. 'Now this one is very interesting, James. Sorry, Clive. Can I start again? Sorry.

Now this one is very interesting, Clive. This is the product of a giraffe, and you can see there by those flies that the giraffe was here quite recently, probably this morning. How was that?' Already mentally rehearsing, for my commentary, a couple of giraffe-related gags about being shat on from a great height, I told him that it was fine, and that he should just keep it coming, not worrying about any mistakes because we could always edit them out later.

'Sorry. And over here we've got some Thomson gazelle dung. Quite delicate, isn't it? A refined beast, the Tommy. And these bones here are Thomson gazelle bones. Lion kill, I should think. Quite recent. Probably last night.' He was looking at the trees. 'I think we should go back to the car now.' Mike, having sensed that Denis had seen something at the edge of the tree-line, wanted to go closer, but had to content himself with a bunch of giraffes who came drifting through with scarcely credible grace. All they needed was music by Tchaikovsky and they could have been ballerinas auditioning for Balanchine. Mike then set about getting individual close-ups of the various piles of poop until Denis pointed out that what he had seen in the shadow of the trees was a pride of lions and that any of them could get to us before we could get to the car, so it was time to go. Mike lingered over the heap of bones. Imagining my own bones lying in the same position, I kept sneaking glances at the tree-line, but I could see nothing except trees and shadows. Denis, I concluded, must have eyesight like a fighter pilot.

When we got back to the camp and the waiting Helen, I climbed down from the Toyota as if I were the sort of Battle of Britain hero who would climb down from his Spitfire or Hurricane and smile shyly as he walked in, holding up a number of fingers to indicate his kills. Actually, if I had done so, I would have been indicating only the number of dung piles I had seen, but the mere hint of lions had been enough to set my heart racing. Hippopotamus kill more people, and buffalo are more likely to rub you out from sheer spite, but there's something about the big cats that connects directly to your reservoir of primal fear. The fear is well justified in the case of lions. The previous month, an old male lion had come into the suburbs of Nairobi and killed a man who had stopped to check one of the back wheels of his Volkswagen. In the previous safari season, out here where we were now, an Italian banker, in the back of a Land Cruiser with his whole family, was caught short by the squirts. The driver told him to do it in the car but the Italian banker was too fastidious for that. My sentiments exactly, except that I had already guessed, as you have, the next part of the story. He got out of the car to squat behind a bush and his whole family had to listen while the lions ate him. Although the old-man lion, like myself and most of the men I know, has no real ambition left beyond lying around impressively while the women shop for lunch, he nevertheless can live up to his billing with shattering suddenness when he is in the mood.

In theory, there is less reason to be wary of cheetahs. They probably won't go for you. But they do look, even when in repose, as if they could go right through you. Next morning we were in the car trailing a brat pack of young cheetahs taking hunting lessons from their mother. There was a bunch of impala in the distance and mummy took off in that direction, accelerating like a drag racer. There is a beautiful poem by Amy Clampitt in which a cheetah's petalled coat suddenly turns into a sandstorm as she starts to run. I scarcely saw the transition, but Mike said he had got the shot. He was sitting strapped to the bonnet of the Land Cruiser with the camera on his shoulder. (I might be making that sound easy: the camera was a hefty object in those days.) Kungu put the pedal to the metal as we raced towards the point from which the impala had dispersed in all directions. The impala, if I may pontificate for a moment, have been given their beauty only as a reward for being the unluckiest animals in Africa. There are a lot of them, they can run like mad and they might have safety in numbers, but the cats can run even faster over a short distance, and if you're the one impala in a hundred that a cat catches up with, to have been as cute as Natalie Portman is no recompense when the lights go out. When we found the cheetah she was already tearing her victim to shreds. As her young trainees turned up to join her, the gorgeous killer turned to look at the camera. She was divine, but she had blood on her silky cheeks.

For the cheetahs, Denis had allowed Mike to stay outside on the bonnet, but for lions he had to come inside. A few hours later we found a whole pride of lions inhabiting an upmarket clump of bushes and immediately I wished the car had been a tank. Even Mike looked impressed, and he was the one who asked if a lion had ever tried to jump in through the big hole in the roof of a car like ours. 'No,' said Denis, 'but you never know.' Apparently the bunch we were filming were all males, so there wouldn't be any violence, because the females were off somewhere doing all the hard graft, like researchers. A bit further on, we saw the women at work. One of them ran down a junior warthog and killed it with a bite to the neck. There was only a brief pause before the males arrived for lunch. A big male who looked like the one that had the contract for the MGM logo swallowed the dinky little warthog whole. 'Usually,' said Denis, 'lions do most of their hunting at night. So you're in luck.' Mike zoomed in as the last of the warthog disappeared down the lion's gullet, leaving nothing outside but its tail, as if the lion had ingested one of those old field radios with a whip aerial. All the other lions looked around glumly but they couldn't have been less interested in us. Nevertheless the scene was scary enough and we had some good stories for the campfire that night. High on adrenalin, I sat up late with Kungu as he taught me my first words of Swahili. *Simba* I already knew from reading Hemingway. *Simba* meant lion. Kungu told me the word for 'big': *kubwa*. So a big lion was *simba kubwa*. The language was delicious to pronounce, with full syllables like Italian, and no awkward clusters of consonants, as in English. Denis spoke it fluently and he was also a good teacher (the two things don't always go together), but Kungu was the teacher of my dreams, infinitely patient and very flattered that *bwana* should take the trouble. *Bwana* – that was me – resolved to study hard. *Bwana* had visions of himself as an old Africa hand, saving Ava Gardner from the charging *simba kubwa*.

Part of the plan, while we were in the Masai Mara, was to visit the Masai themselves. This took quite a chunk out of our budget, because the Masai were good at business. They still sent their teenage boys out alone to kill a lion with a spear; they still drank cow's blood as a source of protein; but they also, by repute, owned half the taxis in Nairobi, running them on a franchise basis so that lesser tribes like the Kikuyu did all the driving. At home in their huts, the Masai charged serious money even to be looked at, let alone photographed. Recently a German tourist had snapped a Masai warrior without making a deal first. The tourist went home with a hole in his shoulder, made by a spear. He had a good story to tell in Wilmersdorf, but we didn't want any of that, so all the right palms had been well greased before we showed up among the huts for the mandatory scene of me spontaneously joining a circle of warriors as they jumped to impress the women. Propelled by exactly the same impulse from which I wrote lyric poetry, the warriors ascended vertically to a startling height, simply by flexing their feet. Spontaneously I joined in, and after about half an hour we had the makings of a nice sequence about the visitor making an idiot of himself while the surrounding crowd of giggling women failed to be impressed. Some of the younger ones could have been models for Claude Montana's latest collection, so I was really trying. I felt I understood the men. As a consequence I found the animals more interesting, because they were less predictable. When being watched by a cheer squad of young women who look like David Bowie's wife Iman at the height of her beauty in *No Way Out*, a male human being of any age or colour will immediately start auditioning. But you can never tell which way a leopard will jump.

4. ELEPHANT WALK

There was plenty of animal unpredictability on hand when we relocated deeper into the Mara triangle, where a bend of the muddy river was meant to be full of hippopotamus. We were all facing towards this as we filmed, but Denis was continually sneaking a peek in the other direction. When I asked him why, he said: 'The most dangerous thing you can do out here is get between a hippo and the water.' I was still shivering at the thought when a hippo surfaced just in front of the camera and opened its mouth to the full stretch. It looked like the entrance to a candy-floss parlour. Then a whole flotilla of them started surfacing all over the place. They must have been at a meeting down there. The river was palpitating with hippopotamus. Their numbers never grow thin, because nobody wants any part of them. The same would be true for rhinos if there wasn't one part that everybody wants: the horn. Converted to powder, rhino horn is in demand all over East Asia as an aphrodisiac. If rhinos needed the powdered skull of an East Asian bank clerk in order to get their rocks off there would be complaints, but as things are, the rhino is doomed. We filmed a couple of them from our speeding car as they ran, and when one of them turned towards us to indicate that the fun was over for the day, his horn looked awfully big. In today's terms, it would have provided enough aphrodisiac powder to meet the requirements of a whole cinema full of Chinese wage-slaves for whom watching a Gong Li movie had failed to do the trick.

Since it was well known that most of the poaching of ivory, horn and crocodile skin was organized by elements close to the government, the animals concerned were living on borrowed time, but when you saw them in the flesh they looked a lot more threatening than threatened. This particularly applied to the crocodiles, well-armed examples of a primitively savage life form that had flourished for a long time until it ran into us. We did a night shoot on how to feed the crocodiles, who are skilled natural predators but too dumb to realize that any extra food provided by human beings might come with a price tag. Clandestine representatives of handbag manufacturers feed crocodiles on the sly, but we were at an officially sanctioned spot, with floodlights provided. There was a kind of ramp leading down to the water where regular feedings took place so that tourists could get a snap, if that's the word we're looking for. The pampered crocs who hung out near the ramp were reputedly too spoiled to be aggressive. When one of them emerged to collect its free meal, we were told, it would be a model of ambling bonhomie. With Mike and the camera parked off to one side, I hoisted a large lump of raw antelope and edged down the ramp, with a local character at my shoulder to tell me what to do. A croc a block long came boiling up the ramp and I asked the local character – famously wise in the ways of these beasts – what I should do next. But the local character was no longer there. Taking this as a message, I dropped the meat and ran. Back in the car, I needed a nip of Scotch from Denis's hip flask. Mike turned up to say that he had a great shot of the croc eating but needed one of me running. So I went back down the ramp for the minimum necessary distance and ran again, cleverly feigning fear by delving, method style, into my memories of being caned by the Deputy Head Master of Sydney Technical High School. No doubt the finished sequence would make it all worthwhile. When the camera is with you, you have to do the necessary.

The camera was not always with me. There were rest days. Though some of its rules added up to a frustrating curb on flexibility, the union was very right to insist on resting the crew at regular intervals. The programme maker always has reasons for working the crew continuously, and the crew, if left without protection against those reasons, would soon be worked to exhaustion. So you got the odd blissful day when no filming happened, but you had to pray that nothing worth filming would happen either. On just such a day, Denis, with Kungu at the wheel – I sat beside him so he could continue teaching me Swahili while Denis, sitting in the back, explained the finer points of grammar – took us out to get a broader view of the surrounding country, in which the meandering muddy river seemed always to be in view no matter where you went. Equally ubiquitous were the Volkswagen Kombi buses of commercial safaris. In any area of Kenya there were half a dozen safaris going on at once, and most of them travelled in Kombis. As a result, herds of Kombis were almost as common as herds of animals. If a clump of trees was thought to contain a leopard, a cluster of Kombis would form around the clump. We stopped near one of these Kombi gatherings while I watched the tourists do their thing. As so often, the Japanese provided the richest material for a possible commentary. Photographing everything to prove that they had seen it, they photographed the Kombi they had just got out of, photographed each other, and photographed the clump of trees in which the putative leopard resolutely declined to make itself visible. In those days even the most up-to-date cameras made noises. The multiple Nikons crackled like a firefight.

You couldn't blame the Japanese for being mad about their cameras, most of which, after all, were manufactured in Japan, like the Land Cruiser we were sitting in. I made a note that we would have to get this kind of scene on film, because it was part of the truth. We would have to film the photographers as they took photographs. But it was a depressing spectacle. One felt for the leopard, whose instincts were geared up for hunting, not for being hunted. 'Kwenda,' said Denis to Kungu. He meant, 'Let's go.' So we went, driving off to a stretch of river where no Kombi vans were in evidence. 'You sometimes see one or two elephant crossing here,' said Denis. As if on cue, a whole family of elephant showed up, moving out of the trees on our side of the river and plainly bent on fording it. As the family waded in, a few more elephant started arriving behind them. Then there were many more. Finally there were about fifty of them wading across or queuing up to take their turn. Among the adults there were infants, almost fully submerged and poking their little trunks up like snorkels. Some of the old males were yelling with impatience, as old males will in a traffic jam. Denis told me I was in luck: he had never seen anything as good as this in all his time in Africa. Kungu said he hadn't seen anything like it since he was a boy. I had never seen anything like it in my wildest dreams. I didn't need telling I was lucky, but I was feeling exactly the opposite, because we weren't getting it on film. I didn't say that, however: for once the adjective 'breathtaking' had a literal sense. The muddy water was being whipped to a froth. On the far bank, two clumps of Kombis were rapidly assembling to flank the path that the emerging animals would take. A hundred cameras crackled. The storm of photoflash put the herd into a panic. The leading tuskers trumpeted. The whole herd sped up. The ones getting out of the water slipped on the mud. To either side of the beaten path, mothers boosted their babies out of the water with their foreheads. I saw one of the mothers, while she was still hip deep in the water, wrap her trunk around her squealing tot, lift it and deposit it on the bank, where it trotted around in small circles of bewilderment. 'I suppose you're sorry you're not filming this,' said Denis, master of understatement to the last. But I had already decided that I would never mention what we had missed getting on film, and until now I never have. It might have sounded like bitterness.

The film camera is an instrument for creating rain. In Kenya we got lucky with the weather and I did not have to learn this lesson, but it had already become apparent to me that time was expensive. If you did not have a plan B ready for when plan A went wrong, you would be wasting money at a rate that the people supplying it would be bound to notice. A grasp of this fact is the beginning of realism. There are other artistic fields in which you can be creative without being realistic. In poetry there will always be a Dylan Thomas, and he will often do great things, even while borrowing more money than he earns, breaking his bargains, drinking the pub dry, pissing in your fireplace and wrecking every life with which he comes into close contact. But when film or television cameras are involved, you can't lead a bohemian existence even for a week. Flaubert's rule – live like a bourgeois, think like a demigod – applies rigidly. Against my own profligate nature, I was already learning to be parsimonious with my energy. It's half the secret.

The other half, of course, is to seize an opportunity. I was getting better at that too. It was a firm part of our plan that all my commentary would be done later in voice-over, with no 'pieces to camera' on the spot. This principle had been hatched mainly at my initiative, and sprang from my belief that the walk-and-talk was not only something that I was no good at, but something that no normal human being looked sane doing. David Attenborough got away with it when he was walking towards you out of the desert while explaining that the erosion of the topsoil was due to the agricultural policies of the Roman Empire and then a 150,000-ton oil tanker crossed the screen behind him in the same shot, thereby encouraging the viewer to suspect the hidden presence of the Suez Canal. But without the oil tanker he would have looked exactly like a man walking for no reason except to prove that he could. I wanted to do most of my talking over the finished film, which could be cut together far more tightly in the absence of long filmed speeches that had to be preserved no matter what. But this future flexibility entailed a strict discipline of getting plenty of coverage at the top and tail of each sequence, so that there would be space to add the links. These bread-and-butter shots can be boring for young directors, most of whom fancy themselves as Federico Fellini's natural heir. Such journeywork can even be boring to the cameraman, so you have to get him on side, employing gifts of diplomacy that did not come naturally to me. I learned them because I had to. Many a film has been ruined by lack of coverage. Luckily Mike was a workhorse as well as a daredevil. His only real drawback was that he spoke Cockney rhyming slang as if he assumed that I would understand what he was saying.

'Can you,' he asked, 'just hold it there while we get some light on your boat?' The time I took to figure out that 'boat' was short for 'boat race', which rhymed with 'face', could prove important if the other face in the shot belonged to a buffalo sticking its head out three feet away as we toiled uphill in the Land Cruiser on a bumpy track cut through thick bush. The shock of suddenly seeing the buffalo's foaming nostrils and mad red eyes from so very close is with me still. It was like turning over a Sunday colour supplement and finding, on its cover, Donatella Versace after her latest encounter with the collagen. I yelped as if stung. Denis reassured me by saying that the buffalo needed room to run before it did any damage. 'Give him a bit of space and he could take the engine out of this car.' My boat turned white, like a yacht.

Onward to Kilimanjaro, where we camped out in the open with the mountain for a backdrop: a cyclorama three miles high. The mountain had Hemingway's legend stamped all over it. It might as well have featured a giant sculpture of his head, like Mount Rushmore. Possibly as an elegiac closing scene for the film, we did a campfire interview in which Denis evoked the departed spirit of the Great White Writer. Denis did the old boy proud, but while the magazines were being changed he let slip a few things that would have been dynamite on film. 'He couldn't shoot straight to save his life, so he had to wait until the animal was practically on him. Quite daunting if you were standing next to him.' Also it turned out that the master of language had never learned nearly as much Swahili as he liked to pretend. Since *Green Hills of Africa* is peppered with Swahili words, this was hot news. Why hadn't he learned it? 'He wasn't a very good listener. Not like you.' This was the only time that I had been called a good listener and I took it as one of the biggest compliments of my life. From that moment I redoubled my efforts as Kungu's star pupil, and the time soon came when we spoke together in his language as a matter of course. Our conversations were a bit elementary from my side, but they were good for my brain tissue. An awful pity that Swahili is so short of literature, or it would be with me still.

There is a lot more that I could say about my safari but at this rate I would need ten more volumes just to recount my memories of filming in twenty years' worth of foreign places. I have gone into detail about the Kenya film because it provided a foundation course in which I had to learn an awful lot in a hurry. One of the things I learned was the importance of leaving your prejudices at home. The story of the connection between the Europeans and the native Africans had seemed cut and dried in Nairobi: it had looked like no connection at all. But when Denis and Kungu were together you saw something else. It wasn't a master–servant relationship. They were colleagues, working by agreement. Denis taught me a wonderful Swahili expression which had been much employed by the white masters of the old days. It could be translated as 'Why? Because *bwana* says so.' But he also said that it was an expression he himself had never used in earnest, and that it would have been all over for him in Africa if he had ever felt the need.

Near the end of the shoot, there was a day when I climbed out of the old Dakota that had brought us from Kichwa Tembo and I got the news from someone on the ground that the BBC had just announced the death of Philip Larkin. That prince of poets had always been very kind to me and I found the sense of loss hard to take. Kungu asked me what was wrong. Running out of words, I told him that a wise old man, a man who spoke beautifully, was dead. Kungu taught me the phrase for when you miss someone. When I left Denis and Kungu to lead the rest of their honest lives under a succession of corrupt governments, I often missed them both. But I never got in touch. Filming is like that: you get to know people well, and then you don't see them again. And I'm afraid I'm like that: I get busy somewhere else, and nothing connects or continues except in my work, where I put the care and patience that I should have given to real life. It's a character flaw, and filming gave it a licence. Already, back there at the beginning, I was wondering how long I could keep at it before everything else fell apart. I would have liked to have been in England when Larkin died. On the plane back to London I began a poem about him. In fact I wrote it to him, as an address to his ghost, and I included a lot of detail about Africa, which he had never seen. When you have a vision as powerful as his, of course, you can see the world without leaving home, but some of us are lesser spirits.

5. PAUSE TO REGROUP

Back in Cambridge with my family, I strove to atone for my recent absence by telling stories of Africa at the dinner table. To my disappointment, my rare carved wooden rhinoceros aroused only a mild interest, although it is still there today, looming in a small way on the shelf under one of the windows to the back garden. But I scored a hit with my evocations of the charging elephant and the narrow escape from the killer crocodile. People under a certain age go for that kind of thing. Phrases that I planned to use in my commentary were duly tested. I also learned, to my surprise, that a family holiday was due. But first I had to edit the film. I took my tested phrases with me into the editing room and soon found that very few of them fitted. Since electronic editing was still in the process of being invented, all the footage was hanging there in the form of strips of celluloid, a forest of potential. But after the relevant bits had been loaded into the editing table it soon became apparent that several scenes I had thought were in the bag barely existed. The elephant charged and I ran, but we were in different shots, so I might as well have been running on Dartmoor. The crocodile charged and I ran again, but again there was nothing to prove that these things were happening on the same day or even the same continent. It was nobody's fault except mine. I should have realized the necessity of staying close to the camera and keeping it behind me, so that it could pan easily with the animal while keeping me in the frame. Off to the side, the camera would miss the connection. Richard was in charge of the editing and tried hard to convince me that kicking myself was useless.

Eventually I cooled down and started to earn my money by writing a narrative that would tie the fragments together. Most of the raw material was impressive, even beautiful, but I had been counting on the moments of action that made me look all set to take off at high speed when danger threatened. When jumping with the Masai I looked sufficiently silly, but I had always thought that the real story lay in the moments when I was included in the picture along with the prospect of death, so that the viewers would share my impulse to hit the ground running. Those moments weren't there. Richard was very good at getting me beyond what I had always thought and into the realm of fact. He had a phrase, 'Let's see if we miss it,' which made it easier to take the disappointment when a sequence that had required a lot of hard work to shoot had to be cut out. All the scenes set in Nairobi hit the floor. I didn't mind losing those, but when I said that I was sorry we had ever shot them in the first place Richard had the right reply: they would have come in handy if the animals had been rained off. It was a long, hard edit but the results were pretty good. Next time they would be better. There had to be a next time because already I was convinced that writing words to pictures was the most fun that a writer could have when not being handed an Academy Award by Sophia Loren.

One principle I had already grasped was that the words could punctuate the pictures and vice versa. Measuring sentences to fit a sequence or even a single shot, I relished the freedom of not having to say that a charging rhino was a charging rhino. I could say that its horn would end up in an aphrodisiac cocktail glass in Hong Kong if it didn't end up in me first. Windows of opportunity opened up one after the other. It was an interplay. This principle came in handy when we started planning a weekly variety show composed of interviews, with a top section reviewing the news. To go with some footage we had of the Soviet leaders reviewing the May Day parade in Red Square, I wrote a sample fantasy and Richard went for it.

This frivolous approach to world affairs would not have

impressed my fellow regulars at the Friday lunch. At various locations, the Friday lunch was still going on and would do so for some years yet, but increasingly the demands of our respective careers were pulling it apart. When the up and coming are still in the early stages of their ascent, they cling together for warmth, but higher up the mountain, even though it gets colder, they start going their separate ways to the top. They just get too busy. It was our timetables, and not our different views, that put the first cracks in the old camaraderie. Different views there had always been. Kingsley Amis regarded James Fenton as an agent of the Viet Cong, an impression that Kingsley had perhaps gained from the fact that Fenton had arrived in Saigon riding on a North Vietnamese tank. Their contrary opinions did not stop them making each other laugh, and even when they weren't laughing they had the common background of a deep knowledge of English poetry throughout its history. Martin Amis was of the opinion that the mere existence of nuclear weapons was enough to rot our minds with subconscious dread. I agreed with Robert Conquest that nothing except nuclear weapons could have stopped the US and the USSR from going to war. Ian McEwan and Mark Boxer also thought that atomic bombs were bad things and that peace was a principle. I believed that peace was just a desirable state of affairs. Christopher Hitchens thought I was a propagandist for global nuclear war. I gave chapter and verse to prove that I had got my concept of an armed truce from Raymond Aron. Terry Kilmartin, who had known Aron personally and translated some of his major works into English, said that I was overdoing my admiration for a philosopher who had after all, um, ah, ended up 'a bit right wing'. I said I was still a leftie. Peter Porter said I was certainly to the right of him. Russell Davies, speaking in the voice of Sir John Betjeman, said that only the Queen's opinion counted. The clashes of opinion were mighty, but the rule of the table was that you couldn't fight your corner without making it amusing. The ability to quote helped there. Allusions flew like paper bullets. Craig Raine, modelling a hairstyle based on an explosion in an armchair, was so hard to interrupt that I wanted to stab him with a fork. To judge from the way he was waving his own fork, the feeling was mutual. Piers Paul Reid, secure in his Catholic faith, got cooler as the quarrels heated up. He was a Jesuit at a conference of evolutionary scientists, relishing the shades of folly. Julian Barnes, as has always been his wont, said just enough, and it was always good. Otherwise he sat stonily amused, like an Easter Island statue watching a restaurant scene in *Mr Hulot's Holiday*. With the talk as the main dish of the feast, nobody noticed what they ate, and Ian Hamilton, as usual, never even ate it. He just smoked and drank simultaneously. Smoke was part of the landscape, as on a misty moor haunted by voices.

Having realized that some of my best friends were still slow to abandon the notion that the totalitarian regimes in the East, despite their impeccable record of victimizing the common people they were notionally in business to protect, had somehow questioned the validity of liberal democracy in the West, I found myself writing with more urgency on the subject of the totalitarian mentality and its implications. My thesis was that true intellectuals in the West, or indeed anywhere, would have to attain a clear view of the past if they were to work beneficially in the present. My own view of the past was expanded considerably by a recently acquired ability to read Russian. Helped along by the sheer beauty of the language, I had gradually elevated my level of reading somewhat beyond the level of cat-sat-on-the-mat. A big help in coping with the initial stage was that the one thing the Soviet Union was really good at was publishing cardboard-covered teaching aids full of pictures of cats sitting on mats. Since Russian is the kind of language where there is a different verb for cats sitting down slowly, cats sitting down suddenly and cats just sitting there, it is very easy to have your heart broken before you get to the far edge of square one, so I had some reason to bless the Kremlin. But now that I could read the dissident and exile texts in their full range, other reasons for admiring the regime were looking thin on the ground.

Christopher Hitchens, whose sense of humour was of such a quality that he could quote from P. G. Wodehouse and make him a lot funnier than he was on the page, was less cheerful when I quoted Lenin's written opinion that the party must rule by terror. Reacting sharply to the suggestion that the foundations of state terror were already well laid before Stalin took over, the Hitch still saw merit in the revolutionary tradition. Later in his coruscating life as a commentator he modified that view, but at the time he had no trouble in making me feel like an incipient Tory for placing my faith in historical institutions: it was not, after all, as if I, with my relatively poor memory, could easily quote Edmund Burke in my defence, whereas the Hitch, who had a memory like a library, could quote Tom Paine until the cows came home and turned the milking shed into a commune. But I think I was rather better at remembering the words of the dissident Russian sociologist Alexandr Zinoviev, who said that any society which placed collective rights above individual rights was a lawless society, and that was that. The words, in the original language, had cost me almost as much trouble to read as they had cost him to write, so I was unlikely to forget them. (When I met him one day in Geneva shortly after he had been expelled from his homeland, he complimented me on how I had quoted him in an article but asked me why I had found it necessary to make the point. 'Does not everyone think that here?' Bad guess, *tovarisch*.) Thus armoured, I could persist in believing that a naivety based in reality was better than a sophistication based on a fantasy, and I pressed on with my intention of expressing what I felt in the form of connected thought.

As one essay succeeded another, I found I was getting better at it. In the field of discursive, expository writing, practice helps. Time brings fluency, or at least the appearance of it. With experience and accumulated knowledge – I was still reading a great deal, a habit I retain today, although my always unreliable memory has begun to weaken – the actual practice of writing got more difficult, but that was a good sign. (Thomas Mann defined the writer as someone for whom writing is harder than it is for other people.) As a reward for persistence, the finished product became less clotted, more transparent, and therefore easier for the reader to remember from paragraph to paragraph, the unit on which I based my style. (Writers who compose only in sentences, even if the sentences are vivid, soon strain the reader's patience: sensible people are not long amused if they are flicked repeatedly with a wet towel.) The relative success of my first novel *Brilliant Creatures* didn't distract me from my ambition as a factual writer. Some of its reviewers thought that a television performer had no business writing a novel of any kind, but there were others who approved, even if they had to do it through gritted teeth: always the best kind of approval to have. In both Britain and Australia, the blessedly literate educated reading public made up their own minds, and the book, after its honey-moon period as a bestseller in both hardback and paperback, went on to sell more than a quarter of a million copies in the course of its life.

But if I could publish *Brilliant Creatures* again now, I would have to annotate its contemporary references. It was a commentary on the times. Even in the first flush of its vogue I never thought of myself as a career novelist. I sat down every week with people who could do that better. I knew that the best use of fantasy in my writing was to make factual statement entertaining. What changed for me, in those years, was my notion of the range of fact over which entertainment was possible. It could go wider, if not deeper. My first two books of essays, *The Metropolitan Critic* and *At the Pillars of Hercules*, had got me somewhere. The essays I was writing now got me further. A few years later I collected them in my third volume of essays, *From the Land of Shadows*, the first of my books to make my political position explicit. There were many people, some of them uncomfortably close to me, who were ready to insist that my political position was somewhat compromised by the physical position of Japanese game-show contestants staked out on a beach for the crabs, but I was determined to keep going with my balancing act.

It was a balancing act performed on the run. The weekly studio show consumed a lot of energy even before it got to air. It was hard enough just to sell the thing. Jeremy Isaacs, not yet equipped with a knighthood, was at that time still in charge of Channel 4, which he had created from scratch. He agreed to meet me and Richard at the Garrick Club. It was a club rule that you weren't allowed to do business at the dining table. You weren't even allowed to take a piece of paper out of your pocket. When I got elected to the Garrick after the usual wait of several years in the queue, I cravenly allowed its prestige to impress me, and for a long time the place came in useful if I wanted to hire a room for an anniversary party or something like that, but eventually I had enough sense to ask myself what the hell I, of all people, was doing in a club that did not admit women unless they were on a leash. I saw a bunch of sozzled old men camped under the grand staircase, boring the daylights out of each other, and I had a sudden urge never to be one of their number. So I resigned. Hardly anyone ever resigns from the Garrick. I know that my friend Tom Stoppard did after he figured out that he was going there only once a year and therefore paying several hundred pounds in membership fees for a single lunch, but hardly anybody else has ever been on the exit list. Most luminaries are on the entry list, and once they get in they stay there until they have to be carried out in a black plastic bag. But that's exactly what's wrong with the place. It's essentially a well-decorated nursing home.

At the time of this meeting, however, I was still susceptible to the aura of an inner sanctum. Isaacs, whom I now count as a friend and neighbour, fitted right into the Garrick's trad decor. He did quite a lot of quoting in the original Latin. But he listened, and he bought the show. It was still a paper project and we couldn't even show him the paper, but he had imagination. This was the man who gave Verity Lambert the green light to make *The Naked Civil Servant*, which remains, to this day, the single most adventurous television programme I have ever seen. Like Sir Michael Balcon at Ealing or Lord Bernstein at Granada, Jeremy was one of that great line of British Establishment Jews who had been cultivating the nation's artistic garden since the heyday of Benjamin Disraeli. It was not yet apparent that the line would soon lose its confidence and finally die out. What Jeremy said, went. He gave us his word and we knew it was as good as gold. Many years later, when he was in charge of the Royal Opera House at Covent Garden, he took the word of a BBC producer on the assumption that it was as trustworthy as his, and the new boys stitched him up a treat: *o tempora*, he no doubt said echoing Cicero, *o mores*. What times, and what customs. But on the day he met with us the times had not yet changed: the grandee had spoken, and we were in like Flynn. There was still a lot of work coming up, however, so the family holiday would be a welcome break.

6. ALPINE IDYLL

I was lucky it didn't break my neck. For several years the family had gone skiing in Italy, mainly at Bormio and Madonna di Campiglio. At Madonna there was a ski instructor called Italo who was much loved by our daughters and who taught me a lot about life, if never enough about skiing. Taking me out for a solo lesson, he carved a turn on a slope covered with fresh snow and explained the resulting sculpture using a ski-pole as a pointer, like an art critic decoding a doodle by Brancusi. The tiny amount of displaced snow at the start of the curve showed how the weight had been applied in a smooth progression as the knees were gradually bent to push the skis down. But then there was a symmetrically equivalent crescent indicating how the knees had been straightened with similar gradualness to complete the turn, thus maintaining the curve instead of its degenerating into a skid. Done this way, a completed turn would prepare for the next as the unweighted skis floated naturally into the fall line. Though my own turns continued to look like a demonstration of elementary ditch-digging, what he had shown me served as an ideal in my memory of how the application of effort should always be exactly measured: nothing by force, everything by logical progression. Too much disturbance in the medium was a sign of strain. The lesson is still with me today. It serves me like the passage in Johnny Weissmuller's autobiography about how the essence of swimming the crawl is to relax the arm when it's out of the water, so that it wastes no energy. Fully relaxed, it will fall into the water under its own weight, without a splash. The secret of composition in any form is the appropriate application of effort.

The result is an aesthetic effect that should never be aimed at directly, but only reaped as the harvest of correct preparation. If skiing in Italy had always been like that, I could have gone home and written a sequel to Byron's *Don Juan* or a companion volume to *War and Peace*. But at Bormio the whole family traumatized itself by following a less judicious instructor across the slope that had been prepared for the World Downhill Championship.

Trekking cross-country, we came to the edge of the championship slope about halfway up its initial precipice, where the competitors would be riding their hissing skis at full clip in the tuck. If the high-speed *pista* had been covered only with snow the view downward would still have been enough to chill the blood, but it had rained the previous night and the whole thing was a sheet of ice. We were about a mile up the mountain and we had this highway of frozen water diving past us. Everyone else edged their way across successfully to where the soft snow started again on the far side, but I was the one who lost his edges and started down like a crate of pig iron. As I approached the speed of sound, I could only just hear my instructor's voice as he came streaking down after me crying 'Joe! Joe! No, Joe!' He called me Joe because he couldn't manage the name Clive (no Italian can: it comes out as 'Cleevay' if you're lucky), and he was yelling 'Joe, stop! Stop, Joe!' He had the English word for 'stop', but if I had known how to stop I wouldn't have been on my way through the sound barrier on the road to certain death, would I, you dumb bastard? His next shouted imprecation was even more useless. 'Too fast, Joe! Too fast!' Luckily, when he got below me, he managed to get his skis in parallel under mine and bring us both to a halt only about a kilometre below where my family, with varying degrees of compassion, were watching the nominal head of the house revealing his fragility on the path to oblivion. Trembling all over in the nearest I have ever come to liquid fear, I vowed to shake the ice crystals from my heels and never ski in Italy again. Too many people knew me. As I started the long slog of chipping my way back up the glacier there were groups of people on either side of it taking photographs. One of them had a little film camera.

So we went to Davos, which is a bit more swish, and has many slopes kinder to the average skier, as part of the Swiss plan to send every visitor home happy. Even the black runs are less likely to get you killed, and on the red runs I fancied my style. My wife, naturally elegant in everything she does, was a neat skier, but she knew she was no Ann-Marie Moser-Pröll. With her sensible nature, she could take it when our elder daughter, thriving on the advantage of having started as an infant, turned into a notably graceful expert who could slalom down a mogul field like a gull through waves, and even our younger daughter collected a medal for going downhill faster than the other tots in her class, many of them wearing designer crash helmets bought by doting mothers in mink hats. I couldn't take it at all. If you make your start, as I had, by doing stem turns, it is frustratingly hard to persist with a parallel turn when things get sticky: you revert to the stem, as a badly trained singer in a panic will revert to singing from the throat instead of the diaphragm. Still relying too often on brute force – always the main reason why men learn more slowly than women – I bullocked my way down a tight gully when I should have linked carved turns together. Instead of winding a silent, snaky trail down the fall line, I hauled myself noisily though a rough and unlovely zigzag. But there was a long, empty, straight and inviting slope ahead, ending about half a mile down with a set of apparently gentle bumps. With the rest of the family behind me, I went into full Franz Klammer mode and dived down hill with my speed building up all the time, like a P-47 leaving behind a flock of Me 109s. For almost a minute I just kept on going faster until there was no faster I could go. My velocity was far beyond the point where I could contemplate any kind of turn at all. But I didn't have to turn. I just had to negotiate the first bump. I did, but I went airborne, nosed over and, after long enough in the air to mentally rewrite my will, hit the speeding snow with the full length of my body from nose to toe. The quick-reaction bindings worked all right and my skis came off in the advertised manner, but there was no such automatic mechanism to prevent the loops of my ski-poles from practically pulling my thumbs off even before I had come to a sobbing halt halfway up the next bump.

After what seemed an age the family accumulated around my crucified form, kindly asking if anything was broken. Judging from the pain, almost nothing wasn't. After I reassembled myself I was ready to pretend that it had all been planned as a comic routine, but the agony in my thumbs prompted involuntary cries that rather spoiled the effect. Advised to turn myself in at the clinic and have my thumbs put in plaster, I typically preferred to wait until the piercing throb went away by itself. Decades later it still hasn't.

This disinclination to get my medical problems attended to has been with me throughout my life. I would like to think that it sprang from a magnificent detachment from material concerns, but I can't deny that there might be an element of fear. The doctor, like the dentist, is a judge of behaviour, and I quailed at the thought of being sentenced. Even if I had been blessed with moral courage, however, I would probably always have been inclined to just let things go. I lack the time. I have things to do. To the objection that procrastination is bound to cost me more time in the end than prompt attention would have cost me at the start, and that I would have got more done if I had been sensible, I can only answer: don't you try reasoning with me. To be aware of the doomed struggles going on within my soul, however, gives me an edge as a commentator on politics and culture: I know from internal evidence that the capacity of the human mind to fool itself can be infinite. Turpitude, even when it looks energetic, almost always springs from mental sloth. When the real Berlin was burning all around him, Hitler went back to tinkering with the scale model of his dream Berlin which would never now be built. Rather than face facts, he took refuge in his art. Greater artists than him have done the same. Think of Charlie Parker, who must have known that drugs would kill him. He even knew that they made him play worse. In fact he said so. But he went on reaching for the needle anyway. You can see the whole picture and still miss its point.

For the last two days of the holiday I sat alone in the bar of our hotel, working on the opening chapters of a second novel, for which my provisional title was *The Remake*. Perhaps the spasms in my torn thumb muscles had gone to my brain, because I found myself planning a book which was bound to fail. It was going to be a novel comprising all the modernist narrative techniques that I most hated. Thus I would demonstrate that I cared nothing for my reputation. Looking back on the self-immolating folly of this intention, I can't counsel firmly enough against the inadvisability of deliberately flouting elementary propriety, especially for anyone whose reputation is already under threat. Inviting your critics to come and get you is a very bad way of proving that you don't care what they say. But I already knew all that, and planned to put it in the book. It would be a book about the centrifugal multiplicity of a personality. It would even be a book about the monumentality of its author's stupidity. It would be a book with everything, which is rarely a good aim with which to start out, because it courts the employment of overloaded prose. Luckily there was a compelling reason to dictate that the opening lines of my suicide note would at least be carefully composed. With my right thumb useless, I had to hold my pen between the next two fingers. As a result, the dangers inherent in fluency were staved off, at the rate of about one paragraph per hour.

On the plane home to England, with my thumbs held erect, I distinguished myself by transferring the food on my plastic tray directly into my lap. It is always a bring-down when the people to whom you are most closely related can't bear to watch you eat. When I went to the toilet I had a lot of trouble with the zip and what happened next was a farce, as if I was trying to aim an unlit cigar. In cold weather it still happens. Laugh, Pagliaccio. But the new studio show was waiting for me to join it, and the pain in my thumbs was soon sidelined by the pressure in my head. There was a lot to think about.

7. THE WEEKLY STINT

The bulk of the weekly show would consist of interviews, and there would be only two ways of doing those, well or badly. But the top of the show offered multiple ways to go wrong. I had seen too many talk-show hosts struggling in vain with an unpunctuated opening solo spot. Theoretically it should have been interrupted by the spontaneous laughter of the studio audience but all too often it had to be interrupted by enforced hysteria that sounded even more embarrassing than silence, as if Stalin was doing a stand-up routine for the Politburo and the penalty of not splitting one's sides was to get it in the neck. What I wanted was an illustrated solo spot. Such a device had been a feature of American television talk shows since the earliest days. In my time as a TV critic I had mugged up on what the Americans did. Mugging up was harder then than now, because there were no discs or tapes, but when I was in New York on other business I would spend every spare hour surfing the channels on the TV set in my hotel room, looking for re-runs.

Partly I had wanted to confirm my suspicion that the British front-men were getting nowhere, but I would have done it anyway out of sheer admiration. The famous Johnny Carson always had plenty of props he could react to. In a later day, even Dick Cavett, the best solo talker of the bunch, always had other stuff on screen so that he could snatch a few minutes being a voice without a face, and his face was a lot nicer than mine. Such ploys were already in a high state of development before British critics, who often had only a slight knowledge of American broadcasting history, credited David Letterman with inventing them. Invention almost always has a tradition behind it. As with poetry, all the revolutions are palace revolutions. Totally original innovators – Ernie Kovacs in the US, Spike Milligan and Kenny Everett in the UK – are very rare. I had no ambitions as a revolutionary. But there were new things I had seen done that I thought could be further developed.

Fake news was the first. The editing process was getting fast enough to yield usefully short clips. A few of them – only a few, the percentage was vanishingly small – could be given a misleading voice-over that might have a high yield. And perhaps a quick story could be told through a succession of misleadingly explained stills. Reciting the wrong words over the right still: today it is such a standard technique in television comedy that a long-running show such as *Have I Got News For You* will use it as a closing number, but the idea began with us, and like most new ideas it had to evolve from something more primitive. We called stills 'cards' and sometimes we used a dozen cards to tell a single story. During the first series of the weekly show the number of cards got down to three or four, and in the next series it got down to one. Looking back from now, it seems obvious that we should have started that way. Similarly, most of the bits of fake-news footage were far too long, so that I was writing a whole paragraph when a single sentence would have done. To put it briefly, the secret is to put it briefly. But you always think that's what you're doing, until experience teaches you that you aren't being brief enough.

It took a while to get all these gimmicks up to speed. With the interviews there was less to learn. Richard already knew that there had to be a pre-interview, conducted by a researcher. Without that, I would not have been able to go on prepared. More importantly, the pre-interview ensured that the guest would go on prepared. Try to skip that preliminary stage and there was a distinct chance of the whole thing going haywire. Nobody, for example, can answer a question like 'What's the most embarrassing thing that ever happened to you?' if you ask it cold. The guest has to know that you're after the story about the time he forgot his glasses before dinner at Sandringham and stubbed out a cigarette in the Queen Mother's crème brûlée, or the story about how he broke wind during an audience with the Pope. Otherwise the answer will be waffle at best, dead air at worst. Admittedly there can be cases of a thoroughly prepared guest pulling a deliberate double cross, but it hardly ever happens. Unfortunately I think it happened to me quite early on, with results that came close to spooking me for keeps.

One of our earliest guests was the politician Michael Heseltine, by then well embarked on the voyage to glory that would eventually convince him he might successfully challenge Margaret Thatcher for the leadership of the Conservative Party. Still handsome today, in those days he was gorgeous, with a head of hair borrowed from Veronica Lake and the sculpted face of a Viking diplomat. Our researcher came back from the pre-interview clutching her heaving bosom while she breathed in short gasps, like a nymph reviving from the embrace of Pan. *Yes, Minister* was in the first flush of its well-deserved renown and naturally she had asked him if he had seen it. He told her that he had watched every episode. He could quote the dialogue. He thought it was brilliant. So I had my first question all set to go, and half a dozen follow-up questions on the same subject. This was going to be a breeze.

On studio night Heseltine arrived in a succession of fast cars and swept into the building through corridors of throbbing female hearts. The make-up girls had drawn straws to get the job and the winner found that she had nothing to do except tone down his radiance with a light dusting of talcum powder. After I had finished my opening spiel, Heseltine loped into position while the studio audience drew its collective breath in vain, his charisma having instantly burned all the oxygen out of the air. The press, imprecise as always, had taken to calling him Tarzan, but surely this was Siegfried emerging from a quick dip in the Rhine, or Achilles on furlough from the battlefields of Troy. After

a few routine compliments I levered my first softball into the
launching tube and let him have it.

'I know you're fond of *Yes, Minister* . . .'

'Never watch it.'

'Oh, come on, surely, as a politician, you . . .'

'Never seen it. Too busy.'

I could see myself on the monitor, looking exactly like
someone caught in a fusillade of flying shit. Somehow I got
through the next twenty minutes but I was a whole week getting
my brains back. Luckily there was soon plenty of evidence to
prove that preparation was useful, and often crucial. I risk skip-
ping forward in the chronology here, because when you interview
hundreds of people over the course of years the order of memories gets shuffled in your mind, and I never kept a file of the
tapes. Someone, somewhere, will have a list of all the names and
times, but I rather hope that I'm never told. I remember the
stand-outs because they taught me lessons. Basically they divided
into three categories: self-starters, normal human beings and
walking disasters.

A self-starter is someone who could have done the whole
interview on his own. Neither Ruby Wax nor Mel Brooks has
ever really needed to be asked a question, and if they were on
screen together they would probably explode, like matter meeting
antimatter. While he lived, and arguably for a considerable time
after, Peter Ustinov was the supreme example, closely followed
by the young version of Billy Connolly, the one whose goatee
had not yet been dyed purple. (Nowadays Stephen Fry would
be high on the list, but we are talking about a previous epoch,
when the new kids were on their way up but had not yet taken
over.) I met Ustinov quite early on and he was even more
bounteous with his gifts than I had expected, like a Father
Christmas who arrives with a sack full of toys and immediately
sets about manufacturing new ones in case you don't like the
ones he's given you already. As he settled back into his chair with
his cherubic face rising like the sun over the global curve of his

paunch, I only had to press the ignition switch and he was off and away with a stream of memories, impressions, illustrated short stories and sound effects. Russian ballet dancers met German generals. Hollywood producers hob-nobbed with the clientele of a hamburger joint in Nepal. Jet airliners took off. Marlene Dietrich recited Milton. This guy was a universe.

All these miracles were conjured into being while scarcely anything moved except various components of his face. He knew everything about what his features looked like on camera and could control each one of them individually. So you saw the whole history of his film career being reprised: the petulant sneer of Nero, the wearily arched eyebrow of the Devil's Island convict in *We're No Angels*, the infinitely thoughtful pout of Hercule Poirot. Even his nose could act, as when his separately flared nostrils evoked the favourite racehorse of the Maharajah of Cooch Behar. The only drawback with someone who can ask all his own questions is that you don't get much of a chance to ask him anything hard. Ustinov was a frequent guest in the Soviet Union and there were some of us who thought that his cosiness with the Kremlin was a pretty dubious form of détente at a time when dissidents were still getting shrink-wrapped in blankets, but he only had to launch into his imitation of the late Comrade Brezhnev and you saw that it would have been in bad taste to slow him down. He was the most variously gifted man I ever met in my life, but he would have been the first to admit that versatility can be a kind of limitation. Indeed he would admit it unprompted. Prompting of any kind was something he had never needed.

With Billy Connolly you got the same torrentially original effect except that he couldn't stay in his chair. Years later, when I interviewed him again in a satellite link-up from London to Los Angeles, it was the same deal: the material was different but he did the identical imitation of St Vitus winning a break-dancing competition. He was supposed to be standing upright in a tight head and shoulders shot but he kept disappearing sideways and

suddenly returning as a mad British officer, or sinking through
the bottom of the screen before surfacing in the role of Esther
Williams being goosed by a dolphin. In the studio for the first of
his several interviews with me, he used his chair as the merest
reference point while he darted about. A camera on its pedestal
was still a heavy item in those years and the men who operated
them needed muscle. The bloke behind Billy's camera had to do
a lot of abrupt hauling and he put his back out, which must have
hurt worse because he was already convulsed with laughter like
everybody else. The important thing to note here is that Billy
wasn't doing a set routine. It was all coming off the top of his
head, accompanied by a wild stare which suggested that if he
hadn't been doing this for a living he would have been beating
people up at random. One of his best performances in the movies
was as a psychopath hiring himself out as a debt-collector: he
was so frighteningly believable that the film was almost immediately forgotten. It was called *The Debt Collector* and those of us
who saw it are still having bad dreams. There are famous actors
who can't act anything like as well as that, a fact which tells
you a lot about acting. To a great extent it's for people who can't
do much else, and Billy could do everything. The self-starter,
simply by his nature, can give you an idea of the reservoirs of the
human mind, because everything he remembers is at the service
of his powers of fantasy. In more than twenty years I met a bare
half-dozen of them. It was a revelation every time. All I had to
do was whip the top occasionally and I soon learned to confine
my intervention to a single flick. There was only one of them
who made me wish for a supply of tranquillizer darts instead,
and that was Freddie Starr, of whom more later. He popped up
near the end of my television career and belongs in the last
chapter, or perhaps in a separate book, made available in a plain
wrapper to the kind of customer who watches television with his
Rottweiler.

Ordinary human beings could be no less brilliant – some of
them were even more so – but they would stop to think. Joanna

Lumley was such a good actress that she could imitate a self-starter, but as her host I had to think of what to ask next, which wasn't always easy as I sat there in the extra light of her beauty. She was full of interesting opinions and perfectly fluent in expressing them, but she wouldn't just run on. She had been too well brought up for that, and didn't want to speak out of turn. Charlotte Rampling suffered from the same well-bred politeness but was shy as well, so I had to dig, making a constructive response every time instead of just grunting with approval. Peter Cook, who could give you a whole show for an answer, still needed a question. Tom Stoppard was another human being, despite the contrary evidence provided by a creative mind from outer space. I had known him for years and was well aware that I would never meet anyone quite so clever. But he was one of those rare clients who made me wonder whether a pre-interview was any use. He had given the ferret a set of shapely answers but when I reproduced the same questions in the studio he steered clear of giving the same answers again. He looked for different words, which took time, so the hair-trigger effect he gave in real life was slowed down to mere articulacy. He changed the stories because he was too original a speaker to use the same words twice. There was a lesson there. Preparation can be inhibiting.

But its absence could be crippling. The enchanting young actress Emily Lloyd was still a long way short of getting used to all the attention. She became available at the last minute and there was no time to prep her. Richard, always the king of the bookers, booked her anyway, but I could tell he was worried, and the worries proved well-founded. She lost the plot after the first question and took mental refuge in the nursery, doing the on-screen equivalent of hiding behind the doll's house. From her eyes, I could tell what was going on in her mind. 'I'm supposed to be saying wonderful things but I'm being boring.' From my eyes she could tell what was going on in my mind. 'This girl is drowning and it's my fault.' It was agony for both of us, because if I ever had one virtue as a host it was a determination to make the guest look good. What I should have done was take my cigarette lighter out of my pocket, set fire to my finger, and ask her to comment. But I was no longer a smoker. So, as one tends to do in a crisis, I reverted to a bad habit, and started giving the answer along with the question. 'And now that you're established as a star of the big screen I suppose the offers are coming in and you have to choose between them and that must be difficult because some of them are challenging roles but they wouldn't be a commercial success while others wouldn't really extend your range but they could be useful in consolidating your career as star of the big screen who . . .' Nightmare.

In the editing room the wizards saved her life, cutting the interview down to a few minutes in which almost nothing happened except a pretty girl looking bewildered while a desperate man babbled on. Even when she smiled, she looked as if she were trying to conciliate a burglar. I could have shot myself, because she got some of the blame that should have gone to me in its entirety. It couldn't have been as bad as I remember it, but it was bad enough to instil in my bruised mind a deep resolve to be ready, always, for the guest to freeze. When the guest is in command, he can yes–no you and he will still look good. In the old days of *Late Night Line-Up* there was a notorious live interview when the irascible playwright John Osborne answered all of Sheridan Morley's questions within two minutes, saying 'Yes' or 'No' and nothing else. When Sherry had run through the list of questions written on his sheet of paper he had to start thinking of new ones. 'Read any good books lately?' was the first. (Osborne's answer was 'No'.) Sherry, by now no longer with us, was normally a pretty relaxed customer. Later on, in the twilight of his career, he operated as a drama critic and was famous for falling asleep in the first act a few seconds after the lights went down. But I'll bet the memory of that evening was among his death-bed flashbacks. Osborne, on the other hand, undoubtedly never gave it another thought. Bastards have no remorse.

When the guest is not in command, the host has to get in and help or he will have blood on his hands. Determined to avoid that, I gradually extended my range of techniques for helping the guest to be no less interesting than he would have been in normal circumstances. The prepped anecdote helps because if the guest forgets it, or any essential part of it, you can supply it for him. The moment you do that, of course, the audience knows that you already know. So you have to admit it, and make a joke of it. If that sounds artificial, remember that the whole deal is artificial anyway, and trust the audience to enjoy your discomfort. As long as the audience isn't enjoying the guest's discomfort instead, you're in the clear. The first essential for the interviewer is to realize that the conditions in a television studio have about the same relation to everyday life as mechanized warfare. For ordinary human beings it's as freaky as hell and you have to guide them through it, even at the risk of your own skin.

And then there are the walking disasters, most of whom must remain nameless. On radio, the walking disaster is usually the pundit – sometimes of professorial rank – who starts making hand signals to illustrate a point. On television the contrary applies: he is the celebrity who is all words, and can't cut a story short to save his life or yours. Some of the older and more laurelled British actors could be very dangerous that way. There was one patriarch of his profession who, in the standard patois of upper Thespia, insisted on referring to Laurence Olivier as 'Larry' and John Mills as 'Johnny', so that you and the audience had to figure out who he meant. But there was worse in store. When it came at long last to the climax of one of his protracted anecdotes, he would start saying 'Johnny' instead of 'Larry' and vice versa, so that you couldn't figure out anything. As he droned on, the screen filled up with warm, pink fluff, but you could say he had a kind of charm. There was a Welsh white-collar trade-union leader called Clive Jenkins who couldn't have been credited with any charm at all.

Clive Jenkins is dead now, a fact which moves me to only the minimum of grief, because the memory of his sneering whine

and self-satisfied grin is still with me. I promise that I tried, but
the jig was already up before I had finished asking my first
question, because he was fishing out of the inner top pocket of
his suit a document folded thickly as a cosh. After straighten-
ing it out he began to read aloud a list of prepared objections
to something I had once said about him in print when I was
television columnist. Since he would have needed several hours
to get right through it, this was an example of his lack of realism,
but let's not leave out the piercingly unpleasant nature of his
voice, which might have been designed to provoke the English to
subdue Wales all over again and put its every last male citizen to
the sword. There are varieties of the Welsh accent that can bind
you with a spell – Lloyd George was the great example, and I
always love listening to Terry Griffith's snooker commentaries –
but the version spoken by Clive Jenkins wasn't one of them,
largely because it so successfully expressed his personality. In all
my adult life, the human character trait that I have been least
able to understand is a misplaced sense of superiority, and for
some reason it always shows up in the voice first. 'You see' is a
tip-off phrase, meaning 'You don't see but I'm here to help you.'
But there is an intonation that means the same thing, and some
people are never free of it. The mere existence of Clive Jenkins
was enough to prove that the voice, when it comes to broadcasting on television, is even more important than the face. The face
of Clive Jenkins made you want to hit him. But his voice made
you want to shoot him. He was on the air for ten minutes and
we lost a quarter of a million viewers.

It took a few weeks to get them back again, but on the whole
the studio show was a ratings success, and some of its features
were quickly copied, especially the fake news. The trick of identi-
fying full-face photographs of Yasser Arafat as being glamour
portraits of Yasmin Arafat, the Palestinian beauty queen, was
instantly popular. I would still pull the same stunt today, although
I probably wouldn't be allowed to, because political sensitivity
has not only distorted taste, it has become a substitute for it. But

I regarded Arafat not just as a terrorist, which he admitted, but as an enemy of his own nominal cause, which I myself believed in. In common with every liberal in Israel, many of them in that country's armed forces, I thought that the Palestinians should have their own state, and that Yasser Arafat was not a good choice of leader to help them get it. Saying that he had an unpleasant face seemed a valid shorthand for saying that he played an equally unpleasant political role. So the trick was more or less true. My views about the legitimate use of fake news centred on that principle. The fake news had to reflect the reality of the real news. Nowadays, the material presented as real news is often in itself fake news. The consensus of perception dictates the supposed facts. President George W. Bush, of whose acumen no opinion could be lower than mine, never did serve his troops a plastic Thanksgiving turkey in Iraq. The *New York Times*, professedly a journal of record, ran that story on page one. When they found out the story was false they ran their correction on an inside page. The correction probably wouldn't have worked even if they had printed it as a screaming headline. The image of Bush and the plastic turkey proved unstoppable.

Neither did President Bush ever say 'Mission accomplished' aboard an aircraft carrier after the quick defeat of Saddam Hussein's armed forces. The captain of the aircraft carrier hung up a banner with those words on it, and Bush was photographed in front of it while saying something to the contrary, namely that there was a hard road ahead. Similarly with the general perception that Bush said Nelson Mandela was dead when Mandela was still alive. Bush never said it. He was saying that any Nelson Mandela figure in Iraq was already dead because Saddam Hussein had killed him: a reasonable statement. Yet even after it was established that Bush had meant the reasonable thing and not the erroneous one, Jon Stewart, one of the sharpest US television front-men, kept the joke in because it was too good to leave out. This erosion of the concept of objective truth grows more disturbing all the time, but I don't think that our first tentative experiments in deliberate distortion back in the 1980s were the cause. Fake news was for entertainment, real news was for information, and the first thing wouldn't even have been effective unless the viewing public had a firm grasp of the second. Our viewers got the point and we were duly rewarded with their attention. They switched the show on again to get more. Buoyed up by this response, I got better at unifying the show's written material with a consistent style, but it was a hard task to fulfil all on my own. I might have faltered under the load had I not been so convinced that my whole multiform enterprise depended on it.

The studio show's overheads were covered in-house, so it was a cost-effective prospect for the channel as long as enough people watched it. That being so, the studio show paid for the special documentaries like the Postcard programmes, which would have been impossibly non-profitable had they been the only thing I did. The relationship between these two main kinds of production was to hold true wherever we went in the next two decades, from ITV and Channel 4 onward to BBC2 and BBC1, and finally into independent production, by which we made programmes principally for ITV, where we had started off. We would never have had the opportunity to navigate the full circle – or, to put it more crudely, to play both ends against the middle – if the studio shows had not been there to fund the adventure. It wasn't a case of robbing Peter to pay Paul. It was a case of keeping Peter healthy so that he could pay for Paul, his more refined but less employable elder brother.

8. ECONOMY OF EFFORT

This capacity to finance a fragile element by building up a bank with a more robust element was equally crucial in my continuing career as a writer. Jonathan Cape, in the person of its senior editor Tom Maschler, was ready to publish my books of essays, which didn't really make any money, just as long as I went on writing autobiographies that did. My second book of memoirs, *Falling Towards England*, risked queering the pitch: it was set in the 1960s, which everyone supposed to have been a fun time, but the way I told it I wasn't whooping it up at the party, I was shivering outside in the cold with my nose pressed to the glass. Luckily the public went for my story anyway, and Cape had renewed reason to go on publishing my less profitable essay collections just to keep me happy. Maschler was no profligate, but he was canny enough to know that a happy writer might write more books of memoirs and even a couple of novels that would get on the bestseller lists as *Brilliant Creatures* had done. That second hope was duly screwed when *The Remake* came out to be greeted by universal execration. One of the London reviewers kindly said that it wasn't a real novel but it was more enjoyable than most novels. I would have settled for that, but he was the only critic in the country who said anything like it. The critic who said that *The Remake* was a boundary-busting excursion into the ironic formal possibilities of the post-modern novel was working for the *Jerusalem Post*.

None of this would have mattered if the public's reaction hadn't so exactly echoed the critical reception. The book tanked. Later on I was to learn that it had taken away some of the readership I had already acquired for my first novel, so that my third and fourth novels had to start out in a smaller market, populated by those who were not afraid of experimental novels. Most people, very sensibly, were. I remain proud of all four of my novels – indeed *The Remake*, the infectious catastrophe, has some stretches of writing in it that I would have to pedal hard to equal now – but there can be no doubt that as a total effort they barely featured in the black ink of Cape's account books. Still, enough of my titles had been commercially successful to convince Maschler that it would be worthwhile publishing anything more marginal that I might come up with. Both to me and Cape, however, it was important that my books of essays would earn prestige even if they earned no money, because the publisher himself is always engaged in a balancing act: he wants some of his writers to be news stories in the heavy papers, so as to protect the house against the charge that its other writers are only there to please the crowd.

From that angle I was a reasonable prospect. I couldn't complain about the critical reception of my non-fiction books. In the heavyweight journals they were usually given to the best-qualified reviewers and almost always taken seriously, to the extent that there were polite sighs of regret that I should be wasting my time on television. But exactly there lay the problem: a serious man wasting his time can easily find himself regarded as a timewaster trying to be serious. Most of the adult papers had already grown the arts equivalent of a gossip column by that stage and in these new message boards any coverage of my work always began with the assumption that a would-be Hamlet had been stripped of his paint to reveal the clown. Obviously I would be running this risk for as long as I tried to circle the ring with one foot on each horse. But there was no quick way out of it, because the relationship which applied in television between the studio show and the filmed specials, and which applied again, in the literary field, between popular writing and serious criticism, also applied, in my total working economy, between broadcasting and literature.

I was no economist, but even I could do the sums. Taken for all in all, my books did well enough, but if I had done nothing else then they would all have had to do well, and even better. Failing that, I would have been up against it, and my family along with me. My wife was a respected academic who would always be in demand from the leading universities, but an academic salary weighs only so much on the property market. The same is true for books, even when successful: getting overcommitted to property is one of the standard financial mistakes those writers make who get an early hit, and then discover, when the tax bills come in, that they are under fatal pressure to write another. It was television that made a civilized life possible for my family, and made it possible for me to write only from inner compulsion, and never to a market imperative. As a clincher, it was television that made it possible for me to go on writing poetry, ever and always at the heart of my desire. If I had done nothing except write books, there would have been no time for poems, because any poem pays less than nothing even when it earns you a cheque. In 1982, with the kind encouragement of Karl Miller, I had serialized a long ottava rima poem in the *London Review of Books*, of which he was then the editor; and Cape later published the poem as a slim hardback under the title of *Poem of the Year*; but the advance for the book would barely have bought me a sack of apples, and the royalties added up to a resounding zero. I still rate it as my best long poem and have never begrudged the months it took to compose, but financially it was less than a dead loss. Money and time are forms of each other, and there is no poem that does not cost the poet a hundred times what he gets paid for it. Poetry, the centre of my life, has always been the enemy of my material existence, and even now, after fifty years of writing it, it is still trying to put me out of business.

The foregoing disquisition might make it seem that I had

everything weighed up. The opposite was true. I was working from instinct. Nowadays I sometimes get the credit, and often the condemnation, for having invented the idea of a multiple career, but I had no such idea in my mind, or even the time to think about it. Empire-building was the last thing I aspired to. For an empire you need a central stream of royalties and residuals, like Dolly Parton, who could never have built Dollywood if she had not already sold millions of records, and would not now be giving gazillions of dollars away to charity if she had not first built Dollywood. Television paid well, but the era when programmes would go on selling forever on tape and disc had not yet arrived, and we were all paid upfront in what amounted to a permanent buy-out of our rights. (Benny Hill got rich from foreign sales because some condescending executive decided there would never be any, and tossed him the rights as a sweetener.) So it was a good deal but a limited one, and anyway, there was never any question of my having got into television by calculation. I got into it because I loved it, and I was well aware that I had been lucky to be given the opportunity. After all, I didn't look the part.

Despite a rigorous programme of pounding myself into the floor at the gymnasium three times a week, I was permanently overweight by at least a stone. I was never really overweight enough for the journalists to call me 'fat', but when they called me 'portly' I had no comeback. The kind of journalists who think a word like 'portly' has a sprightly, irreverent ring to it haven't really got any opinions worth bothering about, but I did my best not to give them an easy target. Also I thought I owed it to younger viewers not to scare them to death by the way I looked. I was working, however, with intractable physical material. Even had I slimmed to the proportions of Clint Eastwood, nothing would have coaxed my eyes out of their deep cavities: when I smiled on screen, it was the silent agony of a man facing a sandstorm. My hair, thin on top, had to be cut close if my head were not to look like a hard-boiled egg being squeezed in an astrakhan glove. Thus shorn and shaved, my features had the general air of belonging to a bureaucrat whose idea of a thrill might be to install a new accounting system in a regional office. This appearance was reinforced by the blue suit that was introduced for *Clive James on Television* and continued into the studio show. Not through inertia, but from inspiration on Richard's part, it was decided to retain the blue-suit look for the Postcard programmes. Later I coined a term for them – 'blue-suit documentaries' – but as usual there was no defining plan going in, only a descriptive term that we applied later. Wearing the blue suit on location simply made sense. If I wore it in every scene, any shot could be cut into any sequence, thereby providing a useful reservoir of coverage. In hot locations, when I had to abandon the jacket and roll up the sleeves of my blue shirt, we maintained that look in as many scenes as possible, for the same reason. Wittgenstein once told his new landlady that he didn't mind what he ate as long as it was always the same. For the presenter of filmed documentaries, the same rule applies: it doesn't matter what you wear as long as you don't change it. Two identical copies of the blue suit went with me to Dallas.

Of the several American cities we made films in during our first decade, Dallas undoubtedly was the least interesting, but it was a hot prospect for the network, because the executives had not forgotten that I had made a running gag out of the American television soap opera of the same name when I was a critic, and the time was not far in the past when even the BBC made a news story out of J. R. Ewing getting shot. By the time we got to the real Dallas, however, it had left the television *Dallas* looking like a hick town. There weren't many men wearing cowboy boots like J.R. and there were absolutely no women staggering around sloshed like Sue Ellen with her lipglossed mouth working away as if she were giving oral sex to the atmosphere. Instead there was business efficiency on all sides. Here was a sunbelt city as a new model for globalized America. Clusters of tall glass buildings hummed with computers processing electronic money.

Everything was highly organized except us, partly because Terence Donovan was in charge.

Richard had forgiven Donovan for his slapdash approach to our film about the Paris catwalks because the results had been so wonderfully glossy. For Dallas, Donovan, shuffling hugely on Richard's carpet, promised that he would put a clapperboard on every shot, so that the editor would not be once again reduced to dementia as he tried to synch up sound and picture. Donovan remembered that promise but he forgot all the others. He wasn't dishonest, he was simply inspired, but you don't want a director to be inspired until after he has done the housekeeping, and this elementary requirement was one that Donovan could rarely bring himself to meet, because he was so easily bored. About fifty floors up in a glass skyscraper freshly built by the magnate Trammel Crowe, we interviewed one of the sons of Trammel Crowe in his office, which looked out on a panorama of other skyscrapers, many of them also built by Trammel Crowe. The skyline thus provided the perfect backdrop for interviewing the favoured heir of a man who was building a city, but when I looked back to see what Donovan was up to I could tell by the angle of the camera that it wasn't pointing at the buildings. After the first change of magazines, I took a squint through the eyepiece and found out that it was pointing at a bare stretch of Arkansas. While the son of Trammel Crowe took the kind of phone call in which phrases like 'Meet you in Geneva' crop up with no artificiality at all, I whispered to Donovan that we needed the buildings.

'Nar, we don't want that.'

I tried to tell him that we did want that.

'Nar, everybody does that.'

Thus was the problem laid bare, loud and clear. Donovan didn't like shooting anything ordinary. When the footage of the son of Trammel Crowe interview got back to England, Richard took a look at it after it came out of the bath and he went off his head. Donovan got the news down the phone and behaved better after that, but he was always better at capturing the look of the thing than at getting the story. Luckily the look of the thing was a local form of hard currency. The fine women of Dallas spent much of their lives being 'best dressed' for charity events, which took place at the rate of three or four per week. Some of these best-dressed women, notably the beautiful Nancy Brinker, who was married to the inventor of the Chili's chain, had started out as models anyway. But they were all classy numbers and their frocks were beyond belief: Chanel, Givenchy and Dior couture originals were their equivalent of combat fatigues. (Armed with my experience of the Paris catwalks, I got a lot of traction with the women by being able to name the designers without asking, but any advantage was offset by the effect on the men listening in, who automatically assumed that I was a faggot.) The preposterous intensity of it all made for terrific pictures, and satire could not have improved on the endless speeches, in which everyone at the event was thanked individually for her donations to charity, as if people with billions giving away thousands were running Jesus Christ a close second in the magnitude of their sacrifice. I have always tried to be suitably respectful of the way the elite in any American big city centres the whole of social life on charity. A great deal of money flows towards good causes. But those involved, when they are not attending the fund-raising events in the evening, do nothing else with the day except get ready to attend, and there is little energy left over for what you might call the life of the mind.

Most of the conversations were about hair. Radiantly well-groomed women talked strident balderdash about what was happening on top of their heads. Being American instead of English, they talked it louder when the camera was on them. Donovan got the shots. But at a society party held in the hospitality room of the hotel where we were staying – which just happened to be Dallas's number-one boutique hotel, the Mansion on Turtle Creek – he forgot to get the shot which would tie me together with the visiting film star, who just happened to be Sophia Loren. She was in town to help the Crystal Ball Committee judge their best-dressed competition. Her advice could have been obtained in no other way except in return for an astronomical fee, and now here she was at the Mansion doing the social bit that always goes with the paid appearance and helps to make the fee seem smaller by taxing it with tedium. All the women present were dressed at least as well as she was but none of them were making any sense whatsoever as they yelled into her face, updating her on the latest news about hair. We got a few hundred feet of Sophia looking alarmed, as well she might have done. What we didn't get was a single shot to prove that I was at the same party as she was.

The Mansion on Turtle Creek had a hex on us. We were staying there at a discount, but the discount was the only thing that went right. It wasn't Donovan's fault. It was the fault of whoever had decided that Dallas needed a single-storey Hollywood-style hotel of unbelievable luxury. Unbelievable luxury, even when tasteful, is for Arab princes, Russian racketeers and other people with more money than sense. Normal human beings are uncomfortable when the en suite bathroom has enough towels for a symphony orchestra. The hotel was owned by the daughter of Caroline Hunt Schoelkopf, the richest woman on earth. The daughter, who was in town for precisely one day before she flew on to open a new hotel in Bogota, was the one responsible for making the Mansion's dining room the top spot for the best-dressed women to get together for Sunday brunch and eat half a strawberry each while the harpist played 'Stardust' and they discussed whether Trammel should buy Lichtenstein. But it was my idea to interview the daughter beside the hotel's swimming pool. I couldn't blame Donovan for that.

For reasons unknown, I had failed to notice that the hotel was directly under the flight path for the final approach into one of the main runways of Dallas Fort Worth Airport. Perhaps the wind had prevailed in another direction for the previous week, bringing other runways into use and leaving this one out. Perhaps the hotel itself had soundproofing to match its air-conditioning, which maintained the guests at such a delicately judged temperature that it was the outside air, when you emerged into it, that seemed to have been produced by a machine, possibly a blast furnace. Anyway, the swimming pool was out there under the sky. The daughter, looking very fetching in one of Jil Sander's first brushed-cotton trouser suits, sat neatly relaxed in a cane chair, showing the kind of confidence that comes to you when, having been born into a family of enormous financial power, you are encouraged to prove yourself by managing every hotel the family owns, up to and including the Mansion on Cobra Swamp in Kandahar, and, having successfully managed them, you are given them for your birthday.

She also showed patience, which was very good of her, because the planes, with all their flaps out and howling in low gear, were going over every couple of minutes. 'So when did you realize that your family was . . .' Pause for whine of approaching jet, howl of jet going over, whistle of jet sinking very gradually into the distance. 'Well, I guess it was when my father bought the Dallas Cowboys and . . .' Pause for whine of another approaching jet, etc. If we had been filming with two cameras the noise would have mattered less: we could have written it into the story or even made a joke of it. But when you have only one camera, you have to shoot the reverses on to the interviewer afterwards, and unless the background noise of the questions matches the background noise on the answers, you can't edit the results. Hence the advisability of finding somewhere soundproof for the shoot if you can't get into a studio. It was a lesson that I was pleased to learn, but learning it was expensive. A few more stuff-ups like that and we would have lost the movie.

We made just such another snafu when we interviewed Nancy Brinker *chez elle*. She lived in the size of house that you would expect the wife of the founder of Brinker International to own, but you wouldn't have expected the standard of interior decoration to be quite so high. Were there any Gobelins tapestries left in France? There were also cases full of real books, an item of property often absent from the decor of the American rich. The only tip-off was that it was all too clean. As for the chatelaine, she was a dream come true: cultivated, articulate, poised, funny. Donovan was so enchanted he had the idea of linking together the shots of her with suitably ethereal fades and mixes, leaving out the predictable reverses on me. We were short of time so I went along with it.

By the time we got back to London, Richard had already discovered that there was something strange about the Nancy Brinker interview. A beautiful woman was being interviewed by a ghost. On the other hand, the daughter of the richest woman on earth was being interviewed in the middle of an air-raid. But what had really wound him up was the society party where Sophia Loren was present but I had somehow failed to get myself into the same shot. About that he was, in his quiet way, apoplectic. To repair all this damage, we had to park the film for a year until the weather was right and then go back to Dallas, with Donovan conspicuously not in our company. With the same sunlight, and with me wearing the same infinitely valuable cheap blue suit, we got all those tedious but necessary covering shots – arriving at the hotel, leaving the hotel, arriving at the Chili's franchise, leaving the Chili's franchise – which Donovan had so sedulously dodged. We also went back to the Brinker palace, where we discovered that Nancy's pet decorator had repapered the walls of the room where we had interviewed her, so that when we shot the reverses that we needed, the wall behind me would look different from the wall we had already filmed behind her the previous year. It would have been a lot simpler just to ask her to do the interview again, and I'm sure the future United States Chief of Protocol and Ambassador to Hungary would have said yes: gracious diplomacy was among her countless virtues. But she had just been diagnosed with breast cancer and was confined to quarters. So we would have to make do with what we had. Doubtless it would cut together somehow: I could always say that she made a point of decorating each end of a room differently.

But what really counted was that we got back into that hospitality room in the Mansion on Turtle Creek. Richard talked a few of the society people from last year's bunch into dressing up again. Since they rarely dressed down, they found it no trouble to comply. In America, everybody loves being in the movie. They crowded around me while we got a shot of me staring symthetically at exactly the right angle to meet Sophia Loren's haunted glance as it had been captured the year before in the same room. I did a little smile to match a little smile from her that we already had in the bank. Actually she had been smiling in fear at some crazed woman raving about the beneficial effects of having split ends sealed shut by laser surgery and sprayed with ionized platinum, but the viewers wouldn't suspect that, especially after I wrote a suitably wistful line about intimate eye contact. If all this ducking and weaving had been taking place today, the tabloids would have loved to have a story about how I faked a close encounter with Sophia Loren, but in fact we weren't making up the shot, we were just getting the shot we should have got first time around. Much of the final work in a movie shoot always consists of getting the shot you should have got. You have to keep the ethics in mind – rescuing a sequence is one thing, telling a lie is another – but you always have to keep the ethics in mind anyway. To work in any art form requires an ethical decision every five minutes.

When we took the repair kit back to London all the patches fitted and Donovan's name as a director was saved, but Richard refused to use him again. I agreed, but couldn't help thinking it was a pity. I loved Donovan. He was so sweet and funny. But he was a star director, and in a presenter-led documentary special the man with his face on the screen had better be the only one with the artistic temperament, otherwise you will all be very soon be sharing an extended stay at the Mansion on Shit Creek.

9. WE'LL ALWAYS HAVE PARIS

The American cities should have been easy, if only because every American is in show business, so that there is no chance encounter that does not turn immediately into a scene: all you have to do is tone down the volume. But it was a European city that gave us the measure of what the Postcard format could do if it was approached in an orderly manner, instead of as an exercise in what Donovan himself had the grace to call 'kick, bollock and scramble'. Once again it was Paris, but this time there was no question of concentrating on the catwalks. We were out to do the whole thing. There was a lot of planning before we went, and we were better protected against caprice when we got there, because we had both a producer, Beatrice Ballard, and a director, Laurence Rees. Each would go on to a glittering career, but the important thing to note here was that both of them were naturally thorough and quick-witted – two qualities that often get in each other's road. They certainly needed the quick wits, because one of the first sequences on the roster starred Françoise Sagan, once a teenage novelist, now the first lady of the French literary world, and always and forever an *enfant* as *terrible* as they come.

The Renault company had given her a new car for her personal use, presumably on the understanding that they would benefit from the publicity even if she killed herself in it. When she was young she had insisted on driving her brand-new Aston Martin barefoot, thereby to demonstrate her carefree spirit. 'I shall live badly if I do not write, and I shall write badly if I do not live.' Bouncing alternately on its nose and its tail, the car, when it finally came to a halt, was in even worse shape than she was, which was saying something, because very few of her bones were left intact. Luckily her clever head survived to dream up more novels. When we met her, she wasn't so young any more but she still lived hard. Perhaps unwisely, our sequence with her had been planned to take place while she drove. The camera and the sound were in the back seat and I was in the front beside her, asking her questions while she kept on proving that the only way she knew how to drive was to go flat out. It must have been some kind of muscle disease, or perhaps the consequences of her first crash: her rigid leg jammed the accelerator against the firewall. My questions tended to fragment as we switched with yelping tyres from one boulevard to another, threading our way between cars driven by normal people and taking every red light as a sign to speed up. 'So when you first met Sartre what AAAGH! did he say?'

Uncannily she responded with coherent answers, possibly because she knew that the imminent crash wasn't going to happen even though it looked to me as if it had already commenced. It looked the same to the cameraman, who could see the road ahead through his eyepiece and got a lot of footage that trembled all the time even when she was driving on smooth asphalt. 'He say to me, you are so *yong*. He say, when you *leave* a little longer then you will have the *droit*, the *droit*, what is it?'

'You will have the AAAGH! the right.'

'Yes, yes, of course. Stupid of me. Then you will have the right to your despair. You want me to go more fast?'

'No, this is AAAGH! fine like this.'

The man we hit was carrying a briefcase. He was crossing the road, we heard a thump and suddenly there he was behind us, spinning like a weathervane in a storm. We must have hit the briefcase. 'We heat someone?' she asked me. The camera missed the spinning guy but it caught her face asking the question, and I knew that I would be able to put a narrative on it that would be funnier than seeing the bloke spinning on the spot. It was a wonderfully surreal sequence, all the mad speed made even funnier by the sudden stops every few blocks so that the great lady of French literature could scoot into a bar and powder her nose. Her powder of choice was an open secret. Everybody knew, including her friend François Mitterrand, then President of France. She knew all his secrets too. The Parisian elite were a tight crew, somehow made more so because they spoke their own language.

It was a language that I had been learning for years and am still learning now. My assistant Cecile Menon politely puts me though my pronunciation drills but I will never get to speak French well. I love to read it, though, and when we were filming *Postcard from Paris* I spent all my downtime trawling for books in the green boxes of the second-hand booksellers along the Seine. On a rest day for our crew I was bent over the treasure trove of a *bouquiniste* when a stocky figure in a well-cut dark blue suit showed up beside me. The discreet presence in the background of a couple of young men with earpieces tipped me off. It was Mitterrand. Instantly I remembered a river full of elephants, but I remembered also how I had not mentioned them, so that the crew would never know what they missed. We wouldn't have been able to sneak a shot of Mitterrand anyway. The *gendarmes* (the real gendarmes, not the ordinary *flics*) would have moved in and thrown us all into a van. Besides, I liked being alone with the books. When waiting in the car with my driver, I would read to him from Simenon or Maupassant while he winced at every second word before making me read the sentence again. A glutton for punishment, that boy. He taught me the French translation of a short speech that I dictated to him in English. 'The day when I am able to converse freely in French I will be very happy. Unfortunately, that day is still distant.' When I at last managed to memorize the French version in roughly the right accent it was highly effective in convincing any English-speaking people present that I was quite good at French: as long, of course, as they themselves were not.

In the future I was to make a point of learning an equivalent construction in any other language we ran into. Your friends are impressed and the locals applaud you for your eagerness. That, however, is as generous in the matter as the French commonly get. In Paris especially, they don't like to hear their beautiful language spoken in any way except to perfection. Beatrice, being a properly brought-up English girl, had French among her attainments. It came in handy when we were snatching a scene outside the cafe Deux Magots in the Boulevard Saint-Germain, because to turn the passing pedestrians into walk-on players took a bit of explaining. It took little persuasion: even more so than the Americans, the people of Paris want to be in the movie, because they think they might be helping the next François Truffaut, a national treasure, or Jean-Luc Godard, a national idiot but they love him.

But it wasn't enough to talk them into participating. We had to say what we wanted done. I liked the way Laurence Rees attacked himself when he couldn't make himself clear. He would dance on the spot, beat his breast, forget how to breathe. These were good signs, betokening an urge towards self-improvement. Beatrice was summoned from her hotel room full of paperwork, told what I was after, and set about roping in the punters. We were filming the passing parade for a sequence in which I would say that the women of Paris – not just the *grandes dames* but the office workers, the sales girls, everybody – gave a lot of time and thought to looking chic. Half an hour of filming had revealed that a general shot of the passing pedestrian traffic wouldn't do the job, because somewhere in the frame among the scores of glowing visions there was always at least one woman who looked like the captain of a tugboat. The only solution was to get upstream and do a bit of casting. Beatrice came with me while I singled out half a dozen impeccably qualified knockouts. On my behalf, she explained to them that they should each walk towards the camera at a given signal. See the camera along there at the cafe? Don't look at it while you walk. Just let it look at you. I would have sounded very foolish trying to explain all that and might well have been arrested by the car full of *flics* who were taking a close interest, even though Beatrice was armed with all the appropriate permissions. She was very good looking, so they wanted to check her papers.

While they did so, I went back to the cafe, sat down in the right spot, gave the signal and the first woman came swaying along as if she had been making movies all her life. All the others were equally good. In this way we secured a series of clean shots for which I could write a narrative at the rate of one line per shot. It was a lesson learned. If the scene has to make a particular point, assemble it out of particular shots: a general shot won't do the job. What made this sequence a breakthrough for me, however, was that I had spotted the problem beforehand and not afterwards, and had managed to convince the people working with me. There was a hidden requirement in that: they had to be smart enough to see the point. These two were, so we were in business. There were no prizes for spotting that young Beatrice was a class act but with Laurence it took a bit of imagination, because he carried on as talented young men often do, reminding himself of what he had to do next by sticking Post-it notes on everything including people, referring to himself loudly in the third person, dashing his ginger head against the nearest brick wall when he made a mistake. He would have been unbearable if he were not so clearly demonstrating an eternal truth about the arts: talent rarely looks poised early on. The naturally cool customer is seldom going anywhere. As it happened, Laurence Rees was going on to become one of the most significant writer-producers of factual television series in recent times. But he would not have been so effective in that valuable role if he had not known a lot about how to direct, because it meant that directors couldn't fool him. Television is a producer's medium, but the best producers know everything about direction, and a lot of what Laurence Rees knows about it he learned on *Postcard from Paris*, so I feel quite proud.

Laurence's speed on the uptake proved vital when we filmed

an interview with Inès de la Fressange at the madly fashionable
Café Costes. Inès, newly retired as a model for the couture salons
but still the official face of Chanel, was so famous that her mere
presence could reduce a whole city block to silence, as if she had
just stepped out of a spaceship. (The French don't mob their
celebrities but they have a way of revering them from a distance
that can stop the traffic anyway.) The Café Costes was the latest
creation of the designer Philippe Starck, always in the feature
pages for his ability to take some everyday object and reinter-
pret it, or deconstruct it, or generally futz about with it in ways
possible only to genius. Now he had done this to a whole cafe.
The conjunction of the celestial gloss of Inès de la Fressange and
the cutting-edge modernity of the Café Costes was a sure-fire
prospect. All we had to do was bring them together. When it
transpired that the conjunction could not be brought about
until after lunch, we spent the morning filming in the cafe's
downstairs toilet *pour les hommes*. What the toilet *pour les dames*
was like I don't care to imagine, but you can take it for granted
that the men's room had been reinterpreted to within an inch of
its life. Locks on the cubicle doors either didn't lock at all or
locked you in forever, thus reinterpreting the function of a lock.
Concealed in chromium fairings that echoed each other's formal
properties with a conscious play of irony, the reinterpreted soap
dispenser dried your hands while the reinterpreted hand-dryer
dispensed soap.

But above all, Starck had reinterpreted the relationship between
the urinal and the hand basin. He had played with daring semi-
otic irreverence upon their essential similarity. Those of us who
believed in their essential difference were in for a shock, as we
found ourselves washing our hands in the urinal after taking a
piss in the sink. It was at this point that I decided Philippe Starck
was *un ouanqueur* – a French word of my own invention which
has somehow never caught on in France – but I was also grateful,
as if all my Noëls had come at once. You couldn't dream this
stuff up. You had to get some fantasist like him to dream it up

for you. Laurence was already exhausted after the two hours of hard work it had taken to light the place – it is always much harder to film anything when there are reflective surfaces around – so I had no trouble convincing him that we wouldn't need to stage any action. All he had to do was get clean shots of all the naff gear and I could do the whole story with the commentary. Even with the hand basin and urinal combo, we wouldn't need any shots of me pretending to use them. I could just look at them, visibly abandon any intention of using either and walk out looking puzzled. Laurence's vital contribution was to make sure that I didn't overdo the looking puzzled. That much you can learn from your cameramen and directors, if you aren't afraid to ask. Most presenters overdo the facial expression because they haven't been often enough told that the camera can see what you think, so you don't have to act it out. When the adrenalin's pumping, however, hamming it up is difficult to avoid.

You are never more likely to ham it up than when you are registering surprise. In real life, surprise merely makes your face look puzzled for as long as it takes your brain to process the unexpected information. On screen, if you adopt a 'wow' face to convey your shock, it looks hopelessly over the top: better to do nothing. All this, of course, presumes that you are coping with the task of conveying appropriate facial reactions to a surprise you know is coming. Sometimes you get a real surprise, whereupon the problem solves itself, and you will remain nicely dead-pan unless you get the fatal urge to do a 'wow' face after you scrape off the custard pie. When we relocated the camera and the lights upstairs to the bar for the interview with Inès, I didn't immediately see the vaudeville possibilities inherent in Philippe Starck's idea of what constituted suitable furniture for a place where fashionable people might like to meet in order to drink, snack and talk about structuralism. The tables, though tiny, nevertheless had flat surfaces on which such things as drinks, cups of coffee and plates of pastries might conceivably be placed without falling instantly to the floor. The chairs, however, all turned out, on closer inspection, to have three legs. This was Starck's breakthrough concept. Chairs had had four legs each, one in each corner, since civilization had first emerged among the Ashurai people of Mesopotamia thousands of years before Christ, but now a genius was on the case. Still waiting for Inès to show up, I sat down on my allotted chair so that we could get my portion of the establishing sequence. Pretending to be reacting to Inès's shattering glamour – I had a standard stunned-mullet expression to fit that – I lowered my behind carefully into the hard laminated plywood seat of the three-legged chair.

I wasn't pretending at all when I fell sideways out of shot, the chair still magically attached to my behind as if it has been glued into position. On my way down, I was already aware that we would somehow have to capture my transition to the floor. This is where the experience of filming that I had already acquired came in handy. A wide shot that panned with me as I dived would have taken a lot of setting up and would have looked contrived anyway. All we needed was a tight shot of my face as I lay on the floor. In the editing room we could tack that shot on to the first one, in which I fell sideways out of frame. As long as I did a good enough job of looking stunned while I was lying down, it would all click. I remembered the way Oliver Hardy had always made a point of looking merely resigned after the house fell on him. Helping me to cut my performance back – as the stage actors say when they act for the screen – was my apprehension that the beautiful Inès might take a dive too. But when she came wafting in I could see straight away why she wouldn't be falling out of any chairs. She didn't weigh anything. She was six feet tall but she was made of light. This ethereal apparition was famous for never wearing the same kit twice, all the way down to her lucky underwear. For this appearance she had chosen a sort of sailor suit ensemble which would have been appropriate for Captain Nemo's social secretary on the *Nautilus*. During the

interview she told me that she always chose her outfit for the day
on the basis that it must tell a little *storee*. Today her *storee* was
of the sea.

She could have told me anything and I would still have
nodded with agreement, although every nod set me tottering on
my triangular base. Since we had asked the management to let
other people use the bar so that we could have some authentic
background, almost every answer from Inès was punctuated by
the sound of a new arrival sitting down on a three-legged chair
and hitting the floor with his face immediately afterwards. But
I could easily narrate all that. I didn't think that what either
of us said made a lot of sense even at the time, but she was
such a spellbinder that it didn't matter. Correctly guessing,
however, that the ambience would be at least as entertaining
as the interview, I asked the crew for a lot of extra coverage as
we arrived and left, so as to leave room for my comments on
the advanced designer's success in ironically dramatizing the
previously unexamined connection between chair and occupant.
Inès, as advanced a design as a human being could be, sailed
serenely away after assuring me that my blue suit told a *storee* of
– how could she put this? – of a man in a blue suit. 'You are not
chic, yes? And that is your *storee*.'

We filmed for two entire days down in les Égouts, the sewage
tunnels under the city, and after painstaking work we got a lot of
highly atmospheric footage which never made it past the first
fortnight of editing, because, in the end, people trump spectacle.
One of the people was completely unplanned for. The plan was
to track with me as I visited the cemetery of Père Lachaise, did a
tour of the gravestones and ended up at Proust's black slab, but
when we got to Edith Piaf there was already a fan watching over
her who might have been cast by the wraith of Jean Renoir and
sent down to me for just this moment. The fan was probably
in his seventies but might have looked younger if he had not
overdone the black hair dye, the mascara, the rouge and the
lipstick. He had loved her, however, and knew how to say so. He

said so in French, but one phrase at a time, so I could translate it aloud as he spoke. The antiphonal effect was elegiac beyond anything that could have been written and acted. In the trade you call it a 'snatched' moment and there can be no doubt that the snatched moments are often the best thing in the movie, but if you have to depend on them you are in trouble. They reward the diligent, as is proved by how they are always withheld from the careless.

10. KEEPING THE BALANCE

Like a tour of duty as entertainments officer in a nuclear submarine, filming got me away from home, but home was waiting for me when I got back. Leading a balanced life got harder all the time. The first hazard was the fame factor, which seemed to consist entirely of drawbacks even when they were construed, by others, as privileges. Straightforward irritations were relatively easy to handle. In the streets, large tattooed artisans whom one would not ordinarily have wanted to meet shouted, ''Ere! Ain't you that Clive Jenkins?' The temptation to say, 'Go screw yourself, my good man,' had to be resisted. Even the nicest version of this instant familiarity involved a lot of autograph-signing and dozens of involuntary conversations every day. It didn't happen in Australia, where my programmes, because they had been made in Britain, were resolutely kept from the screen by an ABC executive who took pride in protecting the Australian public from my disloyal voice. As a result, Australia was a reality check: when I went there on literary business, I got the mildly enthusiastic reaction appropriate to someone whose books have been read, or at any rate heard about. These bursts of normality served to underline the sheer weirdness of what happened when I got back to Britain and found myself shouted at by a whole building site full of workmen if I failed to stop and answer their questions about 'them Chinese'. (After several aborted interchanges I deduced that by 'them Chinese' they meant the Japanese game-show contestants.) Walking on, instead of stopping, was the only way to save something from the day, but the penalty was to be followed for half a block by loud shouts of 'Aren't we good enough for you any more, Clive?' In Soho one afternoon, Martin Amis was walking beside me when that question came raining down from above and he was fascinated. He still tells the story now, and I remain convinced that the hellish atmosphere of his middle-period novels was partly generated by that momentary revelation of mediatized insanity. One of the most unsettling aspects of being public property on that scale is that you are always addressed by your first name even when the message is abusive. 'Clive, you're a tosser.' At such moments I felt bound to agree, but if I had stopped to discuss the matter I would not have been able to call my life my own.

That Faustian feeling of having sold your life to the Devil is the real explanation behind the self-destructive behaviour of the younger celebrities. They got what they wanted, and it drove them nuts. As an older hand, I was better able to compute the odds, but staying clean wasn't easy. Sometimes wine, women and song look like the only place you can hide. (This can be especially true when you are out on the road, and stuck for the day in unfamiliar streets thronged by thousands of strangers all calling you aggressively by your first name. Any soft, kind voice sounds like a port in a storm, and artists on tour are often trailed by tabloid snoops in the hope that loneliness will lead to folly.) Since I would never have gone into show business in the first place if I had lacked the conviction that I was the natural centre of attention, to be a recognizable face fed a primal urge, but it could sap the very confidence it was meant to boost. 'Why are people suddenly so keen to ask me to dinner?' It must have been a question that nagged even Einstein.

Yet I quite liked being invited out into the beau monde. For one thing, in the border territory where gracious living meets the arts there are invariably more than a few women who are works of art in themselves, and I have always enjoyed the outlaw feelings that come with making a beautiful face laugh. For a heady instant you are Zorro, standing outlined in a window arch. A little less paunch under the cummerbund might have been appropriate, but for the moment I felt up to the part of making the great lady giggle. She didn't have to be a countess. She sometimes was, but the fun was just as intense when the woman on your left or right was, say, Alison Lurie. ('Write a *strange* novel,' she said to me, and I did. I wrote *The Remake*, thereby loading myself into a circus cannon after first having taken down the net.) At higher altitudes, where the British aristocracy hung out with the super-rich, the yield in verbal interest seldom matched the visual splendour. I didn't hear much said that I couldn't have made up after being injected with enough novocaine. On the other hand, there were pictorial aspects that I was glad to file away for future use. Some of the grand houses in London have stretches of garden behind them in which you could land a light aircraft, and you would never suspect the layout was even there just from looking at the front door. One night, in one of these game reserves for the privileged, I saw a vision crossing the moonlit lawn between two marquees.

She was the acknowledged supreme young beauty of the day. In that year her name was Charmian Scott, and her mere existence was a reminder that you can't make that sort of thing up. You have to see it. In fact you have to see it before you can even imagine that there might be something you can't make up. She was wearing an off-the-shoulder ivory and white ball gown and when she turned into profile the length of her perfectly straight nose looked like an echo of her collarbone. Now was the time to quote Keats, but my throat was full of wood shavings. Clearly, radiantly, she had been sent to Earth to marry a duke. A few months later she did, which made me feel better about not having said anything. Not that anything I could have said would have made the slightest impression, which was the real trouble with the whole scene. It was like being in a masque written by Milton, but the level of conversation was usually even worse. There was always some drawling Adonis sitting opposite me who wanted to save me from talking to the women I sat between. 'I must say that the things you get those Chinese chappies doing are a bit ripe.' I could hear better things than that on a building site.

Educated in a hard school to appreciate the fragility of their advantages, the renegade East European aristos were far better value. Nothing could beat a multilingual high-born widow who was ready to show her kinship with artists and philosophers by inviting them regularly to dinner, usually for the only civilized conversation they would have that week. This was far preferable to hearing from the landed gentry about land, or from financiers about finance. The most glittering salon was run by Diana Phipps, whose original surname was recorded in the *Almanach de Gotha*. Tall, stately and uncannily charming, she had a gift for getting the bright sparks together and giving them a taste of the high life without cramping their style. At the same table as David Hockney, Philip Roth, Harold Pinter and Sir Isaiah Berlin, it was flattering to be treated like one of the boys. Lord Weidenfeld was the London host who was most famous for inviting every-body at once, but here he was a guest, and obviously glad to be keeping company with people who spoke his language, which was the cosmopolitan language of the old European cafes – not of cafe society, but of the cafes themselves, the places where the bohemian intellectuals once gathered before the two great waves of totalitarianism washed the brains out of the old cities. Eaves-dropping while he compared notes with Alfred Brendel about the precious wreckage of the culture from which they came, I mentally composed a reading list as they talked, and a quarter of a century later I am still working through it. Brendel, who was just about to launch into his second recording cycle of the Beethoven piano sonatas, had strips of Elastoplast around his fingertips. I couldn't have envisioned that under hallucinogenic drugs. The most startling surrealism is always real. Brendel, whose knowledge of literature is on a level with his mastery of music, told me that I should read the essays of Alfred Polgar. I had never heard of Alfred Polgar, but it was at such moments that I knew I had come a long way from Kogarah. When I was roaming the grounds of some stately home I had merely come a long way from the front door, and there was nothing but a general impression. Here, all the impressions were specific. The names had faces and their mouths were in action. Harold Pinter, an actor to the core, would present his profile even if you were sitting in front of him, but his voice was a thriller: deep, resonant, the rumble of a gravy train. When he found an excuse to quote from Philip Larkin's great, late poem 'Aubade', Pinter would invariably quote the whole thing, to riveting effect. A political tirade, however, would sometimes inspire less unanimous assent, and a discussion might ensue during which his wife, Lady Antonia, who could get that kind of thing at home, would gently go to sleep, right there at the table. Her narcolepsy was a genuine affliction but it came in handy to block out boredom. Philip Roth was wide awake, alert to Pinter's opinions, and hated every one of them. At one point, when Pinter was blaming America for the destruction of Carthage in the third Punic War, Roth stood up and stormed out, taking Claire Bloom with him. It was a spectacular case of 'Darling, we're going home,' and I was there to see it. Noticing everything, I made a conscious effort to remember it all. If I couldn't take out a notebook and jot it all down, at least I could pay attention. But I also noticed the number of writers present who had begun to grow less productive a generation ago, and I quickly figured out where they had been. They had been here, entertaining each other instead of the public. Social life was a trap. Either you had a social life or you got things done. But the woman who taught me that would never have been in a position to teach it if she hadn't known all there was to know about the *douceur de vivre*, and I was glad to be instructed, although sometimes the lessons were painful. 'People don't want to be charmed. They want to charm.' It was a way of telling me to shut up and listen. Learning to keep my mouth closed occasionally as an aid to keeping my ears open, I became more sensitive to nuance, perhaps the most important French word in the English language.

Nearly all the terms in the English language that cover the subject of social grace are French, strangely enough. The British have almost no native vocabulary for the guiding precepts of the sweet life. If you rate *comme il faut* above *savoir faire*, as indeed you should, you will find it hard to say so in everyday English. Luckily I understood the phrases, even if I couldn't pronounce them. At such moments in their careers, men who have risen in the world often consecrate their elevation by starting a second marriage, usually after contriving to demolish the first. As Cyril Connolly – important critic, repellent man – once put it, 'The woman with whom one shares one's early struggles is rarely the woman with whom one wishes to share one's later successes.' The frozen symmetry of the expression is enough to show what's wrong with the idea. There is a certain realism to it – far too many of the marriages in my generation cracked up on that very rock – but the realism is bloodless. Nor was Connolly wise to neglect the possibility that the woman with whom one shares one's early struggles might decide that one is a twerp, and kick one out, being in possession of a mind of her own.

The advantage of having had a taste of the high life is that you are not thrown for a loop when you are offered a whole plateful. As a writer I thought that there were things I had to find out about how the world worked – one of the Devil's opening moves, when subverting the soul of an artist, is always to present the artist's thirst for privileges as a vocational duty – but I was too committed to my stock of common memories to trade it in for keeps. The family holidays continued to provide a steady stream of such treasure. The death dive at Bormio and the throbbing thumbs of Davos were regularly supplemented by the yield of stories from our annual fortnight in the sun at Biarritz. In the glory days of Biarritz, back in the nineteenth century, it probably rained less often. The Empress Eugénie would not have permitted more than a certain level of precipitation. In the early twentieth century, when Picasso was there, none of his paintings of prancing sea nymphs featured rain. For us, it rained almost all the time. The littoral of the Bay of Biscay is always a full ten degrees centigrade less hot than the Côte d'Azur anyway, but when you add rain to the cool, you can wonder why you came. Then the sun comes out again and you remember. On a sunny day the Côte des Basques was pretty without parallel: the *sable d'or* as soft as talcum, the sea like stretched shantung beyond the neatly foaming breakers, the tamarisks at evening glowing gold beside the pathways that led back up the cliff to dinner at Les Flots Bleus, a restaurant where everyone except me ate piles of *moules* six inches high. Our friend and landlord Michael Blakemore still invited, year after year, his actors and playwrights to join him at the beach. You would see Tim Pigott-Smith, still in character as Merrick from *The Jewel in the Crown*, snarling at a plate of *moules*. The lovely Nicola Pagett smiled at *moules* as if she hoped to charm them open. Robin Dalton, agent to John Osborne, negotiated with *moules*. Michael Frayn inspected a heap of *moules* as if the task was to deduce its molecular structure. My wife and Rhoisin Beresford could get through a hundred *moules* between them, the shells piling up like a midden. All these people were fascinated by *moules*. I could not stand *moules*. What else did the damned things do except lie there on the seabed imitating legless cockroaches while they ingested effluent?

But I loved everything else about Biarritz, and precisely because it was so predictable. Despite its grand name, resonant in cultural history, it was as small-time as the pair of warped espadrilles that the pretty girl finds in her cupboard in *Mr Hulot's Holiday*, my nomination for the title of best film comedy ever made. I was Mr Hulot reborn, with the difference that I had got the girl, and right at the start of the movie. Sunning themselves almost naked on the sea wall, there were pretty odalisques to whom less time had happened, but the woman I had married could still remind me, when she stood in the shallows outlined in her floppy hat against the oncoming twilight, of our first day together on Bronte Beach in Sydney, back there when she was hearing some of my jokes for the first time. For all too many men, and I am one of them, the realization can be a long time dawning that you won't really get to meet that beautiful young woman you just saw in the art gallery, because you already met her many years ago, and now you are getting old. With enough power and money you might conceivably persuade the beautiful young woman to become yours, and it will all be new again, but only for a while. It's the oldest story in the world, and what makes it a mockery is that you have missed the point: in a marriage you can't constantly regain the sense of discovery, you can only learn to value what has already been discovered. If it all depends on novelty, a marriage is doomed anyway: it can only work if you both enjoy the subtle shades of the time-worn.

And there were our children, surprising every day, getting bigger each year but always finding new ways of doing the same old things. On the few days of sunshine they added to their collections of pebbles and shells. Where the rocks met the beach below the esplanade, I still built a driftwood house on the same spot every summer, perhaps out of the same bits of timber. The topping out of a driftwood house was always signalled by my stretching a big beach towel over its rafters, to protect its potential occupants from the sun. As if a field gun had been fired at the clouds, the rain would instantly begin to fall. But the children knew what they had to do. In the year that Uncle Martin was there, they could perch on high stools in a bar and watch him play Space Invaders. But in any other year they had to go to the Musée de la Mer and pretend all over again to be spellbound by the exhibits. While I sat alone under the awning of our favourite cafe on the Rue Gambetta and started on a new book, my wife was shopping in Bayonne along with the other wives, and the children were in the Musée de la Mer checking out the current living arrangements of the same old starfish. Even at home in England, the whole family still calls a threatening sky 'a potential Musée de la Mer situation'. At one point we skipped the Biarritz trip for about a decade, having succumbed to the vain illusion that happiness might lie elsewhere, in a climate more reliable. But eventually we went back, because the Biarritz climate *was* reliable: reliably variable. When a family holds together, its members will develop a language to enjoy even the boredom. When a family breaks up, no amount of excitement will compensate. In my time, I have seen an awful lot of good men make the big decision, and I've heard an awful lot of small change hit the floor. But the small change is precious. Perhaps I'm a miser.

Staying married to one person is undoubtedly a lot less expensive than getting married to someone else, but it still has to be paid for, and although we were by then well off, it was never easy street. Nor, however, was the cash flow any longer the chief consideration. My price as a television face meant that I could go on publishing books with low financial yield, such as *Other Passports*, the book of my collected poems that Cape bought out in 1986, and that Picador turned into a paperback the year after. For a poetry book it did well, and the paperback even got into the spinners at the airport, which made me feel better about life as I passed through the terminal on the way to being filmed doing undignified things in some destination not notable for valuing the fruits of the intellect. When you're hauling yourself out of the mud after take six of failing to ride the yak, it helps if you can remind yourself that you have recently published your collected poems. ('His occasional flashes of sensitivity may be surprising to many who have seen him making an arsehole of himself on TV' – *Times Literary Supplement*.) But the satisfaction was all spiritual. Unusually for a book of its type, *Other Passports* went on selling steadily for seventeen years, but when it finally went out of print I did a few calculations and worked out that the total return for the book would have kept my family alive for about a week and a half.

The best thing about my rate of remuneration on television, however, was that it was transferable. On television, recognizability is hard currency, and by now I could think of swapping channels if the need arose. It seemed to arise when Michael Grade, chief executive at LWT, went to the BBC. As soon as

Michael parked his dynamic form behind his new desk, where
his scarlet braces were nicely set off by the shine of the mahogany,
Richard was one of the first people that he called. We piled into
Richard's BMW and headed for BBC Television Centre as if being
simultaneously wooed by the Sirens and chased by the Furies:
not, as it turned out, a bad analogy for our situation, because we
were leaving a scene that could have turned bad and heading
towards another that would prove to be fraught with danger. For
the moment, though, and as always, impulse was what drove us.
Michael was the man: near him, things happened. Wherever he
was, he kept an open door, and if he liked your idea you could
get it on the air. At LWT, though I had achieved such prominence
that my face was hanging in the corridor to the canteen along
with Reg Varney from *On the Buses*, my position had ceased to
be secure from the moment that John Birt was given an executive
post from which he could think of second-guessing Grade. On a
personal level I had always liked John Birt, and I like him still.
I suspect that the man inside the Armani suit can remember
what we both looked like back in the days of *Nice Time* in the
1960s. Writing a few not very successful sketches for that show,
I had been impressed by how the young producer John Birt's
sideboards were even plumper than mine: and mine looked like
two squirrels taped to the side of my head. Birt had a pair of
dead badgers. But now, time having happened, he was the man
in control, and though his temperament was still disarming, his
language was becoming incomprehensible. He had already gone
a long way towards perfecting a version of management-speak
that not even other managers could understand. Using some
formula previously unknown to science, he calculated that there
could be a more efficient utilization of fixed capital resource
flow, or something, if my weekly main-channel show *Clive James
on Television* were to be scrapped. The advertising department
caught him with these computations still in his hand and told
him that the show made more money, weight for weight, than
anything else being produced on the South Bank, so he should

leave his big idea alone. Richard wasn't supposed to be aware that the big idea had even been mooted, but somebody told him, he told me, and I immediately suggested that we should hit the silk. It's a good rule in show business to spot the moment when the suits upstairs no longer regard you as an asset, and move on straight away. Stick around to be merely put up with and your bargaining power is draining away even if you still look like a fixture. Just because that old coffee machine has always been in the reception area doesn't mean that it's part of the furniture. In fact the moment it becomes 'much loved' it's already doomed, because the guy who moves in at the top with a mandate for change will always change what he can if he can't change what he should.

In less time than it took to think all that, we had completed our transition to Television Centre and were sitting down with Michael for a meeting in his huge new office. Instantly the air was full of flying superlatives: little twittering ghosts of dreams and wishes, like Tinkerbell and all her tiny classmates running wild on sports day. Bred from the playpen to be full of jokes and pithy maxims of showbiz legend, Michael is the most marvellous company even though you can never be sure, while he is talking to you, that he still holds the same post he held when he walked into the room. But there he was, apparently nailed into position, and he wanted us. He wanted us so much, he said, that his BBC2 programme controller was ready with a proposition fit to revolutionize arts television. Enter the man in question, looking like the fashionably dressed proprietor of a luxury car showroom in Beirut. Needless to say, his fame preceded him, because the most PR-conscious media executive of recent times had been preceded by his fame since the day of his birth, when he emerged from the womb into a light-storm of photoflash and an uproar of shouted questions about what he planned to do next. It was Alan Yentob.

11. DEALING WITH GENIUS

Over the course of the next ten years I accumulated overwhelm-
ing evidence to suggest that this moment, when Alan Yentob, on
being announced, actually appeared, must have been one of the
few instances of his ever being on time in his life, so it was a
mark of the honour being done to us by both him and Michael.
At this stage of his dazzling career, Yentob spent a lot of time
with Stanley Kubrick, and at any succeeding stage there was
always some comparably important international star who could
not exist without Alan's companionship and advice. Undoubtedly
these *prominenti* all derived spiritual benefit from their association with Britain's leading arts impresario. But the downside was
that anyone else was cast into the role of walk-on, or, rather,
wait-outside. As a truly gifted producer of programmes, Alan had
never looked at his watch while getting things done, and therefore
he'd had some excuse for behaving as if nobody else owned a
watch either. Up until the moment of his elevation to executive
prominence, which proved to be the beginning of a new era in
BBC history – his hagiographers were dead right about that –
manically inspired programme-makers like him always had
sober-sided executives in charge of them. Actually to promote
the manically inspired programme-maker to the status of executive marked a new phase in cultural administration. From the
moment that Alan's reign as a decision-maker began, the producers who had to report to him found him difficult to reach. All
they ever heard was rumours. He was off in the South Pacific,
spear-fishing with Marlon Brando. He was on Sam Spiegel's
yacht somewhere near Sardinia, doing a deal with Zeffirelli for an

all-dwarf production of *La Forza del Destino*. Or he was in his office, but he wasn't opening the door. Waiting in the corridor, producers who had not previously had beards grew them. People died out there, and their bones bleached on the carpet. It was a tribute to Alan's PR skills that if any of these stories reached the press they only served to reinforce his image as a genius. Let me hasten to say that the image was close to the truth. That was just the trouble. As an executive, he was more of an artist than the artists. There are intellectuals who dream of that arrangement as a desirable ideal, and that's what's wrong with them.

Such was the judgement that I formed over the course of time about the Beeb's leading creative mind, but even then, at this meeting where he and Michael were purportedly offering us the moon, Alan had a way of conveying that he could have been talking to Orson Welles instead. Richard, who actually knew Orson Welles, bristled. Richard could be quite scary when he bristled because he ditched the diplomacy. It wasn't that he had forgotten how to be diplomatic. It was more that he had deliber-ately chosen to be blunt. Between them, Michael and Alan were offering us the job of anchoring a brand-new nightly round-up to be called *The Late Show*, which would transmit live and review everything artistic going on in London that night. When Michael said that Outside Broadcast Units would be laid on so that the show could be there for the curtain calls at Covent Garden and interview the stars, Richard said that it was the kind of suggestion that could only be made by someone who had never actually produced a television programme. It was a measure of Michael's confidence that he was able to field this perfectly accurate assessment without bristling in his turn. And Alan, I had to admit, wasn't bad at taking the message that he wouldn't be getting what he wanted. I had spent some time building up a position, under Richard's protection, where I could make judi-cious plans and did not have to react to random events. I didn't want to give all that up just to meet the challenge – that bad word again – of improvising repartee in order to help a chancy

programme sound coherent. The road ahead would roll indefi-
nitely, with never time for rest, thought or proper writing. Kick,
bollock and scramble in perpetuity? No thanks. We wanted to do
more of what we already knew how to do, pushing it forward
only on the basis of established achievement. Michael was ready
to settle for that. Alan seemed not bothered at all. He was a hard
man to disappoint. His day was too full of riches. It transpired
that he had to leave because he had 'an appointment with
Stanley'. In the car, Richard showed his age by guessing that Alan
had meant Stanley Baxter. It was I who guessed that it had to be
Stanley Kubrick. Baxter, after all, could be reached by telephone.
To get anywhere near Kubrick, you had to be Alan Yentob.

So we had started off by not giving our new employers what
they wanted. What we wanted was a developed version of our
weekly studio show, spaced out, between seasons, with more
Postcard specials, to be shot at the increased rate of two a year.
Generously, Michael ensured that the BBC's contracts department
would minimize the obstacles when my agent Norman North
came to them with his price for the package. Michael's open-
door policy paid off in our favour when we walked in to sign the
papers, because within a week he walked through the same door
in the opposite direction. None other than John Birt had arrived
at the BBC and Michael had decided that there wasn't enough
oxygen for both of them, especially since he could understand
scarcely a word of what John said. As twin chief executives, they
would have been roped together on the north face of the Eiger
while one of them mumbled something about facilitating ongoing
contact with a variable interface and the other shouted, 'Bugger
this!' So our protector was gone.

We flourished anyway, more or less. At this point I could start
writing a whole volume of analysis about the sociology of the
modern media, but the main reason why there is always room
for a good book on that subject is that nobody sane would want
to read it. The first and only thing to say about the BBC is that
I managed to get some of my best work done while I was there.

The same applies to ITV. So the executives couldn't have been as bad as I thought. On either side of the porous divide between commercial and public-service broadcasting, the administrative layer was composed mainly of clever people. When they got in each other's way on the bridge, the effects were felt by those of us down in the engine room, but the effects would have been far worse if the executives had been uniformly dumb. There's a crucial difference between a man like Alan Yentob and the executives in the television system of the kind of country he looks as if he might otherwise have been president of. The crucial difference is about fifty points of IQ. If you're making programmes for a man like that and he screws you around, he isn't doing it because he's stupid, he's doing it because he's at least as smart as you are, but in a way you don't like. Hence the vital importance of a free market, so that you can go and work for someone else who will screw you around in a different way, but closer to your desires. Throughout my television career I crossed from one side to the other and back again solely out of the imperative to get things done. If my price went up all the time, it was only because I had been around longer. But I wouldn't have been around at all if there had been only one system to choose from. As in every other aspect of liberal democracy, the freedom is what counts, and I have never ceased to be grateful for living out my life under no compulsions except those imposed from within my numb skull. Therefore, on the subject of the suits upstairs, I am short of invective, because I am insufficiently fuelled by recrimination. When I say that there were people I could have killed, I'm just saying it.

Though Richard took pride in running a cost-effective production unit, it could not manage the managers, so logistics almost always took too much time. But they only seemed endless: it took only a year to get our office running in the BBC's shiny new HQ in White City. Until then we had to make do with a temporary office in the basement of a BBC annexe called Kensington House, on the wrong side of Shepherd's Bush. (Actually both sides of Shepherd's Bush were the wrong side in those days, but the area had been slowly colonized by young media types who could not yet afford to live in Notting Hill, and eventually, when one of these, Nigella Lawson, sprang to overnight fame, suddenly Shepherd's Bush was St Tropez.) Kensington House was a dump full of stuff that the world had forgotten, but the basement was a dump full of stuff that Kensington House had forgotten. After a week of unpacking files, shifting furniture about and failing to get the equipment we had ordered, our arrival was consecrated by a systems failure in the toilet on the ground floor. We were directly underneath and tried not to take it as symbolic when we had to watch the effluent seep down the walls. Anyway, there was no time to brood. The weekly show needed a rethink because by now there were just enough communications satellites up there to offer the prospect of bringing guests in through space instead of by taxi.

Satellite interviews would suit the look of the show, which had come on a bit since its early days. There had always been a stack of TV monitors on the set, each of them showing a different image to give the sense of busy multiplicity and global scope. Directors and designers wanted to jazz up this techno effect by adding bits of girder, but my own instinct was that if the message was about technology, then the technology should convey the message. Design, I announced, was just design, and British television had always suffered greatly from the notion that design could yield spectacle, so that if you had Elaine Paige singing 'Don't Cry for Me, Argentina' it would be more spectacular, instead of less, if she sang it while standing at the intersection of two enormous white polystyrene pathways to nowhere while dry ice fumes were being pumped up her skirt. Designers didn't like hearing any of this and they loathed me for even thinking it. When I at last learned to keep my mouth shut on the subject, they loathed me for the way my lip curled. They reacted in exactly the way directors did when I said I didn't like any shot that drew attention to itself. Occasionally the bad blood simmered for a while, but eventually I would get my way, although I would have soon been overruled if the results had been less convincing. A show is a collaborative venture; in a collaborative venture nobody's opinion should prevail except by the tacit consent of all; and that consent can be won only if the opinion's proponent makes the show the hero. If his motive is self-glorification, morale will soon collapse.

Season by season, however, the show did a more persuasive job of setting the style for television about television. The set was all television: a kind of television heaven. As the software got more comprehensive, it was possible to charge the stack of monitors not just with a different image each, but with a different part of the same image, to get the effect of a churning cyclorama alive with information. In the middle of all this razzle-dazzle I sat in my blue suit: the human element. Other humans came on as guests, but I was the only human who was there all the time. Everything else was electronic, including the far-flung guest who magically appeared up there on the back wall. The effect was of technical know-how carried to its apogee, like a big rocket crackling upwards into orbit. The reality, however, could be dead dodgy, especially early on, when the window for getting a satellite interview was as short as twenty minutes. You had that much time to shoot enough clean stuff that could be edited into a five-minute spot. One to four was an almost unworkably small ratio. Even in the USA, where every big city had hundreds of spare technicians who could be hired ahead of time, it would still take five or ten of the precious minutes just to get the guest rigged for sound. Usually, on studio day, we had to tape a satellite interview in the afternoon, when the time was right for a guest on the east coast, where it was still morning. A guest on the west coast would have to be taped in our early evening, just before the audience came in for the show, which would be taped too, but shot as-for-live. There could be nothing as-for-live about the satellite interviews, which were bound to be full of stops and starts. The trick was to ensure that the stops didn't cancel all the starts until there was nothing left to edit. But at least there was no studio audience to worry about.

So I was free to worry about everything else. The satellite-interview system was a potential ace in the hole, because it was a pipeline to America, where all the best guests were, as they still are. But for just that reason, the system had to work, and it was so expensive that even a single crack-up could screw the budget. Making it harder was the fact that some of the American guests weren't just up-front, they were out to lunch. It occurred to me that I had never known real tension before the day I interviewed Tammy Faye Bakker by satellite. Tammy Faye was the wife of Jim Bakker, the gate-mouthed television evangelist ('Praise the Lord!') who had grown famous for the amount of money he could get out of his enormous congregation, but he had spoiled it all by spending some of it on a woman of easy virtue. The credibility of his ministry was irreversibly undermined. His wife, who had started off as a simple choir-girl spell-bound by the soaring spirituality of her pastor, was reluctant to accept that the dream was over. There was nothing easy about Tammy Faye's virtue, but she had forgiven Jim at the top of her voice, and was eager to do so again just for me and all the wonderful people of Great Britain. Unfortunately she was inaudible, because the clip-on microphone slid off the discreetly scooped neckline of her spangled top and fell between her ample breasts, where it reattached itself to the underwiring of her bra. The microphone needed a designated female member of the Teamsters Union to dig it out. When it was finally retrieved, covered in talcum, it turned out that she couldn't hear anything, because there was something wrong with her earpiece. The sound engineer at our end said that she must have talcum in her ears. Through my own earpiece came instructions from the gallery that I should suggest to the production staff at the other end that they should suggest to Tammy Faye that she might like to scrape her eardrum with a wodge of Kleenex or a Q-tip. You have to imagine that I was looking at Tammy Faye's face multiplied to the size of a squash court, and that she was a pretty daunting sight even from a distance. The conglomerate of false eyelashes and mascara both below and above each eye gave the combined effect of two extreme astronomical events occurring in close proximity, and the weight of the lipstick dragging her mouth downwards gave the impression of too many people clinging to one side of a rubber raft.

You will notice that I make no mention of the physical characteristics underlying her panoply of cosmetic effect. I would like to be able to say that I never broke that rule. Certainly I haven't broken it in recent years, but I have to confess that in my early days I sometimes did, although mostly inadvertently. I only once did it deliberately. A famous British novelist, after a visit to Australia, wrote a feature article for one of the British colour supplements in which she gave the impression that the Australian media had been not quite up to the task of assessing her sophistication. In particular, she described one of her Australian female interviewers as looking anorexic. The interviewer was a friend of mine and did have an eating disorder, so next time I was in Australia I took revenge by making a few disparaging remarks about the personal appearance of the novelist. I made the remarks to a journalist in full knowledge that what I said would soon get back to London: that, indeed, was my plan. My idea was to remind the novelist that it was a small world. The plan succeeded only too well. My remarks were quoted, accurately, in the British press the next day, and I realized very quickly that I was the one who had been taught a lesson, because in cold print they sounded mean and witless. Revenge was laid bare as a very bad reason for writing anything, so I tried not to do it again.

Nor was the lure of accurate evocation sufficient excuse for a cruel remark. I should never have compared Montserrat Caballé to the battleship *Missouri*. The soprano didn't have to look like that – she could have eaten less – but she still had feelings. The same applied to the young American tennis player Andrea Jaeger. When I said she had a smile like a car crash, I was referring to the braces on her teeth. I thought the observation permissible because one day the braces would be removed, so I wasn't really referring to anything permanent. She might have felt, however, that they were there forever, and had invited the lightning. My general defence in such cases was that no journalist was ever quite as pitiless about my own physical appearance as I was myself. But it gradually became apparent to me that the defence would not quite do. If I didn't mind very much about cutting an awkward figure, other people might mind if I said they did, so I tried to rein in the personal remarks, except for those cases where there had been a flagrant display of wilful self-mutilation by someone who was proud of the result. I wasn't calling Barbara Cartland ugly when I said that the makeup so lavishly applied to the area of her eyes made them look like the corpses of two small crows that had flown into a chalk cliff. She chose to look like that. Nor was I calling Arnold Schwarzenegger innately deformed when I said that when stripped for action he looked like a brown condom full of walnuts. He chose to look like that. Both those remarks, however, have remained lastingly notorious as examples of how I am without mercy when pouring carbolic scorn on people's personal appearance. In fact I have always spent most of my time being careful to do no such thing, but a dog with a bad name finds it hard to outrun. Enough of that. Where was I? Oh yes. With Tammy Faye. She was up there on the wall, she was looking as off the wall as hell, and time was running out.

We were within seconds of having to call off the deal, but suddenly, as in all the best melodramas, the machinery repaired itself, and Tammy Faye was ready to do her thing. She did it surprisingly well. She expressed herself almost exclusively in quasi-biblical bromides but it didn't matter. Television gives a general impression. Nobody ever remembers what you said, but everybody remembers how you came over, and Tammy Faye was, well, kind of nice, even dainty. Hence the surprise, because if her personality had fitted her face it would have been like hearing from a candy store reaching critical mass. Instead she sounded

like a good woman coping with bewilderment. The main thrust
of her argument was that the embarrassments visited on her
adorable Jim were unfair but they must all be part of God's plan.
There could be no doubt that she genuinely loved the sancti-
monious little creep. I refrained from asking her the question
that would be on the lips of everyone in the audience: how could
she have ever looked at that whimpering, wheedling face of his
and imagined that he had a religious calling? The reason not to
ask the question was that she was giving the answer with every
word she said. Love is blind, even when its eyes aren't full of
melting makeup. As the satellite image at last winked out, I didn't
precisely have to choke back a sob, but I was sincerely moved.
Plainly the satellite interview would be a powerful instrument. It
was clumsy – there was a full second of delay that made it hard
to keep question and answer from awkwardly overlapping – but
it gave you a close-up. In Tammy Faye's case, it was a close-up
of a wedding cake that had been hit by a hurricane, but the
soul shining through was good, and a useful reminder that there
is a crucial difference between fundamentalism and extremism.
Tammy Faye's beliefs were as fundamentalist as they come, but
she wouldn't have killed you for not sharing them, except perhaps
when she sang.

It took a couple of seasons to streamline the satellite-interview
system and it was always touch and go. We almost lost a spot
with Billy Connolly in Los Angeles because Billy had turned up
in a silk shirt and we found out the hard way that clip-on
microphones react badly to silk. He launched into his first answer
and within half a minute the lurching and skirling image up there
on the screen sounded as if it was being attacked by locusts. The
crew at his end wrapped the microphone with insulation tape
and he launched into his first answer again. This time the locusts
had been joined by angry wasps. It took half a dozen false starts
before somebody figured out that the thing to change wasn't the
microphone, but the shirt. Billy swapped shirts with one of
the American production staff and launched into his first answer

yet again, just in time for his earpiece to start receiving police reports. So he started responding to those. In came the slate, chalked 'Take 16'. Being Billy, he got better all the time. He couldn't control his merriment at the accumulated cock-ups but he is one of those lucky few who are funnier still when fighting their own laughter. Time was running out, however, and I found the tension tough on my cool, although I was steadily getting better at maintaining continuity through the glitches.

Time ran all the way out with Willie Nelson. A beard in a hat, with plenty of hair hanging down from the back of the hat to make him look even more like Wyatt Earp's scapegrace brother, he was somewhere near the rim of the Grand Canyon, and our idea for the set-up was centred on his identity as a taciturn man of the West. He would ride toward the camera on a white horse, lithely dismount, and be interviewed. Willie Nelson is not just an accomplished singer-songwriter, he is a gifted natural actor – watch him stealing scenes in *Wag the Dog* – but the horse couldn't act for a bale of hay. Willie rode towards the camera and the horse screeched to a halt too late, so that the lithely dismounting rider filled the lens with his belt-buckle. Willie rode towards the camera and the horse screeched to a halt too early, so that the lithely dismounting rider had to trek forward into position from the middle distance. Willie rode towards the camera and the horse didn't screech to a halt at all. It just kept going past the camera and disappeared, leaving the lens with nothing to look at. Had the horse, with Willie on board, gone over the edge of the canyon? Where was our star? But wait a minute: there he was again, riding towards the camera. The horse screeched to a halt in exactly the right spot. Willie lithely dismounted and his earpiece didn't work, so instead of answering my first question he merely smiled, a man of the West not just taciturn but mysteriously bereft of the power of speech. Time wasn't just running out, it ran out. We had to book an extra window, at painful cost, so as to get an interview that would marry up to the arrival shot. A regular actor would have had to be paid twice, which would have blown the budget right out. But Willie was a gentleman. He was also, I later discovered, broke to the wide, so he wasn't just a gentleman, he was a saint. As for the horse, I hope it is rotting in hell. We had some good footage of Willie giving it a serious talking-to, but there was no time to put together a sequence of everything going wrong. It would have been a lot more eloquent than the interview, which consisted largely of Willie saying 'Yep' and 'Nope', like Gary Cooper. Once again, however, the words mattered less than the mere presence. Faces from space! It looked fabulous.

12. DESTINATION TOKYO

With the weekly show raking in the ratings, we had earned our upgrade to the shimmering cliffs of White City, where we were given half an acre of the Beeb's unstained new floor-space in which to spread our staff, who revelled in the unfamiliar luxury of being able to sit down without touching each other. Much to my embarrassment, the whole operation was called the Clive James Unit. Feeling a bit overbilled, I resolved to redouble my efforts, but soon found that I was obliged to triple them. Having got our wish for a bumper ration of Postcard programmes, we now had to make them. It was soon clear to me that they would consume the last vestiges of my spare time. If I hadn't learned to write on board the aircraft, and during every hour of downtime on location, I would have got no literary work done at all. By now I was composing the last of the reviews and essays that went into my book *Snakecharmers in Texas*. I got better at writing them in snatched hours, and their range of reference benefited from the second-hand books I bought wherever I flew. On location, collecting books and stacking them up on the cafe table at which I wrote was a way of staying sane, or perhaps just a way of resting from one kind of hyperactivity by burying myself in another. The cafe table could be anywhere, and today I can't always remember which city came in which order, or even whether it was the BBC paying the hotel bills, or else that previous bunch. I never kept a logbook because it would have scared me to look at it. I could phone around all the old staff – half of them are tycoons by now, but they might still take my calls – and I could work out the actual order of events, but there would be no point: things didn't feel sequential even then. As in every other area of my life, simultaneity was the keynote. The places we filmed were all different, but filming itself was just one place on its own. I loved being there, but often felt that I didn't know where it was in the world. It had a hotel where you had breakfast, and there was a car that appeared on schedule, and then you appeared on schedule and climbed into the car, and then the car took you from one sequence to the next until it took you back to the hotel to have dinner and lie down for a couple of hours before staying awake half the night while you mugged up for next day. The call-sheet being always such a killer, it was essential to know something about the country's past before going in, because when you got there you would see nothing except the present.

I already knew a bit about Japan before we flew to Tokyo. I had once been there on assignment for the *Observer*, and since then I had read quite a lot about Japanese history; and lately I had sat through several hundred miles of footage showing young Japanese game-show contestants performing routines out of a cabaret devised by Dante. That last thing, of course, was the principal reason somebody decided that we should make not just one film in Japan, but two of them on the trot. Our advance party returned with a thick folder full of sure-fire suggestions, and off we flew to make them real. I forget what I wrote on the plane. It should have been my will.

Barely had we moved into our skyscraper hotel in the Aoyama district of Tokyo when we made our first mistake. It was decided that I should carry a bag in the first few sequences, as if I was still looking for the hotel after having emerged from the subway system. We thus constructed a needless continuity problem, because when we got back to the editing room and duly reshuffled all the sequences into a different order, the bag mysteriously appeared and disappeared throughout the movie, always needing to be explained. (Memo: it isn't enough to dress the same throughout. Don't carry anything, because you never know if a walking shot from one sequence might not need to be patched into another, and if something even as slight as a hot dog magically appears in your hand, it will need an extra, awkward line of voice-over. 'On my way to the shrine I bought a hot dog which I consumed instantly.' Cue the sound of people switching off by the million.) But that lay in the future. At the time, I wondered if I would ever get home at all. My Japanese game-show expertise dictated that I should participate in, guess what, a Japanese game show. It was called *Takeshi's Castle*: far and away the most popular game show on Japanese television, out-rating even the dreaded *Endurance*. The castle was a pasteboard cut-out standing in a patch of waste land, but it looked convincing beside Takeshi himself, who was dressed like Michael Jackson in the later, militarized stages of his madness and did a lot of jumping about and crouching while pulling the Japanese front-man's standard idea of a subtly threatening face. Imagine Kirk Douglas feigning apoplexy and you've got it.

Hundreds of teenage contestants in crash helmets pretended to feel terrified. They shrank back, they clutched each other, they shivered. In my tight-fitting red tracksuit and white crash helmet, I wasn't pretending. Stretched high above a pond, there was a jungle-style rope-and-plank bridge on which you had to stand while the other contestants tried to eliminate you with soft cannon balls fired by a spring-gun while Takeshi jumped around doing his threatening thing. Twice as heavy as the average contestant, I had trouble keeping my balance anyway. The bridge swayed wildly to either side even when the cannon balls weren't flying. When they did, the very first one hit me in the face and down I went, to discover that the pond had been dug shallow, in order to receive the falling bodies of much smaller people. Dug out of the slime, I was inserted into the castle to be chased by giants. They were small giants but they were good at poking you with a stick. I was propelled out of a doorway and fell into the moat. For our crew, filming the Japanese crew as they filmed me was tricky, so I had to do it again. This time I emerged from the door and did three-quarters of a somersault before hitting the moat stern-first. Anything for the camera. The massed contestants dutifully howled at the marvellous sense of humour of the *gaijin* – the foreign person – while Takeshi mimed jealousy with what I thought was, for him, uncharacteristic authenticity. It turned out that he wasn't miming. He was the one who was supposed to get the laughs. He had lost face.

He lost his temper along with it but we already had what we needed, so it was no great loss to take our leave as Takeshi did the equivalent of a Hollywood sulk. In the Hollywood sulk, the star retreats to his huge trailer and refuses to come out. Takeshi retreated to a very small bus and never stopped coming out, snarling at us, and going back in again. He was probably still doing that for the next fortnight, during which time we managed to prove that most of our planned story was like a game show anyway. I had been in on the preliminary thinking so I can't say that I was double-crossed. The problem of capturing Japanese culture would have been unavoidable however we approached the task, because so much of the old art depends on refinement, which takes a lot of explaining, and only the explanation can prove that you are looking at the real thing. A Japanese classical sword-smith takes a long time to make a sword, you need a degree in metallurgy to appreciate what he does, and the finished product looks exactly like a stage prop from an amateur production of *The Mikado*. In a Noh play an actor takes half an hour to cross the stage. The special walk he is using takes a lifetime's training, but he looks exactly like an old man with arthritis setting out to buy a newspaper. You can fall asleep while he is making his entrance and when you wake up again he is still making his entrance. In Kyoto, at the Geisha training school, the top lady was one of the greatest living players of the *shami-sen*, the single-stringed guitar that has come down through the ages without acquiring any extra strings to compromise its purity by providing it with, say, the capacity to produce a chord. It goes plunk. It goes plink.

But from this woman we had been promised prodigies of

subtlety. We had been reliably informed that there was no one in her class. A ringer for Sessue Hayakawa, she applied her fingernails in various groupings to the string of her instrument, which produced a series of noises astonishing for their lack of variation. The piece she played, which had reputedly driven many a Tokugawa nobleman to hoarse grunts of desire in times gone by, sounded like a tennis racket popping its strings one at a time under intense heat. As I sat there on my crossed legs in the listening position, her display of virtuosity continued without any hint of an ending. She went plink. She went plunk. As she did so, she moaned at seeming random, evoking the last hour of a coyote with its leg crushed by a steel trap. There was a spoken passage which I thought I recognized as a reproduction of a tannoy announcement at Tokyo's mainline station saying that the Bullet Train to Osaka would stop at Nagoya. Then the moaning resumed, until it was finally climaxed, as she hunched with added tension over her instrument, by a virtuoso simultaneous combination of plunk and plink. The attendant trainee geishas politely told me how long it took to put on their makeup but they took just as long to tell me, and there was no way to save the sequence except to shoot reverses on my straining face while I showed the effects – no need for acting – of having to sit for a long time on my crossed legs. I couldn't manage more than a few minutes without getting up for a rest but then I had to sit down again. We filmed me doing this. It was a true story, and to let myself in for ridicule might mitigate any impression that I was setting out to ridicule the culture, which in fact I revered, even for its way of becoming even more incomprehensible as you focused your attention on it.

Ancient Japanese arts were proving a bit of a bust from our viewpoint. The modern stuff was easier. With complete dominance of the global electronics market as a motor, Japanese economic life was booming, the 'salary men' were working themselves to early graves, and it was fun reporting on the way they lived. In Tokyo the men in suits slaved a long day, got compulsorily wasted with the boss in the evening, missed the last commuter train and checked into one of the new capsule hotels. I checked in along with them, changed tightly into the pyjamas provided and climbed up to a capsule on the third tier. All around me were capsules full of salary men, at the rate of one per capsule. They were in there like bees. The crew had filmed then getting in. Now the crew had to film me. With my racked legs still aching from their agony in the geisha college, I climbed a ladder whose rungs were shorter than the span of my hands. But swinging myself horizontal so that I could slide into the flesh-pink plastic capsule was trickier still. For one thing, I didn't slide. I was exactly the same size as the space provided, which was not the idea. You were supposed to be a bit smaller, so that you had room to read a porno comic book one-handed while politely farting sake fumes. But the camera was on my face as I strained and grunted. Again, no acting necessary. The right effect first time. But it had to be done a dozen times, to get the angles and the long shots. Sweat poured from my face, suggesting that I was crammed into a microwave oven. From other capsules, voices emerged, which, our translator explained, were voices of complaint. The bees were being kept awake. All that the scene needed was Takeshi rushing in, jumping up and down, pointing his finger at me and screaming, 'You are keeping our salary men awake, foreign devil!'

We flew down to Kyushu to film me sitting in a pool of hot grey liquid mud dotted with melons and the heads of people who were there for the melon-flavoured hot grey liquid mud. Some of them had been there for years. They were quite tolerant of the intruder, but I couldn't help wondering why I was so often ending up submerged. (In subsequent movies the question would occur to me again: it was a kind of running theme.) The answer to the question, I realized much later, was actually quite simple. Like the wearing of the blue suit, the plunging of my body into alien liquids emphasized the only reason for my central role in the proceedings: I was the wrong man in the right spot. But the films we made in Japan had a bit too much of the wrong man and not nearly enough of the right spot.

We got closer to capturing the traditional Japan when we filmed my participation in the tea ceremony. The tea master was the top guy in the country. Radiating sacred expertise through the paper walls of his little house, he held the tea master's equivalent of a black belt, tenth dan, and he had not arrived at this exalted rank without suffering, as his permanent frown attested. Change his kimono for a naval uniform and he could have been Admiral Yamamoto just after he got the news that four aircraft carriers had been sunk in the Battle of Midway. As we squatted facing each other, I too suffered. At several points during the first hour, while the tea master was still preparing the tea for mixing with water – the leaves had to be pounded, sifted and closely contemplated before being pounded and sifted again – I did not get up quickly enough to rest my legs. Instead I rolled over backwards, to the amusement of the third participant. Her name was Yoko Shimada and she was present at my suggestion. Back in England, I had informed my troops that the actress in the television mini-series *Shogun* was the most beautiful woman on Earth and that if she were present during the tea ceremony her ethereal face might do a better job of conveying its spiritual significance than mine. This proved to be an accurate forecast and I don't apologize for having made it. Some of my critics were scornful about the way my Postcard programmes were populated with good-looking women. A few of my producers, especially if they were female, agreed with the critics, but I thought the audience could use an effective relief from looking at me, and I would still think the same today. In Japan, especially, it was all too easy to fill the screen with brute reality. All you had to do was get a close shot of a sumo wrestler's behind. But if you wanted to convey spiritual beauty in its most refined form, Yoko Shimada's face was just the thing. Decked out in full kimono, she looked truly, deeply interested in the tea ceremony and declared herself honoured to be watching the tea being ceremonially mixed by the number-one tea master currently in existence. The camera could cut away to her divine countenance while the tea master got on with the job of mixing and whisking. The camera didn't have to watch me rolling over backwards.

In the course of about an era, the tea was finally all set to go. It looked like guacamole but it tasted of nothing, which was apparently the idea. A foreigner tasting his first ceremonial tea couldn't expect to get the nuances. Later on I asked Yoko if she had tasted anything either, but by that time she was back outside the house and had been joined by her manager, who whispered in her ear. She said the tea had been wonderful beyond all imagining, but there was a giggle going on somewhere behind that mask of translucent beauty. While she was inside the house and still on the case, however, she did a superlative imitation of someone being knocked out by subtlety. The cup came to her after it had come to me. As per the protocol, I had turned the cup around so that she wouldn't be sipping from the same bit of the rim I had sipped from. She turned it again, so I think her delicate lips ended up sipping at the same spot. If so, it was as near as I was ever going to get to sharing Richard Chamberlain's big moment in *Shogun* when he fell with her to the futon. We got miles of footage but there was never any doubt that it would have been just another slapstick scene if we hadn't introduced an extra element. Yoko was it, and I said goodbye to her with a correctly angled bow as she was helped into the back of her limousine by her manager, who hated me very much. I have often wondered whether he might not have been the reason why she didn't become the biggest star in the world. If so, he was probably right. She was the golden carp, and she belonged in the old imperial pond. In the open ocean, she might have drowned.

We got a lot of good material in Japan and I think the two movies it yielded hold up fairly well – they are still being screened somewhere in the world all the time – but a single movie would have been better if we could have captured the real texture. I had already figured out why it had slipped through our fingers:

not because it is made of silk, but because it is all based on the language. Our fixer on the shoot, an elegant young employee of the BBC's Tokyo office named Noriko Izumi, was a born teacher. I called her Nikki and her spoken English was so good that she called me Clive, instead of the usual local pronunciation, Karaibu. (Most of the gags about the way the Japanese pronounce English are exactly backwards, by the way: it's 'l' that they have trouble with, not 'r', so the famous 'Lip my tights!' sequence in *Lost in Translation* is nonsense, even if amusing.) So well did Nikki speak English, in fact, that she wasn't in search of practice, and could dedicate all her attention, during my downtime, to starting me off on one of the big adventures of my life. I won't try to record it all here. Sufficient to say that during the shoot I learned enough phrases to play my part in the standard everyday conversation that consists almost entirely of saying hello and goodbye, and I even learned to recognize my first half-dozen written words. That second thing, the written language, is what makes Japanese so hard for the foreigner. The spoken language is comparatively user-friendly. It's spoken in a monotone, in complete syllables, so you don't have to worry about your intonation, and the phonemes can be strung together as easily as in Italian or Spanish. In fact Japanese sounds a bit like Italian being spoken in the next room.

But the written language is a different matter. There are three alphabets going on at once. Two of the alphabets are syllabic, but most of the action is in the third alphabet, the *kanji* characters, and it's a brain-burner. The written language, with its emphasis on memory, is designed to be learned by children so as to be used by adults. An adult trying to learn it had better not be trying to remember anything else. Nevertheless, in the following years, during which I spent as much time as I could in Japan, I got quite a long way with reading and writing, but I didn't have to get further than about a yard before I discovered what our filming trip had missed out. The biggest artistic impact Japan makes is all contained within that amazing written language. A

single page of a newspaper is a work of art. The whole population
shares this enormous aesthetic turn-on and if you can't read it,
you're out of it. *Ainiku*, as they say. A pity. Year after year, in
the magic coffee shops of Jinbo Cho, the book district of Tokyo,
Nikki would check my *kanji* characters as I laboriously entered
them in my notebook. Always more keen to form friendships
among women than among men – once a mother's boy, always
a mother's boy – I eventually supplemented her invaluable help
with additional instruction from a bunch of female teachers
who had daringly started a two-room outfit to teach Japanese
to foreign businessmen based in Tokyo. Their little school, called
Business Nihongo, was an unprecedented initiative at a time
when Japanese women were still meant to mind the hearth. I
staked them to a few months' rent in return for free teaching.
Eventually I could write the phonetic alphabets – the sinuous
hiragana and the jagged *katakana* – with fair fluency, but the
kanji characters were always a killer. The upside was that I got
steadily better at reading and a lot better at speaking. I learned
women's Japanese – men would raise their eyebrows when I
spoke it – but it sounds better than men's Japanese anyway.
(Women, even when annoyed, sound like the pattering of a light
rain on a tiled roof. Men, even when discussing the weather,
sound as if they are whipping themselves up for a *banzai* attack.)
Writing, however, was dead tricky, and I never really got on top
of it even before the day came that I had to put it aside for a
while, and then found, when I tried to pick it up again, that it
had all gone away. One day I hope to start again, because it was
one of the big aesthetic experiences of my life, like getting into
the Bach cantatas.

13. PAGEANT CITIES

Rio de Janeiro was tricky too but for a different reason. A water city whose beautiful setting ranked with Sydney and Venice, with overtones of the Himalayas, it looked majestic in a wide shot but when the camera got closer it was a meat market. Such was the cult of the female body that I looked like a sex tourist just for being there. There was certainly no need to jazz up a tea ceremony with a pretty woman. Pretty women were wall to wall even indoors, and out on the beach they were sitting next to each other for miles as they slaved at the endless task of polishing their fingernails. When they were sitting down, their shapely breasts, only notionally contained by bits of coloured string, were sometimes masked by their arms as they bent forward to get started on their toenails, but when they walked, darkly outlined against the sunlight, every one of them, of whatever age, sported a pair of polished, pointed nacelles like the bumper bullets of a 1956 Cadillac. This was the home city of plastic enhancement for the female chassis, a craze that was later to conquer the world. The top surgeon was on our list of interviewees, but first we had to knock off the exterior footage in case it rained. This time Richard was with us in person and he was very strict about that. If we didn't get the beach life we wouldn't have a movie. He was a bit irritable because of what happened at the Copacabana Hotel when we moved in. We dumped our stuff in our rooms, changed into swimming costumes and gathered around the pool to make our plans, sipping at caipirinhas as we contemplated the same stretch of cool water in which the Hollywood stars had once recovered from the heat of secret trysts in the days when the media couldn't afford to fly. It was balm to our jet-lagged eyes, but after an hour the sun was too hot to bear, so Richard went back to his room, there to discover that it had been turned over: wallet, credit cards, return ticket, all gone. It was hard not to suspect the staff but when the cops arrived even they looked like crooks.

One of the immediately apparent things about Rio is that whereas most of the women are out of a good American surfing movie, all the men are out of a bad American gangster movie. The level of crime was doubly unsettling for being instantly obvious. I already knew something about it because I had been there before, to cover the Brazilian Grand Prix for the *Observer*. One of the drivers, as he walked along the esplanade in broad daylight, had been hauled down onto the beach and mugged not only for his watch and wallet but for most of his clothes. Laurence Rees, rewarded for his success in Paris by being invited to direct the Rio shoot, had arrived equipped with a theory that muggers could be deterred if you walked with sufficient confidence. On the morning after Richard got robbed, Laurence walked confidently out of the front door of the hotel and straight into a pack of teenage thieves who kindly left him the clothes he stood up in but took his watch and everything in his pockets. The doorman looked calmly on. After that, Laurence abandoned the confident walk and adopted the same nervous slouch as the rest of us. You just had to get used to the idea.

Laurence was good at the coverage, though, and while the sun shone there was a lot to cover. I cleverly decided that the reverse shots on my face would look funnier if my head didn't turn. We could just shoot a few hundred feet with my head still and my eyeballs swivelling. Back in England, I could do a voice-over line about the strain of not looking, while the cutaways searched all over the place among the sun-kissed lovelies. There was just no end to the supply. Until now I had never supposed that my libidinous imagination could die of an overdose, but it happened. This was going to be as boringly predictable as a saturnalia, or, as we might say now, a successful suicide bomber's first afternoon in Paradise. Actually we can't say that now, lest we attract the bristling attention of some lethal maniac out to demonstrate the infinite mercy of Allah. But these were more innocent times, when a semi-naked female had nothing to worry about except being microwaved by the lustful glances of slavering males, and nobody bothered about the wrath of God, even though He, too, was supposedly a Catholic.

The body worship of Rio took on a more interesting perspective when we did our first night-shoot. There was a fashionable party in one of the old Portuguese colonial buildings and every colonnade was jammed with glamorous women, but these were the social elite and often of a certain age. Even the most ancient, however, had unlined faces joined to trim bodies by uncannily wrinkle-free necks. One of them didn't balk at telling me that she had been worked on by the top surgeon I referred to earlier. Then she started to point out all the others who had been to the same repair shop. Here was a revelation. There was a sorority of the surgically altered. The women of Rio not only looked on perfect beauty as their birthright, they looked on eternal youth the same way.

Up on the favelas above the city, where the destitute lived in hovels loosely plugged into an incipient mud-slide, we paid a guy in white patent-leather shoes – a defiant gesture in a universe of pig excrement – to tell us about the gangs that plagued the poor. He got us into a voodoo ceremony taking place in one of the rare huts that were made of cement instead of scrap. A hundred people rocked and clapped to a slow rumba. There was an altar decked with votive symbols: a shell-encrusted cross, a barber-shop mirror painted with the image of Elvis Presley, a plastic Kewpie doll, a broken blender. Tedious chanting took place while a chicken was sacrificed. The commentary was writing itself in my head all the time. Rich people were paying to go under the knife of a mad scientist while poor people were getting carved up for free. That latter part was underlined later when our guide to the favelas turned up dead. It wasn't our fault that the news had got out about what we had paid him. Perhaps it hadn't, and they nailed him just for his white patent-leather shoes.

Immortality was expensive but life was cheap. Clean-up squads of off-duty cops were kidnapping pavement children even as we set up for the interview with Yves Pitanguy, the pioneer plastic surgeon who founded the trade with the knowledge he acquired when he was rebuilding the burned faces of RAF pilots during WWII. His humanitarian credentials were excellent, and even in his later years he still spent some of his time correcting deformities. But he spent most of it keeping those society women young. His argument that he could never have paid for his charity work without giving rich women what they wanted was hard to refute. But a television interview is always about the general effect, not the logic, and even as the camera turned I knew that the doc's own face was telling the essential story. He didn't have a wrinkle. Some of his colleagues had been turning back his clock. The skin around his eyes gleamed like his teeth. Why, then, did he look like death warmed up?

Because plastic surgery, when its only aim is to stop time, *is* death warmed up. I could hear my voice-over deepening already. There are no empty subjects, there is only empty treatment. Back on the beach, I talked to the granddaughter of the Girl from Ipanema, subject of the immortal song written to a lyric poem by Vinicius de Moraes, whose poetry I later learned to love. He was a great lyricist, Vinicius, and he had been mad for the ladies. Nut-brown in her pale-green bikini, the granddaughter looked heaven-sent. The society women could never look like that again, but you couldn't blame them for trying, because young beauty was the only local currency that could keep pace with the dollar. Such was the inflation in Brazil that they wouldn't take their own money at the airport. It was a barter economy, and bartering began with the body. Or perhaps you could blame them. One of the old-time aristocrats, a member of the Betancourt dynasty, still lived in the family mansion, and no scalpel had ever touched her. Barely mobile any more, she was the voice of sanity, and she could say it all in English, not Portuguese. Untouched by rancour but embodying the sadness of time, she told the story of the old colony becoming a modern ruin. Within the first five minutes of the interview I knew that she would clinch the movie. I was beginning to learn that a documentary special must be built like a poem, first planned, then modified as the texture emerged. Rio was a lyric poem, but all great lyric poems are tragic underneath, because they are inspired by human beauty, and beauty will die from the same force that made it live.

In my downtime I met a woman whose very existence dramatized the whole modern history of Brazil. Her name was Silvia Nabuco. One of her ancestors had been instrumental in the freeing of the slaves, and now her beloved nation was drowning in the chaos of its own liberty. In Rio she had a house like a fortress, and in the green *floresta* of Petropolis she had an estate surrounded by the walls of a valley. When she was a child the great poet Manuel Bandeira had written a poem for her. She was the one who told me where to look first in the Brazilian wing of the treasure house of Portuguese poetry. She was also the one who told me just how far and wide the voodoo cults still spread. To go with her beauty she had a melodious voice, from which it was disconcerting to hear that Brazil's current Minister of Education had been present the previous night at the ritual slaying of a cow. As we sat talking on the terrace of her fazenda in the early evening, men with shotguns patrolled the valley, her safeguards in a country where kidnapping was a recognized profession. What a story Rio was. But our movie would have been merely picturesque without the history. Matching that to the pictures was my job, and I was getting better at it because I had to. Otherwise we would have been making nothing except a travel brochure plus a dead chicken. Unless you are content to use a phrase like 'land of contrasts', you need to put some

background over the foreground if you are to make any sense of
the shot in which you walk away from the beach and trip over a
rotting corpse.

The capacity to dig for the meaning behind the spectacle was
essential even in the USA, where everyone walked around with
the ostensible message blazoned on their T-shirts. In Louisville,
Kentucky, a hundred spherical mothers were crammed into the
Holiday Inn so that their children could compete in a pageant,
one of the hundreds of pageants running somewhere in the US
in any given week. Once they had all been beauty pageants but
now, after too many scandals, they were just pageants, focusing
on Talent. They are still running even as you read. All the
children have at least one Talent and they are all destined to win
a trophy. Everyone involved in our pageant, whether at organi-
zational or competitive level, wore a shirt marked Louisville
Pageant. If it had been a serial killers' conference in Detroit, the
shirts would have said so. We had chosen the subject precisely
because it seemed so trivial but there were occasions early on
when we thought we had overdone it. One girl's talent was to
march up and down dressed as Uncle Sam. The disc she marched
to was Barbra Streisand singing 'Don't Rain on My Parade'. Her
actual Talent was hard to detect at first glance, but perhaps she
earned points for not looking like her mother, who, like so many
of the mothers, was a rolling sphere.

I risk being classed as a Body Fascist by saying this now,
and I certainly didn't say it in my commentary to the movie,
but the time comes when the truth can no longer be dodged.
This wasn't the first time I had seen clinical obesity in America
but it was always a shock to watch a family arguing about how
many elevators they would need to get to where they were going,
which usually meant downstairs to the dining room. Their
talented children were occupying the brief window of life in
which they would not be physically enormous. We were careful
to avoid getting the shots which would emphasize this fact. I
would indeed be evoking a story about a logical development of

democracy, in which everyone must be special, a uniformity of uniqueness. Another logical development of democracy is that the poor get fat, but that would have been a less interesting story, and anyway it wasn't my natural slimness that sent me out jogging every morning. (Every morning I jogged several times around the vast Holiday Inn, which was surrounded by miles of nothing except an approach road to the interstate highway. Families who filled their cars to the brim struggled for room to point me out as they sped by.) Out of my sweats and into my blue suit after a breakfast of blueberry pancakes with extra cream, I sat at the back of the function room working on the plot-line while the camera was getting footage of a bespectacled ten-year-old boy called Elwood who sang a song about his rubber duck as he jumped in and out of a small plastic paddling pool. He clutched the rubber duck while he sang about it. Compared with what we had been getting for the previous two days, he was a highlight.

Elwood's rubber-duck number started looking like a prize sequence when the message came through from London that there was something wrong with the footage. Not some of it, all of it. Mike, our good man in Africa, was in charge of the camera and no one was more distressed than he was to find out that he had been shooting unusable stuff. The pulse of the fluorescent tube lighting in the hotel had been creating a 'bar' on the exposed film stock. I won't go into details because I still don't understand it myself, but you can take it for granted that we were in a bad spot, because everything we already had in the bank would have to be shot again. Cameramen have been known to drink themselves silly in those circumstances, so it was generous of Mike to buckle down and start shooting all the same numbers for a second time, but it's a rule of filming that the boy with the rubber duck will not be quite so enchanting when asked to repeat the same routine. Elwood concentrated hard but his genius was under strain. There was something mechanical about the way he clutched the duck. Two entire days of my life disappeared as we laboriously went back over the same ground. The little girl who marched to Barbra Streisand marched again. As an impatient man, I tried to tell myself that I was getting only a fleeting taste of what it would be like to be in jail. Why had we persuaded ourselves to come here in the first place?

Richard reminded me. We were sitting in the bar one night listening to the cocktail piano player sing 'Desperado'. She was a good-looking woman but no great beauty, and she sang quite well but she wasn't Blossom Dearie. In her quiet way, however, she was giving it everything. 'This is the story,' said Richard. 'They all want to make it.' Right there I had my big idea. In another week or so, at the end of the pageant, the trophies would be given out. There would be hundreds of them. Everybody would get one. There would be a trophy for Best Holder of Rubber Duck Jumping In and Out of Plastic Pool. The trophies must all be in a room somewhere. Why couldn't we snatch a preview? The women in charge of the project were delighted by the idea, and next day we were filming in the trophy room. Standing on the floor with their plinths touching, the trophies were in there like a tinsel forest, trembling gently to the chug of the air conditioning. The women handed me trophy after trophy, explaining what each one was for. The women, however, were not, in this case, the story that mattered. It was the trophies. They didn't weigh anything. They were on the scale of small skyscrapers but they were made of some intermediary substance between metal and plastic that gave you about a hundred cubic feet of material to the ounce. A trophy whose pinnacle came up to your chin could be picked up with one finger. Suddenly the whole movie snapped into focus. It was a movie about a world of symbolism, where everyone could possess the signs of privilege, because signs were all they were. All I had to do was find a snappy way of saying that.

Thus it was that the Louisville Kentucky Holiday Inn, a tritely veneered breeze-block building parked out of town beside the interstate, proved to be the setting of one of our best movies. We had made something out of nothing. There were no trophies for making something out of the big American cities, although sometimes you could be led into trouble by the obligation to dodge the obvious. Chicago was like that. I wanted to avoid following the gangsters down memory lane to be blasted by a phantom hail of lead. 'But time was running out for John Dillinger . . .' I preferred to concentrate on the architects, but I soon found out why there are so many movies about John Dillinger and so few about Frank Lloyd Wright: even the memory of action is more gripping than no action at all. I was also determined to tell the story of how the industrialists of the nineteenth century had not only turned millions of head of cattle into a river of fat that stunk up a whole corner of Illinois, they had also turned Chicago into a world centre of contemporary art by purchasing the best of Lautrec and Seurat straight off the easel in Paris and bringing it home to their houses. Eventually their well-chosen treasures were bequeathed to the Art Institute, where the masterpieces lining the wall of a single great room are a permanent demonstration of just how awesome American financial power can be.

But Chicago's expatriated European art would have been an unduly quiet story if it had not been offset by something noisier, and our candidate for that was the blues. Unfortunately, much as I loved jazz, I had only a limited tolerance for the kind of blues number in which the singer sings the same not very inspired line twice (or, even worse, three times) before capping it with a third (or, even worse, fourth) not very inspired line, followed by a peremptory wail from that least disarming of all jazz instruments, the amplified harmonica. I spent a long, harrowing night in a blues club where I had to look fascinated by the cacophonous remains of a famous blues shouter called something like Slow Dirt Buncombe (I remember his real name but his lawyer might still be alive) while he gave a string of examples of how a song with less than a minute of material could be stretched to thirty minutes if you made the same line and stanza sound different by mangling them a different way each time. Yelled at cataclysmic amplification, 'Well mah woman she done leff me' was a recurring motif. 'No bloody wonder' was the obvious continuation, but he never sang that. Thanks to the unnecessary volume – the sure sign of inadequate music – I was never completely clear what he was singing, but I could rely on a maximum air of drama when he pulled back from the microphone, slanted his polished ebony head to shield it from the blaze of the heavenly splendour he had created, and suddenly leaned forward again to give a long blast on his hellishly resonant harmonica. The desirable and necessary ideal of racial equality should, in my view, allow us to say that there is the occasional blues artist whose parade of desolation amounts to an acute pain in the neck. Slow Dirt Buncombe was one of these. Unfortunately Nobby, the deaf sound-man who was once again on the case, caught every line of Slow Dirt's act with perfect fidelity, and some of the results got as far as the final cut, accompanied by cutaways of my enchanted, lying face.

The Chicago shoot was carefully planned but somehow we missed the story. On the south side, whose housing projects scared me rigid, Barack Obama was working as a community organizer at about that time, but we didn't dig deep enough to find him. You can't see the future: you can only hope that the present might be different, and one look at the housing projects was enough to tell you that the present was intolerable. We shot some of it, but we might as well have been in a war zone. I sat in a patrol car with a cop who told me that the tract of the Cabrini Green project we were looking at was a free-fire zone in which children regularly got shot just for target practice. We got some of that theme, but we missed its essence, and we even missed the city's undoubted magic. I would like to be able to say that there was no magic to be caught, but there was at least one moment that we might have snatched had I been faster on my feet, or at any rate stronger in expressing my wishes. We were shooting late at night beside the lake, catching the strolling traffic as the locals, after a Friday night out, made the *paseo*: always a good sequence in any city, but even better when you can see water in the background. Often a good story shows up unexpectedly in those circumstances, and so it did here. A pair of preposterously lovely young women in scoop-necked tops and hot pants came rollerblading along the esplanade as if in fulfilment of some adolescent boy's midnight fantasy. With each lazy sideways stroke they travelled another twenty yards. The laws of friction had been suspended. They were twins. It was American teenage heaven, twice. I wanted to collar them, rig up some extra lights and bring them past us again, but Helen, with arms folded, did the standard, 'Oh, Clive, you're impossible,' reaction that some of the female producers tended to trot out whenever I showed an urge to go for the cheesecake. She might have had a point, but I wasn't just doting on the jailbait, I was seeing the extravagant perfection of their skating, whose skill was underlined by the fact that they were both doing it. (The same point is made by synchronized divers.) I could have put a good line over that shot: only in America, never in Blackpool. But the possibility raced away into the dark, leaving us there with an impeccably worthy movie.

Worthy meant dull, however. Years later my friend Ruby Wax, who was born and bred in Chicago, said, 'Boy, you really missed it with that one.' Her remark hurt, because she herself was the supreme exponent of the documentary special. There has never been a better example of the form than her movie about Russia, which depended throughout on her ability to seize the moment. Similarly, in her special starring Imelda Marcos, Ruby might never have been able to snatch the famous scene with Imelda's collection of shoes if there had been a producer deciding what was serious and what was trivial. Sometimes the trivial is the serious. But I fluffed the moment. It wasn't Helen's fault – she usually indulged my more questionable inspirations if I insisted with sufficient fervour – and I make such a song and dance now only because I never quite got over missing the shot of the twin skaters. Get the shot first and then decide. In the same way, a poet never gets over what he lost when he failed to write down that perfect line that came to him in the night. For once unarmed with pen and paper, he is sure that he will remember it in the morning. When he finds that he has forgotten it, he never forgets that he forgot.

14. THE HOUSE HAS THE EDGE

But there was no point going wide if you didn't go deep. Our Las Vegas movie was closer to the mark because I knew what I thought about gambling. Brought up within earshot of the Australian two-up schools and poker machines, I already had my underlying idea for a commentary that would hold the footage together without sounding preachy. It would have sounded preachy if I had set out to condemn the gambling as an unforgivable extravagance, an insult to the world's poor, etc. But my own conviction was that these *were* the world's poor, and were proving that if the poor had enough money they would cease to be materialist. It only sounds like a paradox. Las Vegas is high culture for people who have no other culture but kitsch. They really do think that a hotel shaped like a pyramid outranks the pyramids in Egypt because it has twenty-four-hour room service. As long as you bring your money to town, you are welcome to explain why they are wrong and why that matters. As so often in America, the amount of mental energy being put into the worthless was a marvel. The smartest man we met in Vegas was a security director in charge of the large staff watching from the ceiling of the casino in one of the biggest hotels, on the lookout for cheats. He showed us how cheating was done. Not only could he deal any card he wished from any part of the deck, he could neatly explain why the trick had taken half a lifetime to learn. He could also explain why the odds were better if you were the man in charge of security rather than the world's most skilled cheat. I could have listened to him for hours and I knew our audience would feel the same. But we still wouldn't have had much of a movie without the fast cars.

Louisville had taught us a lesson. It helped if you could pin the visit to an event. There was nothing else in Louisville except the pageant so the stratagem had been compulsory, but even in the big cities there was a risk of disappearing in several different directions if there wasn't a central happening. So we had timed the Vegas trip to coincide with one of those rare American flirtations with Formula One motor racing. The Americans are never going to get the point of F1 because the cars rarely race beside each other, so where's the race? This is a question that only a petrol-head can answer. That year, however, the managers of Caesar's Palace Hotel in Las Vegas played host to a Grand Prix on a track laid out in the hotel's car park. If that space seems insufficient at first thought, remember that an American hotel's car park is usually a hundred times the area that the hotel itself stands on, because even though the people who have checked into the hotel don't mind being arranged vertically, they prefer it if the cars they arrived in are arranged horizontally. Many acres of tarmac were available for concrete boundary walls to be laid down in the requisite pattern, and the whole occasion was done due honour, with nothing skipped. Caesar's Palace, after all, had a distinguished association with motor sport. It was in the forecourt of Caesar's Palace, in the long driveway leading up to and away from the porte cochère, that the great Evel Knievel had jumped the fountain on his motorcycle. Or rather, he had failed to jump the fountain, descending at the wrong angle and breaking, yet again, bones that had already been broken many times, and were held together with metal pins. At Caesar's Palace he broke the pins.

It could be said that an international Grand Prix had inherently more dignity than a lonely madman in white leathers soaring on two wheels into the jaws of death, but I, for one, was honoured to eat in the same hotel whose fountain had made rainbows in the tent of light through which the daredevil had once plunged, ringed with chromatic mist, to yet another disaster. The Grand Prix would have to be going some to top that. Eager to do so, the whole travelling F1 circus came to town and started providing us with footage, not all of which we could use, for legal reasons. My compatriot Alan Jones was World Champion at the time and he gave himself a champion's traditional reward. One of his mechanics, in uniform and tight cap, had strangely little to do except stand about, but was suspiciously well developed in the area of the chest. From close up I recognized the actress Susan George. Similarly, one of Alain Prost's mechanics filled the uniform too well. It was Princess Stephanie of Monaco. It was hell leaving that sort of thing out but the actual racing gave us some valuable action to set off beside the gambling, which was all psychology. Globular people ingesting carbonated drinks from huge paper cups marked GULP while they crank their money irretrievably into slot machines might be ravaged by interior tragedies of an intensity unknown to Aeschylus but it doesn't photograph. I didn't find gambling in the least interesting – when I was young I had too often seen my admirably thrifty mother in tears at not having won even a token tenner with her single, dearly bought ticket in the Opera House lottery – but I found the way it was organized in Vegas fascinating. The people running the place knew all there was to know about how the gamblers' minds worked. In the big hotels, a tinge of baby powder was pumped into the air-conditioning system because older people gamble more when you evoke their infancy. Did you know that? Neither did I.

But the people in charge of Las Vegas know everything like that. Their founding father, Bugsy Siegel, was an expert in the uses of fear. His descendants are experts in the uses of desire, including the desire to return always to the comfort of a fresh new nappy. Armed with such knowledge, they would probably get your money anyway, even if the odds weren't rigged in favour of the house. By nature averse to having my mind read, I was glad to get out of there. We got some watchable interviews. The best of them was with George Hamilton, an actor I had always admired, not least because he was too cool to care about his career. I talked to him in a sky lounge and had the sense to tell him, before the camera turned, that I thought his Evel Knievel movie and *Love at First Bite* were both wonderful. I wasn't lying and he could tell I wasn't, so he opened up. Quite often, when an actor does that, you wish he hadn't. But Hamilton was enchanting. As well as being hilariously full of showbiz lore, he looked like a million dollars, with a Palm Springs tan that might have been designed to go with his tuxedo. The camera ate him up like a crème caramel. There was also a dazzling few minutes with a blackjack dealer who could talk like your basic American dream girl: sassy, wise and quick. But even she was part of the apparatus. She taught me how to bet big only with the house's money or I would never beat the grind. The expression 'beat the grind' is still among my favourite expressions today, but I knew even at the time that the grind of Las Vegas was unbeatable. From all directions, like a hydraulic effect from the lower reaches of Dante's *Inferno*, you could hear the soft roar of the cataract as money poured from the pockets of the punters into the maw of the system. Under that kind of pressure I would have tunnelled out of Alcatraz with a spoon.

Alcatraz sat in the middle of our San Francisco movie like a cliché aching to be filmed. Every steep hill with a trolley-car heading upwards was screaming for a line about Steve McQueen's Ford Mustang heading downwards. Golden Gate Bridge? Very long bridge. I could have talked for an hour about the second-hand bookshops at Berkeley but nobody would have watched. Without a central story we would have been flailing. But a year of diplomacy had secured access to the San Francisco football team the 49ers, coached by the legendary Bill Walsh. Like the legendary Tom Landry of the Dallas Cowboys, his rival for the title of most legendary football coach in a country where all football coaches are legendary, Walsh was legendary for keeping the media at arm's length. Luckily the 49ers' press office was sufficiently impressed by the BBC logo to lower the barrier. They would not guarantee, however, that Mr Walsh would speak to us for longer than half a minute, or indeed speak to us at all. We still would have got the movie without him, because the footballers were good material. The star quarterback Joe Montana was out of action through injury at the time but he was still on the scene. Worshipped by all, he was universally congratulated simply for being alive. 'Way to go, Joe!' Looking rather like Barry Manilow on a quiet day, Montana spoke with similar straightforwardness, assuring me that a positive attitude was better than a negative one and that it was the team that mattered, not the individual. These impeccable sentiments were in no way undercut, of course, by the fact that he earned ten times as much as anyone else in the team. Since they all earned millions, there was no warrant for envy. One of the tight ends – how I would like to have been, or even to have had, a tight end – had a personal collection of aircraft. Not model aircraft: real ones. As I recall it, his name was Scott Clark, or it could have been Clark Scott. He was as tall as Charlton Heston but looked like Tom Selleck. We filmed him climbing into his navy blue Hawker Sea Fury and taking off to do stunts. His girlfriend, who was studying for a Ph.D. in comparative community relations, or perhaps comparative related communities, assured me that Scott, or Clark, favoured a positive attitude over a negative one and believed that it was the team that counted, not the individual. While she was enunciating this principle, her tight-end hero passed low overhead at about five hundred miles an hour upside down, riding in a clap of thunder. After his return to earth he strapped me into a parachute and boosted me into the front seat of his Stearman two-seater biplane trainer. Noisily we gained altitude. All the bay area was there below us. The camera was in another plane and pointing at us when my intrepid pilot turned the plane on its back. All the bay area was there above us. This guy simply loved being upside down. I liked it much less but tried to smile into the slipstream because I knew that the camera was on me.

The level of intelligence among the players was even more startling than the level of wealth. You soon cease to be amazed by squadrons of American athletes all driving Ferraris but when they start talking in epigrams it's hard to get used to, because elsewhere in the English-speaking world it just doesn't happen. Australian cricketers can quite often be funny but they wouldn't send you rushing to write down what they say. One of the defence team (playing in the position of secondary half-back if not half-track) gave me two minutes to camera about knee injuries. You could have put it on television as a fascinating little medical programme all by itself. 'A lot depends on the surface you're playing on. If you're playing on grass and your knee gets hit from the side, your foot will skid. If you're playing on carpet, your foot will stick. The lateral pressure has to go somewhere. If you're lucky it cracks the bone. A bone can heal. A displaced muscle might never come back.' His name was something like Brick Loadstone, he was about seven feet tall with a neck the size of my waist, and he could talk like Oscar Wilde. He took us to see the therapy pool. On the way he explained that he was only just back on the team after an injury, and that he was replacing a colleague who had suffered a similar injury. What I hadn't counted on was that the colleague who had suffered injury was also a replacement for a colleague who had suffered injury. Stretched across the bubbling surface of the therapy pool was a whole line of half-tracks the size of Brick. In the reverses on my face I had no trouble looking stunned. There was something frightening about the degree of specialization and duplication. The 49ers had tiny men, barely my size, who could run fast; they had large men who could stop small men; and they had men the size of dump-trucks whose job was to run a single yard at the crucial moment through the massed bodies of the opposing team. There was a man who rose from the bench only to kick goals; there was a man to replace him if he got tired of sitting down; and there was another man to replace the replacement. There was probably a man with two heads whose only job was to count the rest of them. He would have needed a computer. People who could grow a team like that could grow an army. The

49ers' star wide receiver, Jerry Rice, was a multimillionaire. Looking at his magnificent black body as he took a shower, I thought: 'Well, there he is, the white man's nightmare.' It didn't occur to me that he might be the black man's nightmare too, because if equality depended on inborn ability, then it was all a lottery. He was rich, respected and adored because he was a weapon.

The warfare metaphor was my way into a conversation with Bill Walsh. One of the ferrets had unearthed – without benefit of Google, remember – an article about Walsh's interest in the American Civil War. Walsh owned a library of books on the subject. I didn't, but I had read the whole of Shelby Foote's three-volume treatise, which counted as a library in itself. A man of classic military bearing whose alert features gave him a striking resemblance to Admiral Nimitz, Walsh sat behind the rosewood desk of his large office as if he were the CEO of a large company, which was indeed true. With our camera behind me I sat looking at him, and while we were still fiddling with the preliminaries I mentioned how the Civil War generals had dealt with the concept of a war of attrition between two equally balanced forces. Instantly Walsh was off and running. With the camera turning, I got a perfect interview which I wish I could screen as a separate programme even now. Walsh explained why a strong running game was basic to the passing game, because if you were forced to go to the air, instead of choosing to do so, the opposing team would still be too strong in the pass-rush to allow your quarterback his freedom. He even dealt with the tricky subject of injuries. He said they were bound to happen and that the certainty was reflected in the pay-scale. I asked him whether that idea wasn't ruthless, like saying that Hollywood studio heads got paid so much because one day they were bound to get fired. Walsh said there was a difference between ruthlessness and realism, and that the difference could be expressed by the result. 'A coach who cares too much about keeping the players from getting hurt will never reach the Super Bowl. A coach who cares too little will never even reach the play-offs.' Something like that, but better.

Only a few minutes of what he said got into the movie and I can't bear to think of all the rest that didn't. But we included enough to show America's central paradox in a nutshell: the ingenuity and energy it could afford to lavish on what didn't really matter.

That paradox arose in more awkward form when we flew to Playboy Mansion West in Los Angeles to interview Hugh Hefner in situ. It might have been more instructive to interview him in flagrante, even though, in that earlier phase of his dotage, he was sleeping with his 'ladies' only one at a time, instead of, as later, by the bunch. In the course of his career, Hefner had been notable, among his fellow entrepreneurs of soft-core pornography, in having done more than all of them to raise the status of their field to that of a corporate business – and, beyond that, to a Philosophy. When a football coach talked about his 'philosophy' it was usually a matter of how he rationalized, often with daunting articulacy, the necessary balance between physical aggression and mental finesse. But Hefner's Philosophy was meant to be the full, capitalized thing. Over the course of hundreds of monthly issues of his magazine, he had expounded, in his editorial column, a Philosophy of hedonism that took in every pleasure, including his pleasure in printing the latest work of Vladimir Nabokov and Mary McCarthy. (Very few writers, no matter how exalted their names, could resist the sort of money *Playboy* offered: an instructive example of the sheer power of the cash nexus.) But the Hefner Philosophy, multiform in scope though it was, depended on his basic notion of absolute sexual freedom. If you thought, as I thought, that no such thing was possible, the Philosophy was simply bound to fall apart. I thought that Alan Coren had said all that was necessary about Hefner's promotion of sexual freedom: it advertised something that was not for sale. The neat shape of Coren's remark was still in my mind later on when I defined religions as advertising campaigns for a product that does not exist – a crack that is still widely quoted, although not always by people I approve of. Just because

I don't like militant believers doesn't mean that I find militant unbelievers palatable. But Hefner's central belief, the motor of his extravagant life, I found impossibly solemn even in its moments of humour. I have to admit that I arrived on location with this prejudice in mind. The ambience of Hef – everyone, down to the Mexican gardeners, called Hefner 'Hef' because this wasn't just a democracy, it was, to use Hef's favourite word, a 'family' – might have been designed to show me that my prejudice was antiquated.

If that was the aim, it failed. Hef's feudal estate was indeed teeming with voluptuous young women, but they were vacuous almost without exception, and never more so than when they effervesced, each striving for individualism as they trilled variations on the theme that a positive attitude was better than a negative one. The dining room where free hamburgers were available twenty-four hours a day was indeed impressively populated with Hollywood male notables who had been given the run of the place because they were 'family', but it was sadly apparent that most of them were superannuated lechers. The film director Richard Brooks was typical. He hadn't directed a film in decades, and one of the reasons was that he had been here, chomping the free hamburgers while he eyed the women. He had written *Elmer Gantry*, he had directed *The Brothers Karamazov*, he had married Jean Simmons, and now he was in Hef's Hamburger Heaven, sizing up the poontang on his way to a final resting place in Hillside Memorial Park. This being America, there was plenty of conversation to be had, and it was all fluent; but, this being Playboy Mansion West, none of it was interesting, except when they talked about something else. All the women saw a future for themselves in the movies and of course none of them had a chance, simply because residence at the mansion was the principal item on their CV. The lucky ones got to be Playmate of the Month, and one of those married Jimmy Connors, but none of them was going to be a film star, not even the innocently pretty Dorothy Stratton, who caught the eye of my

friend Peter Bogdanovich. I can't blame him, but she would have
had little chance as an actress even if her jealous ex-boyfriend
hadn't murdered her. Hanging around Hef's playground was bad
training for any serious activity. In days gone by he had worked
hard for his first hundred million bucks, but now he was resting,
and he wanted everyone else to be resting too. The work ethic
was entirely absent. For most of the younger female inhabitants,
getting up in the morning was an obstacle course. Under their
compulsory ebullience, they were somnolent by nature, with
dialogue to match. The veterans, mainly men, had been burned
out for years. Some of them had good war stories but they might
as well have just handed you the script, and none of them had
anything gripping to say about Hef.

There was a good reason for that, as I was about to discover.
None of the attendant bores was quite as boring as Hef himself. He gave me a lot of his time, and I have to say he spoke
honestly. We filmed for hours and I never caught him fudging an
issue once. I had a key question: if this wasn't commodified sex,
what was it? He had the right answer: everyone was a volunteer.
But even when he spoke a useful and subversive truth, he had a
way of putting it that sent you to sleep. Uniquely among all the
American talking heads I ever interviewed, he couldn't say the
simplest thing in a way you could remember. You couldn't
remember it even while he was saying it. The middle of the
sentence had already left the beginning of the sentence lost in the
distance, and the end of the sentence was slower to arrive than a
school holiday. We were in desperate trouble. This interview with
the proprietor was our main event, and it was dead on arrival.

The only way to save the movie was to up the emphasis on
the local colour. Hefner's current 'lady' took us to the gymnasium
to show us how she stayed in shape by working out. She ran
slowly for two minutes on a treadmill. She lifted a couple of tiny
barbells. Hefner, in a silk robe, was in attendance to tell us she
favoured a 'positive attitood'. Struck by a frightening burst of
clairvoyance, I could see our audience falling senseless out of the

couch as if their television sets were emitting nerve gas. Thus it was that I dived into the giant outdoor Jacuzzi to join three of the *Playboy* gatefold girls for an en masse interview that yielded almost no verbal information beyond the fact that they were almost as harmless as I was. On top of that, or rather on top of those, they were wearing both halves of their bikinis. One of the three was quite bright, with a sardonic streak. By no coincidence, she came from England. Even she, however, was keen to point out that it was the team that mattered, not the individual. The whole aquatic encounter couldn't have been more anodyne to the ear. To the eye, of course, it looked as if I was offending against the most cherished tenets of a whole swarm of male television critics, paragons dedicated to the defence of civilization against the rising tide of frivolity. I was no longer in business as one of those, but there were plenty of hungry young men who were, and when they saw the finished movie they combined to give it a drubbing. I had spent the whole movie arguing that Hef's dream of sexual liberty was irredeemably childish but here were the pictures to suggest I shared it. The sequence was used as a stick to beat me with for years afterwards. My only defence was that I had thought the whole notion of joining a trio of Hef's glazed inflatable nymphs for a pointless plunge in the bubble-bath to be self-evidently ridiculous. When they saw the programme transmitted, even my family agreed with that. One at a time and in unison. Of all the Postcards we ever shot, this was the one most patently short of material, and we would have been better off scrapping it before it left the editing room. But that option was never open. Too much money had been spent going in, so it was just too bad if I looked stupid on the way out.

I shouldn't give the impression that everything we did happened in Postcard form. There were other formats asking to be developed. One of them was the star interview special, filmed abroad like a Postcard, but on a far smaller budget. It was a logical development, springing, as developments so often do, from lessons taught by an earlier project that had gone wrong.

While at LWT we had done a Postcard programme about the opening of a new resort called Sanctuary Cove, in Queensland. The show had been mostly a dead duck, a condition proved by the only part of it that came alive. Frank Sinatra had flown in for the opening-night concert and I had briefly interviewed him. Access was tricky. It would have been a lot easier to approach Colonel Gaddafi. Sinatra's lawyers checked out every item in a contract an inch thick. There was a clause saying that the red carpet between Sinatra's Portakabin dressing room and the stairs to the back of the stage had to be fastened down with fasteners not more than six inches apart. One of the lawyers got down on his knees with a ruler. My job was to do the public-address announcement just before Sinatra went on. After hours of drafting, I had a brilliantly compressed and poetically cadenced couple of paragraphs ready in which I evoked his stature and significance. Another of the lawyers read my document, handed it back to me, and then handed me a piece of paper. 'Say this,' he said, 'and only this.' There was a single typewritten line. 'Ladies and gentlemen, Frank Sinatra.' (The lawyer was right, incidentally: as I found out much later, a solo performer, if he is introduced by an enthusiast, is robbed of the opportunity to start at his own pace.) But before I said my line I was granted entry to the star's dressing room for an interview which, I was told, would last exactly five minutes. It was a daunting prospect but I asked him the right opening question. 'The words of the songs have always mattered so much to you. Is that why you don't sing many of the songs being written now?' He said, 'Good question,' and he was off. It was the right five minutes and it turned the rest of the movie to dust.

15. FOCUS ON THE NAME

It took us years to realize that this hard lesson presented a new opportunity. If the whole show could be an interview at that level, we wouldn't need anything else. At the BBC we began to put this principle into practice. With only one location, filming could be all over in a couple of days, although the format took a great deal of preparation, so as not to waste the time of the stars with any questions that they couldn't answer, or, more important, wouldn't. Contrary to received media opinion, there is no point in needling celebrities with awkward questions. The adversarial approach hardly ever works, because the subject can see it coming, and switches to automatic defence. With a forbidden topic, an indirect approach is more likely to work, or at any rate look less intrusive when it doesn't. Katharine Hepburn became available for the usual reason – she had a stiff movie to push – and we flew to New York to interview her in her house in the Turtle Bay area of the Upper East Side. It's the kind of district where Stephen Sondheim is your next-door neighbour and all the pedigree dogs hang out at the same deli. We had been told in advance that the two no-go areas were Howard Hughes, who had once loved her, and Spencer Tracy, whom she had never stopped loving. Ruling these two out left us with almost nobody to discuss except Nick Nolte, her co-star in the stiff movie. Even there, there were things I couldn't say. 'Have you noticed his close facial resemblance to the Duchess of York?' It would not have been a good question.

But the question I did ask proved to be the right one. I put it in the form of a statement, which she could take or leave. 'I'm not going to try to draw you on the subject of Howard Hughes, but some people say that falling in love with you was the only sane thing he ever did.' She liked that, and told me some of the story. I was the first ever to find out that when he took off under the bridges of the East River in a seaplane with only one passenger, she was at the controls. 'Did you know how to fly?' 'No, but he told me what to do.' She also told me why Hughes was so defensive. 'Howard was deaf.' Privately I thought that Hughes had been a particularly noxious freelance fascist, but Hepburn's insistence on his qualities was touching. After that, a direct question about Tracy seemed only natural. 'Tracy had everything, including you. So why did he drink so much?' Her answer – 'Tracy found life difficult' – was the start of something fascinating, a description of how the high living standards of the star system were designed to hold people prisoner. She expatiated without effort on the whole subject of how the declining bargaining power of an actress, due to age, could be offset only by the kind of leverage she was the first to achieve by actually owning the rights to the Broadway version of *The Philadelphia Story*, so that it couldn't be filmed without her. Katharine Hepburn was a very interesting woman. At that stage, the possibility that Marlene Dietrich and Mercedes de Acosta had been among her lovers was not generally known, and I wouldn't have asked her about it anyway. While people are alive, their private life is private if they wish it to be: it's a principle that was already vanishing from the world, but I believed in it, and still believe in it now. The great lady had been generous with her time and thought. We had enough to go on. While we were packing up, she finished making a batch of chocolate brownies and gave me a paper bag full of them to take away, having once again judged her man well. How lucky they all were to have been loved by a woman so brave, brilliant, funny and still beautiful even as the last of her youth melted into time.

Katharine Hepburn was a study in how to age gracefully.

Roman Polanski was a study in what not to do when you never want to grow old at all. Still preferring domicile in Paris to the stretch he would have had to serve in jail if he had returned to Los Angeles, Polanski had just brought out an autobiography which stated explicitly that he had indeed had sex with an underage girl, but that it had been consensual. It was interesting that he seemed unable to get his clever head around the concept that if someone is under the age of consent it doesn't matter if she consents or not. But it was much more interesting that this man had directed a string of important films, one of them being *Chinatown*, which I had judged to be a political vision of the modern world. I couldn't help feeling that we were all better off if a man like that was living in comfort near the Avenue Montaigne rather than bouncing off the walls in Chino prison. There was plenty of anecdotal evidence to warrant his billing as the five-foot Pole you wouldn't touch with a ten-foot pole. But his pint-sized frame was packed with talent, and – a rare thing, this – he had a mind to match his gift. (The memorably tragic ending of *Chinatown* was his idea, not the writer's.) We flew to Paris to set up the interview in L'Amis Louis, a tiny bistro much favoured by Warren Beatty, Jack Nicholson and others among that intellectual elite of Hollywood stars who never flew in a commercial airliner and always regarded the menu as an incitement to order something it did not contain. Interviewing Polanski over lunch was, as I remember, my idea. If it was, I was dead wrong. Always at the least desirable moment, different dishes arrived for hours on end. Polanski was very funny when he showed me how to hold a snail with the tongs provided. I sort of knew, but it was more fun to pretend I didn't. 'Would you like me to eat it for you?' He was directing me. What he couldn't do was follow the movie into the cutting room, where, predictably enough – so why hadn't I predicted it? – the order of our conversation had to be rearranged to make sense. So all the action was rearranged along with the conversation, and we ended up with a sequence of events in which the audience didn't have to be eagle-eyed to notice that the great director and his interviewer had begun a meal with coffee and ended it with snails for dessert.

But Polanski played the awkward question straight. 'I knew you were going to ask that,' he said, and very plausibly argued that if I had seen the girl in her make-up I wouldn't have believed that she was under age either. He rather spoiled things, however, by further contending that all men are switched on by under-age girls. Speaking as one who isn't, and who doesn't like the men who are, I have to say that I found him hard to admire for that. But unless the results were on the public record – which his California case most decidedly was – then his feelings were his business. I felt able to say, though, on air, that I could quite understand how anyone who had seen, as he had seen as a child, his own mother being taken away to be gassed, might be quite likely, in adult life, to be on the lookout for all the love he could get. But the idea that his personality might be entirely determined by his past was not one he seemed ready to entertain. (At this distance, having been subject to the attentions of a few amateur psychologists myself, I am inclined to think he was right.) I didn't think, however, that there could be any doubt that his childhood had affected his creative outlook. I had no idea that Polanski would one day make one of the great films on the subject of the disaster that had formed his vision. Neither had he. But you can be sure that *The Pianist*, a towering achievement for both him and its writer, Ronald Harwood, would never have happened in such a magisterial form if Polanski had stayed put in California to face the music. At best, he would have resumed his interrupted Hollywood career, and the man playing Chopin in the Warsaw ghetto would have been Keanu Reeves. Competent no doubt, but not quite the same thing.

In Paris, even with such a short schedule, there were still a few hours of downtime. Sitting outside my favourite cafe in the Rue de l'Université, where I still write at least part of all my books, I found myself working on the opening chapter of a novel about a young man from Tokyo having his life wrecked by a wild young woman in London. Perhaps Polanski's story had something to do with that, but really the hero, as usual, was myself. The best way to disguise yourself when creating a fictional hero is not to play down his abilities but to play them up. Give him prodigious abilities and nobody will believe it's you. The hero of *Brrm! Brrm!* (bad choice of title: in America it was called *The Man from Japan*, which didn't help either, but at least people had some idea of what they weren't buying) had prodigious abilities in martial arts, which I definitely have not, although I once chopped a milk bottle in half by accident. A key theme in the book was the role played by sexual desire. The plot turned on the fact that every attractive woman in London wanted the hero. I have no direct knowledge of what that's like, but I do have direct knowledge of what it's like wishing it to be true. I think most men have, and especially when they physically don't look as if they should. One such man was Luciano Pavarotti. In his earlier incarnation he had been built like a footballer and the girls had gone for him. In his later incarnation he was built like a housing development but he was still going for the girls.

This was common knowledge but nobody sane thought less of him. For one thing, the continuing power and beauty of his voice made his amatory pretensions very plausible: intelligent women fall in love through their ears, not through their eyes. For another, he was a charming man. When he appeared on television he converted viewers to opera fans by the thousands, just from the way he sang, and millions more loved him just for the way he spoke. He was especially adorable when his command of English showed its limitations. Broadcast to the world, his personal tribute to my compatriot Dame Joan Sutherland was characteristic. 'Thank you, Joan, from the heart of my bottom.' But there was nothing approximate about his intelligence. Full of stories and self-deprecating wisdom, he made a perfect talk-show guest if you could get him. Getting him, however, took strategy on a military scale. We booked him as a guest on the weekly show by conceding to a set of requirements that made sense only if you saw the question of his bulk from his angle, i.e. from the inside.

Pavarotti happened to be in the UK at the time so he wouldn't be needing a private jet. But he would be needing to get to the studio. A BMW 8 series was specified. (He could get in and out of a 7 series but he thought he didn't look good doing so.) The dressing room would have to be of the stated dimensions at least. (A blueprint of an aircraft hangar was duly appended.) Since he was currently on a diet, no food except fruit would be required for the dressing room, but there would have to be enough for a regiment. (From my own experience of dieting, I recognized the foible by which, restricted to certain foods, one eats twice as much of them, so as to diet more seriously.) When on set to be interviewed, he would have to be seated behind a table. We tried to get around this last part by making it a glass table but Pavarotti's minders spotted the trick and demanded a table of full opacity, the assumption evidently being that if the bottom half of their client's bulk were to be concealed, the upper half would take on a closer resemblance to Mel Gibson. But when we finally got him into position he was terrific. His fellow guest was the maestro Zubin Mehta, an equally sharp intelligence and fully articulate in English. Mehta did an entertaining job of helping Pavarotti answer questions about the opera business, and I could have listened to them both all night. Judging from the ratings the audience felt the same. This was a long time before Mehta conducted Pavarotti, Placido Domingo and José Carreras in the first Three Tenors concert, so we were in at the start of the whole thing. It was a festival. It would have been an even bigger festival if the star guest had sung something but you couldn't have everything. 'Clivay, I enjoy it various much.' That went down well at home, where my family were mad for the man.

Pavarotti had the invaluable gift of making you believe that he was giving you everything anyway, even when he wasn't deploying the attribute which made him famous. The soul of his art lay in his generosity and he gave you that every time. In a social role, I was actually present at Covent Garden for the Joan Sutherland farewell gala. My younger daughter usually makes a point of having me ritually slain if I drag her into the story, but I forgive myself in advance this time because the story is more about Pavarotti than about her. Justifiably daunted by the very idea of a big starry night out, she had agreed to attend on the understanding that she would see her hero close up after formative years of worshipping him from afar. During the intermission Pavarotti was behind a table in the Crush Bar holding court. I took my daughter over to meet him. He held up his hand for a handshake and she made the shy, nervous young person's response of failing to notice where her own hand was going. It knocked over a glass of red wine into his lap. He had a lot of lap to soak but there was more than enough wine to do the job. At that moment the great man would have had to show only the slightest sign of impatience and he would have destroyed her confidence for ever. But he did more than merely not doing that. He smiled like a happy grand piano and said that in the town where he was born, having wine spilled on you brought good luck. Then he kissed her hand. In what prayers I have left to me, I always make room for him.

Some of the Postcard programmes were taken up by individual American PBS stations but they rarely made it to the network, and the total PBS audience for them would have been only a tiny minority even if they had. Australia, however, unexpectedly increased the dimensions of our little world. The ABC executive who had devoted his career to keeping my programmes off the air abruptly died, perhaps from exhaustion at the magnitude of what he had achieved. He must have had a warehouse full of our unscreened shows. The man who took over his desk had a different agenda. He put all my programmes on the air at once and I became one of the most familiar faces in Australia practically overnight – a nice study in just how meaningless celebrity status is. The weekly show made a particularly big impression because people like Pavarotti were sitting there talking to the

local guy. The Kid from Kogarah was on at Covent Garden! The
ABC immediately asked us to come to Sydney and do a series on
the spot, with an all-Australian guest-list. At the time it seemed
like a good idea even to us, especially when we considered that
if we turned it down the new occupant of the desk in question
might start emulating his predecessor. So Richard and I flew to
Sydney to meet our executive producer, Michael Shrimpton. It
was immediately apparent that he was a smart man, and equally
immediately apparent that I now had a pair of smart executive
producers, which is rarely a profitable duplication. I was lucky
that they hit it off, but in other respects the luck showed quick
signs of being under strain. Richard got through the welcoming
party all right but it was a near-run thing. The ABC boardroom
was jammed with executives, many of whom would have quite
liked to be in charge of the show, or else, preferably, of a different show without me in it. I think one of them was the dead
executive, propped up from behind. He certainly had a fixed
smile. Everyone rapidly got smashed on the Chardonnay, a variety
of hair oil whose popularity among my countrymen I have never
been able to understand. Still on the wagon, I was soon the
only person in the room not leaning on someone else. On the
boardroom table there were numerous platters of edible refresh-
ment including a magnificent Frog in the Pond, a standard
form of festive comestible uniformly provided at any Australian
celebratory occasion from a children's party to the opening of
Parliament. I had made a serious mistake in not warning Richard
of the possible presence of a Frog in the Pond. I should have seen
it coming. This was a Frog in the Pond on the grand scale, about
ten square feet of green jelly surrounded by scores of chocolate
Freddo Frogs with their snouts buried in the verdant slime.
Richard had never seen grown men and women in proper clothes
pulling chocolate frogs out of a pond of jelly and sucking the
green gunk off the frogs' heads before biting the heads clean off.
For a moment he looked like a young British officer in India

suddenly realizing that his first suttee ceremony was going to be climaxed by a widow being burned alive.

But this Frog in the Pond *de grand luxe* was a sign that the bigwigs of the ABC top echelon were ready to pull every string on our behalf. What they couldn't do, however, was make the Australian audience tune in to watch Australian guests. Never before had there been an Australian talk show with such a roster. Nowadays, you can get that effect from the solo stars booked by the brilliant Andrew Denton, but in those days it was almost unheard-of to have such people on the air even one at a time, and we had them in bunches. We had Lloyd Rees, the great artist, and Les Murray, the great poet, sitting there next to each other. It should have sent the ratings through the roof, but the reverse happened. Finally the critics, of all people, told me what was going on. They didn't mean to, but all I had to do was read between the lines of some of the most contemptuous notices I have ever had. Their message was: he does his first-rate stuff abroad, and then he comes here to earn a quick bundle by doing second-rate stuff for us. The underlying assumption was not true – we had worked hard on every aspect of the show – but it was indicative. The assumption was that local achievement didn't rate on the international scale, and that I had reduced myself to the status of a local again simply by being present. We were shocked, but Richard, typically thinking faster instead of slower when he was up against it, quietly suggested that we might hoist the ratings if we booked Australia's Own Peter Allen, currently making a concert tour of his homeland. One of those versatile performers whose various talents are held together by nothing but ambition, Allen was famous in Australia for having written and recorded a song called 'I Still Call Australia Home', an anthem which somehow gained extra prestige from the evidence that he did no such thing. But at one stage he had been married to Liza Minnelli and for the Australian press he counted as being Big in Las Vegas, even though the majority of Americans couldn't recognize his face. They were lucky, incidentally, because he was one of the most unpleasant men I have ever met in show business.

After Peter Allen died of Aids it became infra dig to speak ill of him but I am glad to break the rule. In television, at the end of an interview, there is nearly always a bit of homework that the guest, no matter how illustrious, is called upon to do – a few extra angles, a wide shot, etc. – and you can measure their real stature by the grace they show in doing it. The true stars will turn the homework into a little extra show for the studio audience. Robert Mitchum, sitting still for a wide shot, said, 'You forgot to ask me what happened after I left the trailer door open while I was fucking the producer's wife and a dog came in and tried to swallow my balls.' A woman sitting in the fourth row fell into the aisle. Mel Brooks would slip into his Thousand Year Old Man character and tell the studio audience that 'many years ago, many, many millions of years ago, there was very little heavy industry, and the main means of transport was fear.' But some of the lesser stars soon showed you why they weren't any bigger. They would get impatient and make sure you knew it. Peter Allen was like that. The interview, during which he had been no more interesting than any other cheap hustler with a collection of personal jewellery, was mercifully over, and he had been asked to hold on while we got a wide shot. 'Can't you put that together from what you've got already?' I put my hand over my lapel mike so that the studio audience couldn't hear me and explained to him that no, we couldn't. He writhed, snarled, and finally said, 'Jesus Christ, what am I doing here?' Then he was gone. A long time later, I realized that he was really asking himself what he was doing in Australia, the land he still called home. The answer was that he was robbing the bank.

I suppose I was too, but the money wasn't really all that great. The ABC, perennially strapped for cash, has never been able to fork out the kind of salaries that the commercial channels lavish on male anchor-men with improbably youthful hairstyles who can reliably generate the same air of vigorous portent when presenting a report on a massacre in Rwanda or the story of the baby crocodile in the bishop's bathtub. ('And finally, for more on that baby croc that threatened the bishopric, let's go over to Raylene Trotter. Raylene?') But I had other motives, although I was still in the process of figuring out what they were. The process is incomplete even now, but early on I was groping in the dark. The initial thing that had got me going, however, was fairly clear to me. It was something to do with national pride. I wanted to make it clear that I still possessed it, and I thought I might have less ambiguous means of doing so than marrying Liza Minnelli, although I would have been flattered to be asked. (She was the most marvellous studio guest, by the way, full of funny, self-deprecating stories about celebrity, as its most helpless victims so seldom are.) I was shaken by the way Australia's own arts stars had been regarded as no great event by the very critics who made most fuss about national identity. Had I but known it, this was a foretaste of an argument fated to go on for decades and bear little fruit even yet. Some of my best friends still believe that Australia is being denied its national identity, so I have to be careful when I point out that they were lucky not to have been born in, say, Poland. It was quite evident to me, even back there at the time of the Bicentennial in 1988, that a country which could produce a poet like my old classmate Les Murray wasn't short of a national identity, it was only short of people with a proper estimate of poetry. Nationalism, as a state of mind, is all fervour and no judgement. National pride, however, is a different and better thing. To have counted on it, and found it lacking, was a bad blow. But it might have been my fault. Perhaps I had been too long away, and had missed the moment when the land of my birth had graduated to a state of self-consciousness even more nervous than my own.

16. THROW TO AUSTRALIA

After two hundred years of European settlement, Australia was understandably preoccupied with its own story. There was a momentum going that was hard to buck. The country's most powerful television company, Kerry Packer's Nine network, wanted an enormous Bicentennial programme that would last an entire evening. It would have three anchors. Two of them were Australian household names – Jana Wendt and Ray Martin – and the third, the ring-in, was to be me. All I had to do was say yes to a preliminary tour of inland Australia so that I might sound as if I knew what I was talking about on the big night. The tour was a wise precaution because like most expatriates of my generation I had never been out of my home state before I went to Europe. Travel within Australia was expensive when we were young. Only the rich flew interstate, and usually because they owned the airline. Fast-forward to a new era, in which Richard and I climbed out of aircraft of various sizes all over Australia for two weeks on end, under the leadership of the show's producer. Peter Faiman had directed *Crocodile Dundee* and still owned a large piece of it, which was like having a tap in his kitchen that ran liquid gold. Blessed with the personal cash-flow that enabled him to do anything he wanted, he sincerely wanted to make a TV programme that would help to give Australia a sense of itself, on top of the sense of itself that it had acquired already from sending Paul Hogan abroad to charm the world out of its pants and Linda Koslowski out of her underwear. That sounded good to me and I happily allowed myself to be wound down the shaft of an opal mine in Coober Pedy by the town's Greek mayor in person. Fifty feet above me he shouted, 'Is beautiful?' down the hole. It was beautiful indeed. The opal seams in the walls glowed pink and azure in the torchlight. I was in a bubble of loveliness.

In the flood plains of Kakadu I was in a puddle of danger. Being paddled in a shallow boat through a club-land for crocodiles was nasty enough but a helicopter ride along the escarpment was nastier still, because crocodiles are reasonable creatures compared with helicopter pilots, none of whom, in my experience, can be trusted. There was a whole generation of them who either pined for the great days in Vietnam or else were ashamed they never went. Making the passenger aware of danger was their mission, as if any passenger in his right mind ever doubted the danger: I mean, just look at a helicopter. If God had meant that thing to fly he would have given it wings. We shaved the escarpment so close that I saw a snake pull its head in. Hence the puddle of fear. Not that I wasn't enchanted by the flood plains on those occasions when I wasn't being shown off to the crocs or flown by a maniac. Kakadu reminded me of the Masai Mara. Here, surely, the African animals would be safe. Couldn't they be flown here two by two in an airlift version of Noah's ark? In years to come I tried the idea out on the PR representatives of several billionaires but I always got the same answer: the quarantine laws would never allow it. The quarantine laws had, however, allowed the importation of the cane toad, which was already, at the time of which we are speaking, taking over the country. The first cane toads had been brought in so that they might eat beetles inimical to sugar cane, but the cane toads quickly proved to be far keener on eating everything else, after poisoning it first. Leopards, I pointed out, wouldn't do that. Nobody listened.

Research had revealed that there was a town in upper South Australia consisting of one house with two people in it. When we arrived by Land Cruiser at the front door, only one of the people was at home. A large, soft woman who looked comfortable to sit in, she told us that her husband had driven to the next town because a pig was going to be killed. Were she and her husband stocking up on meat for winter? 'Nar, he just didn't want to miss the fun.' On the big night there would be an earth station camped in her front yard to watch her celebrate, so I gave her a firework to let off. When I asked her what she and her husband were doing out there – the desert stretched away on all sides until the world curved – she said they liked the simple life. So do I, really, but the world comes crowding in. Anywhere you set yourself up to be alone, a crew will arrive with a satellite uplink and ask you why you're there. Death is the only escape. In that year a lot of the Australian billionaires had died of terminal cash deprivation. One of them had sold all his Sidney Nolan desert landscapes to a gallery in Alice Springs. Off on my own during an hour of downtime, I strode into the tiny gallery, stood on the colourful carpet and bought one of the Nolans straight off the wall: a potentially useful gift for a wife who was starting to notice that I was at home far less often than not. It turned out that the colourful carpet I was standing on was an unrolled totemic painting by Clifford Possum Tjapaltjarri. Every mark on it represented something tribally important except the two footprints in the corner, which represented my size-nine desert boots. I bought it out of embarrassment but it is still in the family, growing in wonder with the years. Listen closely to it and you can hear the music, that delicious throbbing buzz that the great Aboriginal painters somehow get into the paint.

There was more, much more. About three million square miles more. We saw a lot of Australia. But apart from the gallery in Alice Springs, which had not been on the agenda, we saw nothing of the Australian arts, with one conspicuous exception. He was a painter called Pro Hart who was included in the schedule because of his impeccable Australian credentials. Like Crocodile Dundee, he wore a bush hat. Unlike Crocodile Dundee, he did not throw knives. But he did throw paint at the canvas in an uninhibited manner. Sometimes he fired the paint from a gun. Always ready with a few quotable banalities, he had been written up in the *Women's Weekly*: still, in those days, among Australia's

most influential periodicals. Faiman and his staff regarded Pro
Hart as the essence of democratic free expression. After a demonstration of his irrepressible spontaneity – he created a masterpiece in a matter of minutes, though the results made me wonder
why it had taken him so long – Pro Hart was duly signed up for
a satellite link on the big night. My suggestion that we ought to
be including singers, writers and real painters in our purview
fell on deaf ears. Peter Faiman was a nice man and a capable
organizer, but he had little knowledge of the arts and cared less.
His idea of an important writer was Colleen McCullough. I don't
hesitate to record this, because she had the same idea herself. It
was agreed that in the programme she would read out a passage
from her own prose which was meant to be a hymn to the
Australian identity. Back at Faiman's headquarters in Melbourne,
before Richard and I left for England, I argued that if we could
get Les Murray to write a special poem and read it to the camera
at his house in the bush, we could get the whole story about
Australia's new international literary status in five minutes. It was
promised that this would be considered.

Back in Cambridge I was gratified to discover that I was
recognized almost instantly by my family, but they soon noticed
that I was further perfecting my trick of disappearing even while
I was there. My essay collection *Snakecharmers in Texas* came out
and I had to push it in the media. Profile writers skated through
the book's themes in jig time before getting down to the business
of talking about the supposed tensions of fame. It occurred to
very few of them that the press profile *was* one of the tensions of
fame. Television interviewers didn't even pretend to be interested
in anything beyond television. Even more unsettling, radio interviewers also wanted to talk about nothing beyond television.
Increasingly I felt that I would have needed only a flex with a
plug to turn into a television set myself. But some of the reviews,
although careful to warn me that my visible presence among the
massed breasts of the *Playboy* gatefold girls might possibly have
eroded the authority of my opinions on the poetry of Eugenio

Montale, were thoughtful enough to convince me that I might still be some kind of writer. This was lucky, because there were several articles due that I had had only a limited time to sketch out while banging around in the outback. On top of those, a vast amount of draft script for the Bicentennial show arrived from Australia via fax, the new world-shrinking machine which, like every technical advance nominally calculated to save labour, actually increased labour by blocking all routes of escape from incoming requirements. The links and speeches that would be expected from me were presented in draft form. Dutifully I set about injecting them with argument, historical background, rhythm, syntax and grammar. Back they went to Australia, only to return immediately with a lot of yellow markings to indicate bits deemed to be either superfluous or too abstruse. Without exception they were the bits that I considered vital. I found myself fighting to save not just phrases, but whole lines of thought. Snatching a Friday lunch with the London literati as a drowning man who had fallen off the back of a liner might snatch at a trailing rope, I bewailed my existence. It was universally concluded that I had asked for it. There was no denying that. Halfway through the main course, a limo driver walked in, tapping his watch. He had come to take me away. Some of the blokes looked sideways. I couldn't have agreed with them more. There is a wonderful sentence in Philip Larkin's poetry that gets the feeling exactly. 'Something is pushing them / To the side of their own lives.' That was the year when we, the men who were Friday, were forcibly reminded that we were lucky to have lives at all. Our beloved Mark Boxer was diagnosed with a brain tumour. The thing was inoperable, and he wasted quickly to death, but there was time to visit him. Martin Amis and Ian McEwan paid calls right up to the last minute. It bothered me, and bothers me still, that I couldn't bring myself to go. There is a possibility that when I was very young I got a permanent overdose of whatever antibody is released into the bloodstream when we lose a loved one. Anyway, that's what I wrote in my letter, which he sent word that he had been glad to receive.

When Richard and I flew back to Australia to do the actual programme, my idea about Les Murray writing us a poem was still being considered, but nobody at command level of the huge show could get past the idea that Colleen McCullough must be a greater writer than Les Murray because everybody had seen *The Thorn Birds*. I suppose there was something to it. Anyway, the amount of airtime given to Colleen McCullough's assurance that only Australia could have given birth to her unique vision made me feel less wretched at having so much of my own prose cut from the script during rehearsals. Visiting my mother in a spare hour, I warned her that her beloved son would be making only a token appearance. She always had radar for any hint of discontent on my part. Having provided biscuits with the cup of tea, she could tell by the way I bit through a custard cream that I was 'in strife', but really that was too brave a term. There is such a thing as a level at which you can't compete. Besides, all the anchors, including even the mighty Ray Martin – justly revered for his ageless hair arrangement and his mastery of the uniquely Australian media attribute which might be defined as sparkling social concern – had to be cut to the bone to make room for the 'throws' from which the marathon running order was largely assembled. At this point I should explain what a 'throw' is. Look away if you already know. If you do, you probably work in Australian television. Nobody else cares, but everyone in Australian television persists in the belief that a throw is the most exciting thing that can happen on screen, the essential technical trick that defines the medium.

In the throw, the studio anchor hands over to the roving reporter on the spot, saying something like, 'And now, to give us a close-up of how the Prime Minister feels about these new allegations, let's go back to Mike Treadwell at Kirribilli House. Mike?' At which point, Mike says something like, 'Well, Ray,

the Prime Minister hasn't come out of the house all morning but
I gathered from the milkman earlier on that the general atmosphere in there is pretty subdued, pretty gloomy, pretty depressed.'
In a more elaborate version of the throw, the person who has
been thrown to does not throw back to the studio at the com-
pletion of his spiel. Instead, he throws to someone else who is
also out on location, perhaps standing in front of a stretch of
ocean which yesterday had been lashed by a freak storm. 'It might
look calm here now, Ray, but yesterday it was a seething cauldron
that spelt deadly danger to Steve Hewitt and his visually impaired
brother-in-law Hugh Stewart. Yes, this is where two men and a
dog met their fate.' As the reporter turns to look at the stretch of
ocean where nothing is happening except water behaving normally, we go back to Ray in the studio. 'And we've just heard that
those two men are still weak from exposure but ready to be interviewed. We'll be going to them later. But for now, the dog is with
me in the studio. Bluey, how did it feel when . . .' Multiply that
whole rigmarole by a hundred and you will have some idea of the
pace, structure and lexical ambition of the achievement in which
I was now involved. The gigantic, hideously expensive, technically
epoch-making and potentially identity-creating Bicentennial TV
spectacular consisted almost entirely of throws. We threw to Kakadu, to Kalgoorlie, to Wagga Wagga, to Woop Woop. We threw
to a hut in the Antarctic where three huddling meteorologists
assured their watching countrymen that their indomitable Australian spirit was proof against snow, ice and the inability to view
Neighbours on the day of transmission. There was meant to be a
satellite dish parked somewhere near Uluru so that a nationally
famous television correspondent – every reporter out in the field
was more recognizable to the Australian viewing public than Her
Majesty the Queen – could expatiate on the mood of the Aboriginals, this mood being detectable mainly by telepathy through the
walls of dwellings from which the indigenous people, understandably cheesed off by the idea of celebrating two centuries of white
domination, sensibly declined to emerge. The satellite dish was

mounted on a truck, the truck had fallen sideways off the road, and the dish was damaged. The correspondent was there anyway so that he could report on the condition of the dish. 'I'm afraid it's out of action, Ray.'

At this point I looked at Jana Wendt – never a hard task – and could tell she was thinking exactly what I was thinking. Well informed and highly cultivated, Jana is one of those beautiful women who become even more beautiful when they concentrate, and right then she was concentrating hard on the mystery of how, while not having heard from a single person of imaginative achievement in any field, we had managed to throw to every ephemeral television personality in Australia in order to be told, in most cases, next to nothing. Watching the monitors with a growing sense of dread as one fatuous episode after another swam into view, I was unable to exclude myself from the category of well-known faces with nothing to contribute. My last remaining mini-monologue, the one about Australia in war, had been reduced to a paragraph in order to make more room for Colleen McCullough's gruff assurances that Australia's barren interior landscapes had somehow got into the rhythm of her prose. Well, that was believable, but why were we listening to her when we could have been listening to Joan Sutherland telling Jana abut the richly sophisticated Australian musical background that had launched her on her flag-carrying international career? What was Jana doing there, she who had interviewed every prominent creative figure in Australia and was now allowed to mention none of them? And what was I doing there, saying nothing, when saying things is the only thing I know how to do? The lady in the desert let off her sparkler. That had been my idea, and the only one to have reached the screen intact. Otherwise, there was nothing of mine on view except my grimly eager face. Eventually, after several different kinds of eternity – there was a short speech from Prime Minister Bob Hawke that was a killing reminder of how a boring speaker needs only two minutes to evoke the concept of geological time – the thing was

over. Respectful of my hosts, who had paid me well, I was careful never to be drawn on what I thought of the show. But now
that a full twenty years have gone by I think I can risk saying that I was less than proud of having been in it. If we
Australians couldn't do better than that then we had an identity
crisis indeed, but not of the kind that the intelligentsia was complaining about. Australia's creative and scientific life was teeming
with specific voices, but what was missing was the general voice
to place them in context. The general voice is the historic voice,
and in Australia historic voices were in thin supply, despite the
fact – or perhaps because of the fact – that the whole of world
history could be viewed as having taken place precisely in order
to bring about a society so prosperous, multicultural, egalitarian
and politically well equipped to deal with even its most intractable
anomalies.

Still, there is no free country that doesn't churn out trivia,
and it might even be possible that the liberal democracies – of
which Australia is among the most advanced examples – are fated
never to reach a true estimation of their own stature. To do that,
they would have to be fully aware of what it is like not to be free,
and it is hard to reach such a harsh awareness without being
born and brought up in a country that isn't free at all. To that
extent, a liberal democracy is dreamland. Most of the people
engaged in public argument have no real idea of what it might be
like to be officially persecuted for holding an opinion, instead of
being merely vilified by those whose opinion is to the contrary.
As a student of history, I had at least some idea, and was able to
keep my head when I was attacked for being a monarchist.
Knowing that there had been a day when you could have your
head cut off for being anything else, I was able to be grateful that
I had only paper darts to dodge, instead of the axe. The matter
had already come to a point before I went out to Australia to
make the Bicentennial programme, because Prince Charles's staff
had roped me in as one of his Australian advisers on the matter
of whether his Bicentennial speech, to be delivered in Sydney,

should mention the Aboriginals. The Foreign Office, with what I thought to be typical stupidity, had advised him to make no mention of the subject. I advised him to mention it. I doubt if I was alone in this. I imagine Barry Humphries, to name only one other Australian with his name in the papers, advised the same thing, and Germaine Greer certainly would have. (Charles loved Germaine: shyly aware that he could be a bit of a stick-in-the-mud, he was switched on by her coruscating fire.) But among Charles's numerous virtues is a knack for making you feel that he is listening to you as an individual, and not just as the representative of a group. I met him and liked him. More than that, I admired him: I thought he handled his difficulties well. As yet it had not become apparent just how difficult his marriage was going to get. It was easy to be blind on the matter because the Princess of Wales was so attractive that it was hard to imagine, on slight acquaintance, how any male with red blood would not want to follow her around like a puppy. I met her when I went down to Cannes to host a black-tie dinner for Sir Alec Guinness. Charles and Diana were both there, and afterwards Diana came swerving through the crowd to park her radiant face in front of mine. (I mean her face was radiant: mine was just a face, no doubt looking more than usually sheepish.) 'I do think it's awful,' she said, 'what you do to those Japanese people in your programme.' Even if she had called them Chinese, I still would have been enslaved. Perhaps a bell of warning should have rung. It should have been clear to me that she could do this to anyone in trousers.

But she was doing it to me, and I was immediately on her team. In mitigation, I can say that she and Charles still had, or appeared to have, a team going too, and it still looked as if their team were playing for Britain at world-championship level. On that basis, I thought that the future for the monarchy looked secure for a couple of generations at least. But even with a less promising couple waiting in the wings, I would have been in favour of the monarchy anyway, because of my conviction that

the United Kingdom – and, by extension, my homeland – benefited from having a head of state from a family which had no
interests beyond preserving its own continuity. Charles was going
to be that head of state one day; he had few disqualifications
beyond an excess of thoughtfulness and concern; and I was for
him. It was an opinion shared, tacitly at least, by a great majority
of the British people, but there were penalties to be paid for
endorsing it. At some awards ceremony or other, when I followed
Charles to the microphone and complimented him on what he
had just said – he had indeed said it well, but he seldom gets
high marks for doing that, especially from professional commentators who would say it worse – Auberon Waugh was in the
audience and immediately decided, doubtless prompted by a gift
for mind-reading, that I was a raw colonial truckling for honours.
He went into print with this opinion as often as possible and
included me on his list of Australians who should be sent home.
Bron (everyone called him that, even his victims) either didn't
see the historical irony involved in recommending that a miscre-
ant should be forcibly transported from England to Australia,
or else he did, and promoted the idea in order to further his
reputation for outrage. He was a fluent, original and funny
journalist but the shadow of his great father Evelyn might have
frozen him into a mental condition of self-contempt by which he
thought it didn't matter what he said because it was only him
saying it. Certainly he was not one of those journalists who,
lacking the means to make reasonable opinions interesting, must
resort to unreasonable opinions in order to get the reader's
attention. He was more talented than that, so it must have been
from some reservoir of anger that he wrote articles attacking the
author rather than the work. My friend Lorna Sage – dead before
her time, alas – suffered for years from his calumnies. It could
be said that she should have known how to defend herself in
print, but there was no prospect of self-defence for the British
and Australian prisoners of war who had suffered so cruelly in
Japanese hands during World War II. Bron said, in cold print,

that their sufferings had been exaggerated, and that the survivors, and the families of the dead, had been making capital out of stoking the memory of an event that had been largely the creation of Allied propaganda. As the son of an imprisoned soldier I found it hard to forgive Bron for that. But after his death I met one of his charming children and realized that he couldn't have been all bad, if he had brought up his progeny so well: the failings of Evelyn Waugh as a father had not been echoed by the son, possibly because the painful memory was so acute. Anyway, to harbour a literary grudge is time wasted. Your opponent isn't going to kill you, because he isn't allowed to. He can write all the denunciations he likes and you will suffer nothing except the strain of raised hackles. In a society without laws he needs to write only a single denunciation, and you are a gone goose. Literary figures who question the value of a free society should try to spend some time in one that isn't, in their imaginations if not in reality.

17. SHANGHAI EXPRESS

In Shanghai we spent only two weeks, which wasn't enough. But it was a start. An ancient Chinese curse runs: 'May you live in interesting times.' June 1989 proved to be more interesting than even the Chinese leaders had bargained for. In Beijing, Tiananmen Square filled up with protestors, often billed in the Western media as students. The same sort of people filled the Bund in Shanghai and it was clear that they weren't all students. Everyone who could read and write was out on parade. Had we been a news crew, we could have filmed nothing else all day. But we had a carefully prepared movie to make, so we knocked off the sequences one by one. We went to the circus and watched incredible feats of skill until our senses were numbed. How many people in silk pyjamas can stand on the head of the person below? The number is astonishingly high, but not as astonishing as the shape of the head of the guy at the bottom. Either he had been born with a cranium like a foot locker or, more likely, he acquired it under pressure. A fixed smile went with his flat skull but he seemed happy to be interviewed, although he would probably have seemed equally happy if we had set fire to his toes.

We went to the opera and watched men pretending to be women pulling faces while other people of various sexes and sizes turned midair sideways somersaults to the rhythm of garbage-tin lids being struck with sticks. Our numbed senses were benumbed all over again. A man behind me in the crowded theatre blew his nose onto the floor in the standard Chinese manner and I lifted my feet so that the river of snot could slide by unimpeded. The river of snot wasn't all his: a couple of hundred guys had contributed to it. As I sat there with my knees around my ears, I reflected that the commentary for this programme would be no cinch. A whole society was being shaken to its foundations in the streets outside and here we were, stuck with this stuff. Even when the topic had a bit more heft, there was a limit to the extent we could explore it. A woman at the music school told me what it had been like to be included in a representative sample when the Gang of Four sent people of suspiciously elevated accomplishments (the policy was called Three Famous, Three High) off to the fields to have their hands ruined and their pride broken. ('They would lecture us all the time. That was the worst part.') But she wasn't allowed to say that it was all Mao's idea. Nobody was allowed to say that. We talked to a young man called Yi Bin who had managed to assemble a small collection of ancient ceramic fragments and who had published a paper about them. He kept all his collection at one end of his parents' bedroom, on shelves around 'my little bed'. The bedroom was divided by a thin curtain. The thin curtain looked heavier to me than any iron curtain I had ever heard of. Yes, I knew what I would say when I got home: but there was small prospect of saying any of it on the spot, or even of setting up a scene that might imply it. The spooks were watching, or else listening to someone who reported to them, perhaps the guy that drove your van. They didn't have to watch or listen very closely because everyone else knew they were watching or listening. This was a society that was censoring itself. Except, of course, for the demonstrators.

Every night we were in Shanghai, the crowd on the Bund grew bigger. Since the whole mile-long sweep of road was already jam-packed the first time we saw it, growing bigger was a hard thing for the crowd to do, but somehow yet more people were always managing to fit themselves in between the people who were already shoulder to shoulder. Many of the banners were decorated with little bottles. Our interpreter – a nice girl who dressed up to the nines Western style, with an expensive pair of imported shoes – explained that the little bottles were a pun on the name of Deng Xiao Ping. My remaining hair stood on end when she told me that, and I told her to be careful what else she told me. But in her quiet way she was high on a sense of adventure like everybody else: whatever their age and walk of life, the people in the streets were ecstatic. Many of them thought our film camera was a news television camera and they struggled towards it to deliver their message, which was mainly about freedom. They thought I was a reporter. One of them thought I was Winston Churchill. Even if our footage was not impounded, it would be an age before it got to London, so there was no news value in any of it. Nevertheless I thought myself quite the ace. Some of my friends had a knack for getting into the historical action. (Saddam Hussein, when he dived into his last funk-hole, was lucky not to find Christopher Hitchens already down there holding a notebook.) This was my moment in the crucible of destiny. I was as high as a kite from Weifang in Shandong province, where the best kites come from.

Euphoria crashed when the manager of our hotel told us what would happen next. He was a Dutchman. Like everything else in the hotel except the service staff, he was imported. The hotel was the Shanghai Hilton. It was a modern building that had been dropped into the decaying city like a shining probe from space, complete with its own water-recycling system. Even the food was flown in from Hong Kong. (These were still the days when the last place you could safely eat a Chinese meal was China.) The standard of service in the hotel was fabulous. When I opened the door of my suite, there were always a couple of young ladies in black pyjamas crouched outside ready to rush in and change the flowers, the toilet rolls, the wallpaper. They called me, in their language, One Fat Important Man, and equipped me with a tiny cup of red wax and a jade seal (called a chop) on which the name was carved in Chinese characters. They also joined in the task, gladly shared by every local we met including senior members of the Communist Party, of teaching me quite a lot of the Mandarin dialect: a very pretty way of speaking Chinese, as opposed to the

Cantonese dialect, which is impossible to mimic unless you have the vocal equipment of a dying dog. Today, if you're asking, my Mandarin vocabulary has shrunk to the words for thank you, goodbye and One Fat Important Man, but for a while there, surrounded by these glowing sylphs as they corrected my grammar while rebuilding my room, I had visions of myself conversing fluently in their musical tongue. Alas, it never happened, but they behaved as if it was already happening. They were world-class flatterers, that bunch, and no doubt they went on to help organize the Olympics in 2008. But in 1989 all this Eastern-Western luxury was definitely a message from the far future. In the present, the manager told me, the demonstrations could end only one way. In Beijing, he said, Tiananmen Square would be cleared by force, and then everyone in Shanghai would go home. 'There, they will kill a few people. Maybe not here.' I was reluctant to believe that there would be a crack-down. But then the eerily lacklustre Li Peng appeared on television and started to speak. An hour later he was still speaking, even though he hadn't said anything except that the counter-revolutionaries, if they did not disperse, would be suppressed by force. Next day, in Tiananmen Square, they were, and everyone in Shanghai did indeed go home. The Bund emptied in a matter of minutes.

We went home too, on the last plane before Shanghai airport closed. At the time, I would have said that nothing could ever break the monolithic grip of the Chinese Communist Party, and in fact, even now, nothing yet has. But the Shanghai Hilton had already started to change the country. It just never occurred to me that the hotel we were staying in was the real story. Blind to the implications, I felt that our only course was to make the best possible movie out of what we had, and I was all too conscious of the subjects we had been unable to explore, for fear of getting innocent people into trouble. We had met a wonderful young woman who ran a small theatre company. I can't be more specific than that even now, just in case some sharp security officer gets the urge to track her down and re-educate her. (If you think it unlikely that someone could be punished for what they might have said out of turn twenty years ago, you have a very rosy view of how a police state works: the spooks are never off the case, and they have nothing else to do.) When I was safely back in England I got a letter from her saying that she was in despair for her country and wanted to leave. I was all set to send her a reply and an air ticket when a Chinese refugee I knew said: don't. 'They' might conceivably have not read her letter on its way out, but they would certainly read any reply on its way in. I managed some direct help for exactly one person out of a billion. Our amateur archaeologist Yi Bin got a scholarship to London and he defected when he arrived. My family made a friend of him and I wrote the occasional reference. In return he gave me a set of Chinese classical poetry anthologies which are still on my shelves, closed books that I will never now learn to read.

And that was it. Apart, of course, from the movie, which turned out to be a crowd-pleaser. There was plenty of comedy as One Fat Important Man rode around on his bicycle, its tyres dutifully bursting when the scene required. And there was the resolutely cheerful yet infinitely sad face of the music teacher, back from such a living hell under the Gang of Four that she thought the China of 1989 a miracle of liberalism. Beyond help, beyond hope, her tired eyes were a reminder that pity was useless: and she would have been the first to say that she was the lucky one, when so many of her friends had died of heart-break, pounded into despair by Madame Mao's insane vision of the future of mankind. And behind Madame Mao had been the old man himself, now long dead but still preserved in his full corporeal splendour inside the mausoleum that occupies the centre of the same square where that lone student faced down a tank, immortalizing himself in a stretch of footage which has since been screened a million times everywhere in the world except China. The significance of that last fact didn't become fully evident until somebody invented the World Wide Web. The Chinese leaders had kept the pictures out because they were scared of the possible effect. It followed that if the day arrived when they could not keep the pictures out, they would have to modify their behaviour. They still do everything they can, however, to slow the pictures down: the Web routes into China are more closely guarded than the Great Wall ever was. As of this writing, the Great Helmsman's shining corpse is still the touchstone of authority for each new batch of gerontocrats preaching modernization. Until they melt that waxwork down for candles, you can't trust them for a thing.

Being a good Samaritan is a calling for some, and truly they shall see God; but I have always been too selfish with my time. There are occasions, though, when keeping yourself to yourself will shrink the space that you are trying to protect. As the weekly show's satellite interview slot became more flexible, we got into Russia, where the system, agitated by the benign example of Gorbachev, was breaking up with increasing speed. A stocky young journalist called Vitaly Vitaliev became our regular correspondent from Moscow, and quickly earned the love of the British and Australian public. Vitaly's English was pretty good but it never modified the inexhaustibly abundant personality that so many Russians bring to the task of celebrating victory in war, or the birth of a new baby, or just a new day. He always looked and sounded as if he drank vodka for water. He could throw an arm around you from three time zones away. From a clapped-out Moscow TV studio still decorated to match Stalin's personal warmth, Vitaly grunted, chortled and gurgled the story of what was really going on. It was better than anything on the news. After the Chernobyl disaster he walked into the area without a protective suit and still came out glowing with energy, although by rights he should have been glowing with radioactivity and lying on a stretcher. It seemed remarkable how much he was able to say, but it soon turned out that the new freedom of speech under glasnost had its limits. The KGB was phoning him in the night, and in their fine old style they reserved their most obscene threatening calls for his wife and little son. Vitaly was hard to scare, but anyone can be scared by a threat to his family, and the day arrived when he felt it prudent to do a runner. When he came to us in Cambridge on the weekends he was a huge hit with both our daughters. He made 'avuncular' sound like a Russian word, but then, he did the same for every word in the English language. His accent was so catching that even I caught myself wishing him Myerry Chryistmas. Like the refugee dissidents of the old regime, however, those who fled the new one were bound to encounter employment problems. For a while Vitaly was in demand by the BBC and the upmarket press for his opinions on the new dispensation in Russia, but it soon emerged that his opinions did not suit. Nobody knew what he was on about when he said the next big thing in his homeland would be gangsterism, not democracy. He would be proved dead right in the course of time, but for now he was thought to be a bit of a crank, and he soon decided that his chances might be better in Australia. At this point my celebrity status came in handy for once, because I was able to get him fast-tracked through the immigration process. My recommendation read like science fiction but it was all true. Off he went to the future, from which we were later saddened to hear that he had started another family along with another life. It often happens that way: when the pressure that a couple faced together relaxes, it turns out that they were never quite as together as they thought.

Since the majority of divorces are instigated by wives rather than husbands, a man with feminist sympathies – I count myself as one such, despite my Neanderthal instincts – is bound to take a liberal view of the subject, and try to believe that the liberating effects often outweigh the destructive ones. By that time, a lot of the people I had known when I was young were moving into their second marriage, leaving the first in ruins. From a philosopher's viewpoint, this could only be a welcome development in the propagation of human rights. But I couldn't help noticing that my own children cared little for a philosopher's opinion. What they wanted was reassurance from their father that they were living in a proper house and not a bouncy castle. Divorce was getting so fashionable that it wasn't a surprise even when Charles and Diana showed public signs that all was not well. Young people couldn't be blamed for wondering if their parents might not catch the fashion too. I did my best to sound like a man who would always come home no matter what, but it's not an idea that can be very convincingly projected from a distance, and all too often I was away. Being away when I had to be away was perhaps forgivable, but being away when I didn't have to felt like treason even to me. I had become so caught up with learning to read Japanese, however, that I would stop off in Tokyo even if I was flying home from Valparaiso. In a Jin Bo Cho coffee shop I would sit down with my latest batch of second-hand books about the Pacific war and transcribe characters until my eyes bled. Why was it so hard, and how would I ever get anywhere unless I gave it everything?

Somewhere about then, I was having my portrait painted by a prodigiously gifted young artist called Sarah Raphael, daughter of the writer Frederic Raphael, who was of an age with me, which meant that Sarah was not all that much older than my elder daughter. I had seen Sarah's first exhibition and written a piece in which I said that for her to be called Sarah Raphael didn't quite meet the case: she ought to be called Sarah L. da Vinci. She liked the joke and offered to paint my portrait as a reward. After a long taxi ride I arrived at her far-flung studio to discover that she was good-looking far beyond the job description. She had all the intelligence and wit of her famous father, but they were contained, if he will forgive me, in a more disarming package. Married, with a couple of children of her own, she was pushed for time if she was going to get any work done, but I soon learned to value every visit. I hoped the portrait would take forever, like Penelope's tapestry or the tale-telling of Scheherazade. My admiration was apparent but she sweetly put up with it. She'd had plenty of practice. Quite apart from her suitably handsome young husband, her admirers were countless: William

Boyd, Terry Jones, Tom Conti, Daniel Day-Lewis, the list went on and on, all of them helplessly, hopelessly doting on her beauty and genius. That last word was, for once, not excessive. Clearly she was going to be a great painter. She was well aware of this – the great always know they are, because they are never unaware that their gift comes from heaven – but she could be charmingly apprehensive about the burden of her duty. 'You really think I'm quite *good*, don't you?' I did indeed, but I loved her for the question.

Stewing in the turmoil of a Platonic vision was made easier by the fact that my family loved her too. My wife owns more pictures by Sarah than I do, including the portrait of me, which I have to ask permission to look at. When, a few years later, my elder daughter, after taking a Ph.D. in molecular biology, turned from science to painting, she made it clear that Sarah's towering example was one of the reasons. Sarah brought out the best in everyone who knew her. Her father and I had been literary enemies before I met her – the quarrel had been my fault, not his – but when I became a proponent of her work he forgave me my sins. For me, apart from the intoxication of her delightful company, the example of her dedication to her art was a constant lesson in how to focus every tension of your life into a single task and make something of it. She suffered terribly from migraines but she found a way of working even through the pain. When one of her daughters needed eye surgery she would put down her brush, take the patient off to hospital for a harrowing day and pick up the brush again when she got back. She valued everything that happened to her because eventually it would go into her work. Time had improved me anyway: when I was at home, I was of more use around the house. But Sarah's example made me happier about pulling at least part of my weight in a domestic context when there was no camera present to watch me doing so. When my younger daughter and I set off every Saturday morning to do the weekend shopping – a ritual expedition that we still pursue today – I felt blessed, and doubly blessed because it gave my wife a vital extra hour at the computer to nail some crucial point in Dante's *Monarchia*. No wonder she and Sarah adored each other: they were of the same stamp.

Playing the stalwart might have been easier if I had always been on the spot, but even if my temperament had allowed that, my trade seldom did. From that angle, a new format called the End of the Year Show had the merit of pinning me to the ground for the three months it took to write. The weekly show had always been a taxing job to script, to such an extent that a professional had finally been brought in to help me. His name was Colin Bostock-Smith and he was an inspired appointment on Richard's part, because he wasn't only a fountain of skilled gags, he had a practical sense that kept me to schedule. An awareness of timing, in the show-business sense of putting words in the right order, and an awareness of time, in the horological sense of little hands advancing around the clock's face, are two things that very rarely go together in the one personality. Bostock, as I immediately took to calling him, could do both. In addition, he was hilarious company, and we both looked forward so much to being locked away together in my inner office that some of the women in the outer office started to wonder if we weren't getting our rocks off in there – the snorts and giggles sounded like a bath-house bacchanal. I never met a man who entertained me more. More important, what we wrote together entertained the public. I still took the responsibility for the script. My power of veto was unquestioned, and if something unsuitable had threatened to get into the script I had the authority to keep it out. But it was an authority I never needed to use because Bostock's taste was impeccable, like his ear: working together, we created a complete grammar for putting words to images that is still, today, in such wide use throughout the industry that it is taken for granted, and although modesty dictates that I should disclaim my share in its invention, duty demands that I credit Bostock with his painstaking ingenuity. It was meticulous work, but in short order we were motoring at such a rate that Richard started wondering whether we might not need a bigger format to soak up all the scintillation. Hence the idea for an annual round-up was born. The show would be broadcast on New Year's Eve, ending as Big Ben struck twelve. It would be built around all the news footage that we could rake in and suitably misrepresent. Computers could already do a lot but they couldn't yet sort images. If you wanted to choose the right (i.e. wrong) moments from the recent history of Ronald Reagan, you had to collect miles of footage and look at it in real time. Elementary calculation revealed that it would take at least nine months to process the footage and the actual writing would have to start in September.

Entrusted with the mission of framing every prominent villain, buffoon or misguided celebrity, a whole team of ferrets was assigned to tracking down the last potentially usable frame of such natural stars as our old friend Yasmin Arafat. That mission, though huge, had a clear aim. Another aim was less clear, but potentially just as rewarding. If Bostock and I could build a sufficiently portentous context, a perfectly banal statement from one of our gallery of the questionably famous could yield rich results. We wrote a test link about the ending of the Cold War, speculated as to the identity of the single historical voice that had brought this desirable termination about, and followed up the paragraph with some footage of the deeply beige Australian pop star Jason Donovan declaring that there would be less war if people stopped hating each other. The results were uncanny. But the idea was very hard to research, because the ferrets would have to see, in an incongruous historical context, the possible resonance of statements that otherwise meant next to nothing. Statements or actions: any footage of Ronald Reagan walking through a doorway, or just picking up a glass of water, might be the start of something: so fill out the forms and get hold of it. We expected such prodigies of endeavour from the re-searchers that it was sometimes easy to forget they were a bunch of kids. Their den-mother, who I shall call Jean Twoshoes for purposes of respect, was a whiz at digging stuff up and getting the permissions, but she had a tendency to witter on. Richard made a gag out of looking at his watch while she wittered, and it made her witter worse. But she could do the business and I loved her for it. An excess of zeal is exactly what you want from a researcher: too great a sense of proportion and they come up short.

Months before it went to air, the first New Year show felt right, and I even got home on the weekends, radiating the contentment of a balanced life. Or I would have done, except there was always a new Postcard to be prepared for early the year after. It had been noticed that my lack of ability to drive a car could sometimes be a limitation when we were filming me getting about in a foreign capital. Riding on the subway system looked OK in Tokyo or Paris – in either city, only an idiot drives – but it would be a problem if we ever went to Los Angeles, which obviously we would one day have to do. How to find time to have driving lessons was the question. I had always had a theoretical interest in cars – provided I don't have to fix it, there is almost no form of technology that doesn't fascinate me, garbage-disposal units included – but for some reason I had never learned to drive. Probably the reason was a sound professional instinct: a writer might possibly read at the wheel, but if he did much writing at the wheel there would be a crash. From the practical viewpoint of filming, however, the inability to drive was a severe handicap. How to eliminate it?

18. WHEELS AT SPEED

The obvious answer was to buckle the learning period into the subject matter of a show. The chance to do this came when someone proposed a Postcard programme called *Clive James Racing Driver*. The Adelaide Grand Prix had invited my participation in the Celebrity Saloon Car Challenge race, one of the sideshow races to the main F1 event. The Adelaide organizers had been inspired by the knowledge of F1 that I had demonstrated when narrating the annual FOCA (Formula One Constructors' Association) video round-up for Bernie Ecclestone, who more or less owned the whole GP circus. Richard, who had known Bernie since he was only a millionaire, had rowed me in on the narration job before Bernie had a chance to find out that I couldn't drive a golf cart. But I must have talked a good game. The Adelaide people clearly had no clue. Without bothering to disabuse them, we worked out a format where I would qualify for my road licence in England at the start of the programme so that I could move straight on to the racing-driver school in Adelaide, there to learn track technique along with the other celebrities, who had all been driving ordinary cars on the road ever since they were teenagers. It would be a good joke to watch me learning what they learned, provided I didn't kill myself or anyone else when we zoomed around the speed bowl. But before I did any zooming in Adelaide, I would have to learn to drive an ordinary car in England, and the question arose of how we could make my driving lessons visually entertaining. Who would do the teaching? Richard, searching further into his contact bag, came up with the answer: Stirling Moss.

I thought this a brilliant idea until Stirling came shouldering into the office and said, 'How in God's name did you get this old without learning to drive a car?' He was one of those intensely confident men who, slightly shorter than average, are always the tallest person in the room, so that you find yourself looking up to them with your head bowed. I was only partly lying when I told him it had all been his fault. When I was at Sydney University in the late 1950s Stirling had come out to New South Wales for a one-off non-championship Grand Prix. The local media contracted its usual case of severe backwater fever and turned the event into the biggest story since Frank Sinatra had been blacked by the Australian trade unions after referring to the women of the local press as a pack of hookers. Suddenly it was social death not to have an international racing driver as a dinner guest, with the suave Stirling as the top catch. At fashionable tables he would tell tales of the Mille Miglia, the great race in which, at the wheel of the Mercedes 300SLR racing sports car, he had *averaged* a hundred miles an hour over a thousand miles of ordinary Italian roads. The society ladies had no idea of what he was talking about but they could smell the heady cocktail of fame and danger and they leaned towards him like falling flowers. On the big day, the entire stratum of Sydney high fashion decamped to the circuit as if it had been Royal Randwick. With the side-panels of his car removed so that he could cope with the heat, Stirling won the race in such an heroic fashion that I resolved on the spot never to bother with doing badly what he could do so well. Also, I reminded him, he had cynically capitalized on his glory to get off with the University's leading beauty of the time, who had proved tenaciously resistant to my poems but had given herself to him five minutes after she smelled the petrol on his breath. 'You mean Veronica Minestrozzi? What a cracker. I did the whole race semi-conscious.' He gracious in his dominance, I flattering in my respect, two blokes had bonded. A rapport had been formed, which came in handy when I proved to be an unusually inept pupil.

Luckily he was an excellent teacher. Experts rarely are, but Stirling was one of those people who enjoy the discipline of putting hard-won knowledge into terse form. With a cameraman, a sound man and a lighting man all crammed into the back of our Mini, Stirling came up with one line after another that we could put straight to air. I don't even have to refer to the finished film: I can remember everything he said. 'When you come to a turn, get your changing down done first. Keep the clutch out and do all your braking in a straight line. Then let in the clutch and you're already accelerating into the turn.' It was just like Bill Walsh talking about blitzing the quarterback. I love that kind of talk and even today I still store it up whenever I hear it, because it all applies to the making of art: the economy of means, the concentration of effort, the exploitation of momentum. Stirling would have laughed at my suggestion that he was a natural philosopher, but he was. (At the time of writing, he still is: whenever there is a big crisis in F1, the press go to him for his opinion: he's the Old Man.)

When I took my test, the examiner was rather startled by my velocity from point to point and told me he would have failed me if I had hit anything, but I didn't, so now I had a road licence. Our next move was to the old racing circuit at Donington, where Stirling got me started on a bit of speed. Nissan was in on the deal and provided a nice little number that really went. Stirling was in the passenger seat and was telling me not to overdo it at the very moment that I overdid it. We went off the track at about ninety and spun on the grass for some time. The camera got a shot of Stirling's profile while he was in the very act of remembering the spin at Goodwood which had ended his racing career. Although his bones were successfully put back together he came out of the hospital with double vision: not bad enough to keep him off the road, but no more racing. He had had nearly died that time and clearly thought that this time might finish the job. When the car came to a halt in a cloud of steam I started apologizing and am still apologizing today whenever I see him. But he agreed to show up at the racing school in Adelaide to give me a few final tips before I went for my certificate of elementary competence.

In Adelaide all the celebrities congregated at the old speed bowl to get their first taste of the real thing. Flameproof overalls, visored helmets and thin-soled driving shoes led to a lot of posing before we even got into the cars. I particularly liked my driving shoes and took to wearing them to breakfast at the hotel. The retired World Champion James Hunt caught me at it and sent me up. 'Breaking them in, are we?' I liked Hunt, but my fond-ness could have had something to do with the fact that he was no longer in control of his life. We are usually relieved when somebody with great abilities loses the thread: it does something to lower the standard by which we are asked to live. Hunt had been a wonderful driver but never truly dedicated, and now, in the twilight of his career, when he was picking up small change by hanging around the circuits and decorating the set, the knack for dissipation which had led him astray in the first place was visibly trying to finish him off. One of the airlines had banned him for pissing in the aisle. His fans applauded this action as an example of his supposedly maverick nature, but it was more likely that he had just let go because the toilets were occupied. Anyway, even in the wreckage of his glory he still had his authority as a genuine champion, and I kept the memory of how he mocked my shoe-modelling moment as a reminder that posturing seldom goes unpunished. They were great shoes, though. I've still got them somewhere, at the back of a cupboard.

The cars, too, looked quite serious in their numbers and decals, and when the engines fired the atmosphere got all charged up with the cheap rhetoric of derring-do. Actually the cars, Nissans again, weren't as fast as they sounded. The Pulsar model can be dauntingly quick on a public road after it has been stolen by your daughter's bad choice of boyfriend, but for this occasion, on the batch of Pulsars assigned to us, the taps had been screwed down even further than the exhausts had been opened up, so that the cars would sound like the crack of doom while going quite slowly. But they would still cruise on the ton, and when you went into the long banked asphalt turns of the bowl you had to keep the car balanced or it would bounce off the outside wall and came back across the track at just the right angle to T-bone one or two of your fellow students. Stirling's instructions about straight-line braking proved useful. Having been taught from the start to do it right, I didn't know how to do it wrong, while some of the celebs who had been driving on the road their whole lives were suddenly all over the place. Fiercely competitive in this as in everything, I was proud of keeping up, but I also, uncharacteristically, kept a sense of proportion: it was clear that Rowan Atkinson, for example, could really do this kind of thing. In civilian life he had a collection of Aston Martins and had made a point of learning to drive even heavy goods vehicles to a professional standard. (Has there ever been, in all of history, any other headline comedian with an HGV licence?) The racing instructors didn't have much to teach him as he flew around without a squeak or squeal: nothing spectacular, just smooth precision. As in a ski class, I made a point of watching only the best students when I wasn't watching the instructor himself. The instructors were all veterans of the old-time speedway when the cars went sideways through the dirt corners, and I was a bit awed by their tips on how to ride the brakes: it was an offence against the gospel according to Stirling, but I thought they must know something. After all, they were still alive, and some of them must have chased gangsters with the Keystone Kops. When Stirling dropped out of the sky and climbed in beside me, he was horrified by my new bad habits and chewed me out right in front of the camera. 'Christ, who taught you this? Are you trying to kill me *again*?'

I slept badly that night and when it came to race day the Grand Prix circuit looked awesomely twisted, with hard concrete edges and a main straight long enough for a Boeing 747 to get airborne. I made a mess of qualifying, partly because I couldn't make my mind up about the brakes but mainly because, let's face it, nearly everyone else was faster than me except the marathon runner Deke Castella. The gauntly laconic Deke could do quite well on foot over a distance of twenty-six miles or so but he hadn't done much more driving than I had. Up at the front of the grid were people like Rowan and at least one of the insanely aggressive Australian cricketers the Chappel brothers. After you name-checked your way through a couple of dozen people who were all celebrated for baring their capped teeth on national television you got down to the dregs at the end, and finally to me and Deke. It felt good to leave him standing when we all took off. For several laps I wasn't bad through the turns and I had learned Stirling's trick of relaxing on the long straight when the car is going flat out. ('The engine is doing all the work, dear boy, not you. So that's when you take it easy for a bit.') The little Pulsar was barely doing a hundred knots but it felt like contour-flying in a jet fighter as the concrete wall raced by only a few feet away. When a bunch of cars are all going at full chat in the straight they seem, relative to each other, to be floating like jellyfish, and there's the clue to what you should do: nothing. Let the car do it. Adjust your helmet with both hands if you want to. The car will steer itself, the speed holding the wheels nice and straight. At the same point, the F1 drivers, when they were racing tomorrow, would be doing a lot more than double the speed but they would all be peeling their vision-strips, wriggling their gloves to get more comfortable, writing letters home, etc. I was doing a bit of the old casual devil-may-care attitude myself when unexpectedly Deke's car appeared out of my blind spot and floated past me.

That wasn't supposed to be happening and I was mightily cheesed off. After the usual frenzied braking at the end of the straight he dived into the blind right-hander well ahead of me at what seemed an inadvisable speed. It was. A few hundred yards further around and I discovered his car in the middle of the track, facing the wrong way and emitting steam. He had rammed

both walls in succession and shortened his car by several feet at
each end. Luckily the bit that he was sitting in was a strong cage,
but everything else was crumpled up. As I went skating by, now
assured of not coming last, I had visible cause to remember that
a stunt race like this one was no joke. In the inaugural event the
year before, Mark Knopfler of Dire Straits had banged himself up
badly enough for the rest of the band to gang up on him and ban
him from racing, lest he put a crimp in their earning power,
which was larger than that of most small countries but would not
remain so if the star turn had to play the guitar with his teeth.
In my race, now mercifully winding to an end, a few other cars
slowed themselves down by hitting something or each other and
I went past them too, gaining the places that the timid earn when
the bold get wrecked. Our cameras were there to see me finish,
ingloriously but safely. Actually we didn't need the footage. The
Australian TV channels covered the whole event and pictures of
me at the wheel had gone out all over Australia, to remarkable
effect. Nobody was impressed and the women were particularly
indifferent. Except, of course, for my mother, watching the race
in Sydney. She passed out cold from fright while the cars were
still revving on the grid.

Even the most well-behaved woman can lose her head when
she meets a proper driver, but not when his car is no more
powerful than her lawnmower. It isn't judicious competence that
switches on a sensible female's baser instincts: it's the taste of
danger. The apparently glib expression 'only the brave deserve
the fair' is validated by an underlying truth. Danger evokes the
reality of death, and when death is in the room women of
otherwise impeccable decorum can be visited by a sudden urge
to reproduce the human race. (In more recent times, after the
World Trade Centre collapsed, firemen found themselves being
approached by women out of the social pages of *Vogue*.) I went
to Adelaide several times in those years, but unless I have lost
count, that was the year when Ayrton Senna won the heart of
Elle McPherson. Hero of Brazil and messenger of the gods, Senna

was so impressive he didn't need to say anything. Elle was a well-brought up girl and not easily carried away, but those are the very women who decide to go briefly crazy when they run into a man whose overalls smell of high-octane petrol and carry a certified written guarantee that he will plunge for their sake into the gullet of oblivion. Elle followed Ayrton all the way to São Paulo while every other heterosexual man in the world gritted his teeth like a missed gear-change. Even the other F1 drivers were ropeable on the subject, although without exception they were accompanied by at least one fashion-plate girlfriend at all times except when actually driving. When they drove, they were alone, which was, of course, part of the attraction. Given a whiff of that magnificent solitude, women with astronomical IQs revert to the thought processes of a butterfly: impregnate me *now*. The whole F1 atmosphere is as sexy as hell despite the fact that almost nobody understands the technical details. The standard of engineering is always way ahead of the current state of missile technology but the basic deal is as elemental as chariot racing. Once you get interested in the mechanical aspect as well, the GP circus can be hard to leave alone, and some surprisingly eminent civilians become dedicated petrol-heads.

One of them was George Harrison. At Adelaide I saw him trying to be inconspicuous in the depths of the McLaren pit. Some upmarket rubbernecks with pit passes – the platinum card form of accreditation – swarmed around him and asked for an autograph. Turning them down, he fascinated me with his answer. 'It's Thursday.' What a perfect ploy! It gave them the idea that he would have fulfilled their request had it been any other day in the week, but that today was sacrosanct, like Ramadan. Always the most thoughtful Beatle, Harrison was a canny operator and I was glad to have his acquaintanceship, however fleeting. Back in England, he read in some press profile that I was teaching myself to juggle. I never got very good at it, but I got past the elementary stage of juggling three balls in a circle and had moved up to four. It takes patience because you continually have to chase the balls you drop, and they all have an insatiable desire to roll under the couch. The answer to this is to train with soft balls that stick where they land. (Readers who are working on their own double entendres at this point are advised to give up: all the jokes had already been cracked by the time Chaucer saw his first juggler, Dickon Dawkins, who also did a show-stopping trick with two starved voles and a pullet down his tights.) Typically, George Harrison had guessed my problem and sent me a set of luxury leather soft juggling balls that flew like real ones but didn't roll an inch when they fell. He also got in touch to ask me whether I would consider playing a gangster in one of his movies. His production arm, Handmade Films, was one of the British film industry's rare success stories, largely because of his perseverance and judgement. (*Withnail and I*, *Mona Lisa*, *Time Bandits*, *Privates on Parade*, *The Long Good Friday* and *Monty Python's Life of Brian* are just some of the films that would probably have never existed without Harrison's nose for a project.) Bob Hoskins had the gangster market wrapped up, but for just that reason he had created a vacancy, because he wasn't always available, even though he sprinted from one set to the next like a Bollywood soprano. Harrison pointed out that from certain angles I looked roughly like Hoskins: bald, thick-necked, patently libidinous. I pointed out that I couldn't act and Harrison said: 'I know that, but your head's the right shape.' He also said something about how millions of people associated my face with merriment, which would make the switch more effective when I dealt with rebellious lieutenants by issuing instructions that they be incorporated into the cement foundations of a building project.

Suddenly I could see it all: me in the back of a black limo, pressing the button to lower the window and smiling in a sinister manner at someone on the outside while threatening him with grievous bodily harm. A bit of the old grievous. I could hear myself saying it. I would have said yes like a shot if an actual role was coming up, but it never did. If it had, I probably would have been unable to do it, because of TV commitments. That was the downside of doing TV season by season: it locked you into vast blocks of time in which you couldn't do anything else. Later on, Jane Campion, the brilliant film director from New Zealand, wanted me to play a fast-talking Australian lawyer in her movie *Holy Smoke*. The part would have required two weeks in the Queensland rainforest with Kate Winslet. It was bad enough having to pass on an invitation from the Princeton Institute of Advanced Studies to lecture about Primo Levi, a gig that would have done a lot to make me feel that I was still, from the literary viewpoint, in the swim. But Kate Winslet in the rainforest! I had to turn it down and I still haven't got over it. In the course of time I interviewed Kate Winslet in the studio – she was, I need hardly note, utterly unspoiled, articulate and enchanting – and when saying goodbye to her afterwards I told her how close she had come to spending two weeks in the rainforest with me. She smiled nicely but there was something in her eyes that spelt gratitude. For those who make a living in show business, regret for what almost happened can be the second most dangerous emotion after envy, and it's a safe rule that if you can't get your disappointments in perspective you will never last. In retrospect I think I have been not too bad at resigning myself to the chances missed. But I would like to have proved to that divinely talented creature that I, too, had a gift for acting, just as I would like to have proved to Ayrton Senna that I was hell on wheels. To do the latter, of course, I would also have had to develop my latent capacity for science, in order to distil an elixir of life that would have made me a few decades younger and a lot braver.

But I really loved it, being behind the wheel of a fast car. I hadn't been back in England long, however, before I proved to myself and all concerned that I had no business being behind the wheel of an ordinary car on a public road. Ordinary cars didn't come more ordinary than ours. By that time we had upgraded from a Mini to a Golf, which, though bigger, was possibly even less impressive in its surge of acceleration. Even my wife, who by nature favours the secure over the spectacular, sometimes wondered aloud whether the Golf had been the right purchase. We would all get into it, wonder why it wasn't going, and then find out, by close observation of the surrounding scenery, that it was. But with me at the controls the Golf became a weapon whose potential lethality was plain to all but the driver. The moment of truth came when I drove my elder daughter to Oxford for the new term. Passing through Milton Keynes, I drove twice around the wrong roundabout while my daughter made muted noises of apprehension. Kindly she waited until we had arrived at New College and unloaded her stuff – as always, I was good for lifting weights under female supervision – before she started reciting a list of all the times that I had nearly got us wiped out along with the numerous innocent civilians who were lucky to be going home in one piece. Shaken, I decided then and there to quit domestic driving on ordinary roads. I would save it for the screen. The whole family voted their assent with such unanimous alacrity that I felt I had no right even to be cast down. I have never driven on an ordinary road again, except when making a movie, which is a different world, where the budget pays for the damage and you are effectively preceded by a man with a red flag.

That being said, my new ability to make a car go roughly where I pointed it proved crucial when we made *Postcard from Miami*. At the time, the American police series *Miami Vice* was a big hit on British television, so our high-level executives were naturally keen to establish a thematic connection for promotional purposes. By that stage Richard's insistence that I attend a gymnasium twice a week had begun to pay off, and it didn't seem entirely implausible that I should be visiting Miami in order to pick up tips on a possible career as a fashion-conscious cop. I would have to be a fashion-conscious cop in a very ordinary blue suit, but at least I was roughly the right shape. My appearance was further enhanced by my reclining position at the wheel of a Ferrari Testarossa sports car, hired for two weeks at a heartrending fee. The *Miami Vice* stars, Philip Michael Thomas and Don Johnson, were always tooling around in glamorous vehicles and I would do the same, thus to blend into the atmosphere of rehabbed Art Deco hotels, fresh-from-the-carton Architectonica skyscrapers, white beaches, blue water and the scribbled dribble of neon on balmy nights. The benefits of having a proper international road licence were now apparent. Without one, I would have been feebly hailing taxis. In the Ferrari, I looked independent. I even looked dashing. The Ferrari dashed at only a fraction of its potential because I didn't know how to get it out of second gear, but since it would do fifty in first there was plenty of speed to play with if I ever needed it. I did my best not to need it. Buses honked at me, impatient to get by. With the red-headed classic engine emitting a frustrated version of its characteristic coffee-grinder scream, I proceeded at the pace of a steam roller. But in my dark glasses and low-slung bright red car I looked the part while we shot miles of coverage to establish me as mobile in Miami and ready for action: lean, mean, dangerous and perhaps a little stupid.

The Ferrari footage was the link material for various episodes, which fell roughly into two categories: dead serious and utter nonsense. It was nonsense when a huge ex-Marine taught me to load and fire a .45 automatic. It was serious when I interviewed an ex-CIA agent who had been firing a .45 automatic for most of her life. An elegant blonde built along the lines of Christy Turlington, she could have stepped out of the annual Swimsuit issue of *Sports Illustrated*. But she would have still been with the Agency if the PR arm of a Colombian drug cartel hadn't blown her cover. Now she earned her living by writing books and teaching people like me to waterski, something she could do at championship level. The desire to show off to her, coupled with my usual urge to dare all for the camera, had an astonishing result. Most first-timers don't stand up on the skis within the first hour, but there I was, upright at the first attempt and skimming along the blue water beside the white wake of the speedboat from which she, bikini-clad, waved back to me in encouragement, and, I thought, admiration. Off to one side, our camera in another speedboat was getting the shot. It was a moment of triumph and it received its due reward. After my skis got crossed, there was a somersault of large radius that ensured the unyielding water would receive my descending behind at precisely the right angle to inflict a sea-water injection of stunning power. Shafted, I was hauled aboard. 'Not many people do that on their first day,' she said. 'Congratulations.' I smiled back, as a man will smile who has just been sodomized by a speeding pillar of salt.

She gave me a revealing interview, though. It was all about drugs, illegal immigrants, Latin American politics and everything else that Washington was spending billions on failing to cope with. She didn't say that last part but it was obvious that the whole thing was out of control. Off camera, I caught her speaking beautiful Spanish and asked her whether she had learned it as a child. Not at all: she had learned it in adulthood, with a self-devised programme of discipline by which she had set out to memorize the words for all the parts of the body in the first week, and then all the colours and seasons in the second week, and so on. I was abashed, and took the tip. From then on I was much more systematic about learning complete sets of words. (Left, right, ahead, behind, up, down: it's an essential early set to learn in any language.) She was lovely, my secret agent, and she was very bright: a tremendous human asset which America was rich enough to waste.

It was amazing, the wealth of gifted people they had on hand. There was a young customs narc who looked like Steve McQueen. He too was careful not to say that the war on drugs was long lost, but he didn't have to say it. He took me out on a fast boat. Fast meant really fast: with two engines bigger than the one in my Ferrari, it could catch the Cigarette boats that ran the drugs into Miami by night. On our day out, he just trailed a big gin palace into the river mouth while he told us why it was worth a search.

'See that guy at the back who's checking gear? It doesn't need checking. He's checking us.' As so often with the Americans, this was dialogue you could put straight to air. We filmed the narcs as they swarmed all over the target boat and came up with nothing. The day before, they had busted anther boat with about ten million dollars' worth of cocaine stashed in its air-conditioning system. ('Don't worry. If this boat had been dirty we wouldn't have let you film it anyway. It would have screwed the case.') With so much powder being picked up, the inevitable inference was that many times as much was getting through, on its way to reducing a few thousand mothers' daughters to snivelling wrecks. It wasn't a war, it was a process, and the most you could do was to dress the process up to make it look reasonably good for the forces of virtue. That, essentially, was what a show like *Miami Vice* was all about: it gave a pastel tone to stark horror. Real drugs do ugly things to people but on television the actors playing the cops make it all look cute.

Looking cute was Don Johnson's cross. With me in the Ferrari and the crew in the van, we called on him one day when he had some downtime between jumping cutely out of a car with a gun in his hand and rolling cutely on the special grass that would not stain his pastel-blue jacket. His African-American partner, Philip Michael Thomas, was invisible in the trailer, waiting for the day, which then seemed impossibly far off, when a brother would become President of the United States. But Don Johnson was available and generously ready to play along. (The ruthless rule is: a big enough star will give you his time for free but the one who calls for his agent is the one you don't want anyway.) Don Johnson was, and still is, a disciplined performer with the full American song-and-dance background, but he already knew all too well that he had the part because he looked so good in lipgloss. I could go on for ages about the harsh laws of an actor's life, but the quickest way of saying it is that while most of them get nowhere, those who get somewhere seldom get what they want. Don Johnson was a seriously accomplished actor and after he got off the pretty treadmill of *Miami Vice* he made at least two movies to prove it. In the reasonably successful *Guilty as Sin* he was very believable as the too-handsome villain and in the almost unknown *The Hot Spot* he was even better as the lawyer ready to kill for Jennifer Connolly. (Though it could be said that Gandhi would have been ready to do the same, Johnson made it subtle.) But he never got out from under his television image. It can be done: it started with Steve McQueen, James Garner and Clint Eastwood, and more recently George Clooney is a powerful example of the TV star graduating to big-screen hero. But on the whole, success on American TV is a straitjacket. Don Johnson's straitjacket was beautifully cut – nobody ever looked better in pastel poplin, light tan chinos and Gucci loafers with no socks – but he was a prisoner. Later in his career he came to the West End to play Nathan Detroit in *Guys & Dolls* and the London critics, who uniformly panned the production, were nevertheless astonished that he could sing. But of course he could. He could always do all that stuff, and instead he had spent his best years jumping in and out of cars and shouting, 'Go! Go! Go!' His example gave me a lot to think about. Somehow, although my working life was theoretically a version of paradise, I was forever planning my escape, like a citizen of Havana.

The biggest story in Miami was the Cubans. Though this was a political theme of such complexity that it could hardly be unravelled in passing, my producer Beatrice Ballard nicely succumbed to my demand that we trawl for vox pops in Calle Ocho, still officially called 8th Street but by now populated exclusively with people speaking Spanish. Calle Ocho was the main stem for all the Cubans who had transferred themselves from the workers' paradise of Castro's imagination to the opportunistic inferno of America's brutal capitalist reality. Her instinct, however, proved right. Among the one and a half million Cubans who had survived the trip by crowded boat, open raft or rubber inner tube, there were too many head-cases with well-rehearsed stories who would hog the camera even if you pointed it away from them. As if the Bay of Pigs disaster had never happened, they spoke loudly and continuously of secret missions to go home in fully armed glory, an eventuality for which they trained in the Everglades by practising unarmed-combat routines against alligators while fire-bombing small areas of swamp with Molotov cocktails. The best way to handle the Cuban-exile story was to interview Gloria Estefan, which we did. A mainstream chart-topper as well as being by far the most popular singer in the Spanish world, she had a smart mind to go with her talent, and – rarer still, this – good manners to go with the smart mind. She couldn't have been more cooperative, but the best part of the story came by impli-cation, just from the setting. We arrived by boat to visit her at home. She was living on a little island with an entry fee of many millions: a community gated by open water. 'I'm hardly ever here,' she told me, 'but when I'm out on the road it's nice to know that I've got this to come home to.' She waved sweetly at an acre of emerald lawn. The only conclusion to draw was that if you were content to play music for the Buena Vista Social Club and eat meat once a month, then Cuba was for you, but if you wanted to be a star singer on a world scale, then you had to go to Miami. The whole of Central America was heading for Miami. That was the story.

America's magnetic attraction for the disadvantaged of the region remained a hard story to tell because of the assumption among intelligent people everywhere that America had caused the disadvantages. This assumption was largely a false one. Mexico, for example, wasn't poor because America was rich; Mexico was poor because an endless succession of permanently revolutionary governments could waste any amount of American credit while pursuing employment policies which ensured the migration across the Rio Grande of every worker with the ability to swim or even wade. But the assumption kept on being reborn because among the intelligentsia of any free country the idea lingered tenaciously that the established order under which they them-selves flourished was essentially a fraud. There had been a time when I had parroted such opinions myself even though not really believing them, so I was familiar with the mechanism by which one can profess a set of beliefs while harbouring contrary desires. This anomaly is prevalent in the field of show business, and especially prevalent in the theatre, where histrionic abilities are plentifully available to facilitate the cover-up. A radical playwright who accepts a knighthood after a lifetime of vilifying every aspect of the society that made him rich will look indignant if accused of hypocrisy, and his admirers will soon learn to go easy on the mockery if they wish to keep his favour. Among the admirers will be almost all the actors, who are scarcely likely, of their own free will, to get on the wrong side of someone who might write them a part. The almost complete absence of objections to his acceptance of an honour will soon strike the playwright as unanimous approval, and any inner conflict is quickly put to rest.

19. IT WOULD BE AN HONOUR

I like to think that there was no inner conflict in my own case, when I was offered membership in the Order of Australia in 1992. The decoration is conferred by the Australian government. Mine, however was to be pinned on me by the Queen at Buckingham Palace. This invitation was bound to confirm me as an irredeemable Establishment figure in the eyes of the Australian media commentariat, but I didn't mind. By their standards I was already an irredeemable Establishment figure, so why fight it? I would have turned the gong down if my family had objected but they were already buying new hats. And my mother was pleased. Back there in Kogarah she was in the process of being moved into a nursing home on a permanent basis but she had more than enough energy still on tap to convey her approval. Always among her chief fears was that I would not be able to earn a living, and here was a new accreditation that might help get me a proper job. There was a certain amount of raucous comment from my Friday lunch cronies about the honour having been conferred for Services to Television rather than Services to Literature, but I could put up with that.

Harder to put up with was the fancy dress. I looked stout in the morning suit but the effect might have been alleviated if there had been no top hat. There was a top hat. It looked no more appropriate on me than it had looked on Hitler when he called on Hindenburg. The women in my family, who could give the effect of a trio of Furies even at the best of times, fought laughter as they took turns being photographed with the pater-familias in the forecourt of the palace. Luckily, once we got inside, they were led away to join the audience of massed relatives while I was briefed, along with a bunch of other recipients, by Black Briefs in Waiting, Master of the Rigmarole. He was admirably succinct. It was the clearest set of rules I have ever had explained to me about anything. One advanced to meet the Queen. The Queen would hang the medal on the hook in one's lapel. The Queen might ask a question while doing so. Answer it. But when she extended her hand, the audience was over. Shake the hand and walk away backwards. Try to extend the acquaintance and you would be hauled off with a hook.

I would like to say that it all went wrong because that would make a better story. But it went like clockwork, which, I suppose, is what's wrong with it. Why lavish so much protocol on something so trivial? But the answer is in the question. It's trivial for her, who has to do it thousands of times a year, and it's trivial for us, who must live for other satisfactions or else be sorely disappointed. But it's not trivial in itself: or rather, the triviality has weight. It stands in as a comparatively benign substitute for all the corruption that might be unleashed if people did their duties for no rewards except those of palpable substance. The great critic and thoroughgoing bastard Cyril Connolly always thought that he was being amusing when he told the story of how he had expected the Queen to know something about what he did for a living when she gave him a medal. But he was mistaken in two different ways at once. The Queen couldn't be expected to keep up with literary criticism, so there was nothing funny there. And if Connolly wanted his listeners to laugh because his expectations had been ridiculous, he must have been very confident that they were interested in what he felt: there was nothing funny there either. On the other hand, literary criticism had been honoured, in the same way that keeping a neat and honest set of housing-transfer certificates gets honoured when a civil servant receives on OBE for thirty years of service. The protocol is the prize. It's a tradition, and has the advantage of not having been invented yesterday. (Some of the British traditions, including most of the coronation ceremony, were indeed invented yesterday, but they were concocted out of scraps left over from the past.)

I was getting my award at just the right time in my own history. Very slowly, too slowly, I had been graduating out of contempt for the inherited order's injustices to gratitude that it was not more unjust. Object to the inherited social structure by all means, but object in detail, and always in the knowledge that an enforced wholesale alteration would be unlikely to ameliorate the condition of those you claim to speak for, and very likely to make it immeasurably worse. That, briefly, had been the story of the twentieth century, by then nearing its unlamented end. My increasing knowledge of recent history, which I never ceased to study even when out on the trail of tinsel glory, has been doing its work, along with the mere fact of growing older, and so less confident in my ability to change the world all by myself. Both for Britain and Australia, the constitutional order looked worth preserving, the Royal family included: the Royal Family whatever its limitations. (The Queen still knows next to nothing about literary criticism.) Unbroken even by the moment of death, the permanent existence of a monarch sets a limit to ambition. If I bend my knee to the monarch, I don't have to bend the knee to anyone else. This knowledge would come in handy if I were ever to meet Rupert Murdoch, who would dearly like to rearrange the established order so that he could have a say in who would hold the office of head of state. He is a baron, and in my homeland there are many barons like him. At Runnymede, the great charter, by putting the monarchy beyond contest, limited the power of the barons in perpetuity, to the inestimable benefit of the common people. Barons are ambitious men. As an ambitious man myself, I know something about what goes on in their heads. They want the world. The wisest of them learn to temper their wish, but the wish is basic.

Perhaps I should explain, at this point, that it was the constitutional function of the Royal Family that attracted me, and not its personnel. In the mercifully brief time when I was occasionally bumping into them – almost always it was at an awards ceremony in which my function was either to present an award or to look brave when I lost – I liked my Royals bright, which cut the field right down. There were many commentators who thought that the Princess of Wales was no brighter than a forty-watt bulb that tinkled when you shook it, but I couldn't agree. I hadn't met her again since our first encounter in Cannes, because the distance between her and Charles had steadily grown to the point where, if you saw him, you never saw her: it was like matter and antimatter. My romantic view of the assured succession took a bit of a bashing on the several occasions when my wife and I invited Charles to dinner and he turned up alone. When he invited us to dinner at Sandringham, he was alone there too. By then even I could hear the hooter announcing that there was trouble at the mill. But though I was pleased and flattered to see the Prince occasionally, and admired his thoughtful concern, I had plenty of intelligent men among my friends, and some of them outranked him, unless you were put off by the fact that none of them would be King one day. I also knew more than my fair share of bright and beautiful women, but none of them outranked Diana for fascination. It wasn't just because of her position, either. She would have been the centre of the action even if she worked behind an airline check-in desk, an effect that could not be ascribed merely to her beauty. The picture of her standing in front of me in Cannes had never left my mind, but it was partly because of the accompanying soundtrack: in two minutes she had convinced me that I was a clever chap, she had enrolled me in a conspiracy to despise Robert Maxwell – looming like a rotting whale elsewhere in the crowded room, he seemed unaware that she had drilled him with a glance – and she had scattered showering sparks of conversational delight. Clearly in love with the whole idea of off-trail chat, she had evinced the rare knack of persuading her interlocutor that he – in this case me – was a necessary voice in her private campaign to stir things up. One of the things that her lovely eyes shone with was glee. It didn't occur to me then that her taste for mischief could have been akin to madness, but I would have been up for more of the same even if it had. She had only been working the room, but not even Jackie Kennedy in her heyday at the White House had worked a room leaving such a trail of charmed lives.

Diana had an even bigger room to work at Buckingham Palace one night. It was somebody's birthday, I forget whose. It could have been Charles's birthday, but it might have been the Queen Mother's: she had hundreds of them. Anyway, all the royals of Europe were there, along with the regulation sprinkling of media celebrities. They had the fame factor of Elton John at the very least, however, so I don't think I was there on that ticket. Perhaps I had been invited because I was bald, and Charles, whose hair was merely growing thin, wanted a few reminders around him that a man could lose the lot and yet retain the will to live. The sheer extent of the shindig I won't try to evoke. If you can imagine St Pancras Station crammed with a cast painted by Alma Tadema and wired for sound, you're getting near it. Sufficient to say that after too much champagne I needed to take a slash and headed for one of the royal men's rooms, which was a second cousin of the Garrick club's dining room and had a line of solid marble urinals stretching for the length of a cricket pitch. Such was the traffic that every urinal was occupied except one. I took up my position to strain the potatoes and was lucky to get most of the job done before I glanced sideways in each direction and finally noticed that I was the only man present who was not a crowned head of Europe. After I washed my hands I was passed a towel by a flunky who must have been a television fan, because he gave me the appreciative smile that he had just withheld from the King of Norway. But equally clearly he was wondering how I had got in.

Back outside in the teeming ball-room, the field of gravity had been altered by the arrival of Diana *en grande tenue*. You could see immediately why she was bound to have, vis-à-vis the standard Royal set-up, the same effect as the invention of the jet engine on the history of powered flight. Suddenly all the putatively glamorous aristocrats looked ordinary. When it was my turn to chat her up, I was doltish enough to say 'Care to dance?' She said no. Already a dead man, I found it easy to take my life in my hands. 'So can I take you to lunch instead?' She said yes, give me a buzz.

It was as easy as that. Explaining my rationale to the women in my family in advance, I said that as a writer I had to know things. At least one of my listeners rolled her eyes towards the ceiling like a judge hearing from a lifetime burglar that he was a student of objets d'art, but there was no veto. Perhaps the sheer incongruity of the project had wrapped me in a mantle of seriousness, as when a man who proposes to ski down the Eiger blindfolded while reciting the 'Immortality Ode' is interviewed on *Newsnight Review* instead of being locked up for observation. My first lunch date with the Princess happened at a Notting Hill Gate restaurant called Kensington Place, one of her standard hang-outs. She was on time to the minute. (In this and every other respect, her manners were perfect: at the end of any lunch her credit card had always to be beaten from her hand, and her bread-and-butter thank-you notes, to anyone for anything, arrived next day and were always more than a page long.) I got cast immediately in the role of funny uncle and had a wonderful time making her laugh. Too few years later, after her untimely death, I said my piece about Diana, and eventually it was published in my book *Even As We Speak*. If I can be permitted the luxury of a cross-reference to one of my own books, anyone interested can find in its pages most of what I am competent to say about her, and after that book was published I never spoke of the subject again until now. But the reader of a book of memoirs has a right to hear, at the appropriate chronological point, anything that the author can legitimately say about his own history, so I should say this much now. I loved her dearly, even though I hardly knew her.

Though I was always apt to think a beautiful woman intelligent until the facts proved otherwise, which they quite often did, I didn't dote on the Princess just for her physical attraction, which was far out of my age-range, and anyway not that remarkable: as someone who had to deal with people like Helen Hunt and Charlotte Rampling for a living, I knew what physical perfection looked like, and Diana didn't have it. For one thing, her nose was on sideways. But what she did have was lit up like Christmas, from an inner fire that was really the fire of curiosity. She was interested in everything. It was as if she had had not just a deprived childhood, in a household where she was groomed for a dynastic marriage by neurotics whose own ideas of conjugal union might have been derived from a horse-breeding manual, but a childhood without any intellectual stimulus whatsoever, like Kaspar Hauser, the savage infant. Released into the world, she was voracious for news about what accomplished people did. She was interested in accomplished artists, accomplished doctors, accomplished coal miners. This worshipping curiosity, coupled with a wicked knack for reflecting a man's ideal self back to him, made her intoxicatingly flattering as a companion. I was slow to see, however, that she was making the fundamental mistake of taking it all personally. With no security of her own, she dreamed habitually of 'becoming herself', as the fashionable saying went; and of doing so in any or all of those fields of achievement that were opening up continually in front of her. You're a sky-diver? Can I go sky-diving too?

I recognized her, because I have the same personality flaw myself. I have been that way all my life. When I first heard David Oistrakh play the violin, I wanted to be him. When I first saw Greg Louganis dive the inward three and a half somersaults from the tower, I wanted to be him. Even today, I would like to be Roger Federer. But I know I can't, and I have something else to do. Diana had nothing to fall back on. Eventually, had her life not been cut short, she might have built a base for herself more solid than that conferred by her ability to make men who could do marvellous things fall in love with her: a base of realism, founded on a more certain knowledge of what she could get done, through her position, by her unusual and true talent for empathy. But at the time I knew her, she was far from being sure about any of that, and it was all too clear that the multiplicity of her yearnings was scrambling her brains. It would have been easier for her if she had been unattractive. But that's just a way of saying that she would have been better at being herself if she had been someone else.

Alas, she was who she was, with all her charm, and so the charm was a deadly gift. I was on the receiving end of it, and I know. Not that she flirted, even for a moment. Older men who say they are no longer attracted to younger women are almost always lying, but a wise older man does not expect that the same force will operate in the other direction. Certainly it didn't in this case. But she was charming anyway. Why was that? When interrogated at home, I wasn't just trying to save my skin when I said that I thought her more than a touch ga-ga. I had heard her tell obvious untruths. She told me that she had not cooperated with her unofficial biographer when it was quite clear that she had. Such whoppers would have been understandable had she been in show business, where finessing the truth is a recognized survival mechanism. But she wasn't in show business, or at any rate was not supposed to be. I had seen her turn the same atomic smile on the waiters that she had just been using on me, and the news was already out that she had been lavishing a ration of her personal magic on every editor in London, in the dangerous belief that men incapable of loyalty would remain servile even if they were fed the whole carcass. To put it briefly, I thought she was childish. But as I loftily explained to the household furies when they grilled me, the days of her eating disorder were over, she was well fed, she would live for a long time, and I thought she had the capacity to learn. She was one of those people who start off with no wisdom at all and have to learn everything by trial and error, but so was I. I got some sceptical looks, but

I suppose the manifest absurdity of the friendship conferred a certain plausibility, and anyway, it wasn't as if she hadn't bedazzled every man she met, with the possible exception of her husband. (And, I might have added had I but known, every other senior Royal who had seen her in close-up long enough to know that she was a ticking fruitcake.)

There was no safety in numbers, however. If she had enrolled, one by one, every man in the country among her admirers, they all would have had their faces in the newspapers. There were even journalists who got their faces in the newspapers because they had been seen talking to her. To be seen eating with her was a signal for a press stampede, and she and I had scarcely reached the second course of our first lunch before a Range Rover full of photographers and reporters arrived outside. It went on like that for what seemed like years. How long was it, really? Not long enough. I would have liked to know her forever. But it was just the occasional meeting. She had an infinity of people that mattered to her more, and I had things to do. But already I could see myself when I was ancient and doddering, summoned to the palace when she was Queen, no longer in her first youth but still insistent on hearing my jokes. Though there were rumours about the possibility of a divorce, I didn't see how it could happen. And there would surely be an accommodation. (In the *Spectator* I published several articles about the necessity for this, presuming to speak as one with authority, and not as the scribes.) There would always be time. I already knew that time was finite for me, but for her it would be infinite.

To know her took an hour a month at most, and every other moment was crowded. There lay my real anguish. It was too crowded. Television was eating me alive, but I couldn't back out of it, not just because it paid the bills but because I was still trying to get it right. More cursed than ever by the desire to practise everything as an art form, I was trying to give shape to a storm of light. It can't be done beyond a certain point, but I was still keen to know where the point was. Anything else I could do would have to happen in the wings while I did that. The weekly show and the End of the Year show were based in London so I could always write in the back seat of the car on the way to and from the office or the studio. The travel programmes were less forgiving. For writing poems, it was easy enough to find some downtime while I travelled to the location and sat around between set-ups. One of the poems, about the life of W. H. Auden, took months to assemble. I wrote pieces of it all over the world. But Tina Brown, the latest editor of the *New Yorker*, took the finished thing and gave it a whole page to itself, with the opposite page occupied by a Richard Avedon portrait photo of Auden that made the whole splash look very grand. So I had got the thing done. Writing essays was harder, especially if they needed research, but since I travelled light I could always carry a few books with me in my hold-all, and I was steadily getting better at keeping the thread of a prose argument in my head until I could get back to the notebook on the desk in my hotel room. Keeping the thread was sometimes difficult when I had been stoked up by the action during the day. The action was seldom dangerous but it could be unnerving, thereby inducing an adrenaline squirt that doesn't agree with the sedentary process of nutting out an essay about Gerard Manley Hopkins. And just occasionally it *was* dangerous, though it was never meant to be. My producers had a vested interest in keeping me alive, and some of them could barely be restrained from tasting my food before I ate it.

20. WHERE ALL ROADS LEAD

On *Postcard from Rome* the producer was Elaine Bedell, who had come to us from radio and proved a natural at dreaming up pertinent action. A trim brunette so good-looking that she could enslave her presenters by just standing there, Elaine was also an excellent dancer: invariably a good sign, because it means that the person doing the dancing can think in pictures. When I told her that one of the reasons I liked the Castel Sant'Angelo was that Tosca had jumped to her death off the battlements, Elaine instantly had the idea of filming me in a helicopter as it hovered above the castle, thus to provide the perfect shot for a vertiginous voice-over. Though my dedicated hatred of helicopters had only increased after my high-speed horizontal close-up of the escarpment at Kakadu, I saw the point and said yes, but with conditions. If the camera was shooting past me as I looked down, the door would have to be removed, so I wanted a bar across the doorway. And I wanted a six-point harness. (A six-point harness has straps over both shoulders and both thighs as well as the strap at the waist, the whole assembly secured with a circular buckle that will open only at a firm whack from the wearer's hand.) Elaine got on the blower and the guy at the helicopter pad said yes, yes of course, how could it be otherwise?

The Italian way of saying 'How could it be otherwise?' is *senz' altro* and it's a phrase you should watch out for, especially when filming. This merchant had obviously been saying *senz' altro* to everything all his life, because when we got to the pad there was no bar on the doorway and the harness was only two-point, meaning that it was no more substantial than the thing you fasten

over your lap in an airliner so that you won't injure yourself
from the shock when the voice on the public address system tells
you that you have only ten more minutes to choose from the
wide range of duty-free items. A two-point harness with frayed
webbing and a rusty buckle: I had premonitions of diving from
the door at the first lurch. The helicopter stood there in a pool of
its own oil and the strenuously rejuvenated pilot looked the way
Silvio Berlusconi does now, with a hair arrangement suggesting
that any other qualifications he might have had – a pilot's licence,
for example – had also been obtained by mail order. But Elaine
was up for the trip and I would have felt weak if I had downed
tools. (In such circumstances, one should always say, 'I feel weak
and I'm downing tools,' especially if your interlocutor is a young
female you are trying to impress. Why are you trying to impress
her?) Up we went in a rattling roar of loosely arranged machinery,
and in due course we arrived over the Castello at a height of only
a few hundred feet. The cameraman wanted the chopper to tilt a
bit towards the side where I was sitting, so that he could get both
me and the castle in the same shot. I shouted, 'No tilting!' Elaine
shouted, 'What?' I shouted, 'Keep it straight!' and somebody
must have thought I said, 'This is great!' because suddenly we
were canted over at forty-five degrees and I was looking straight
down into the castle's circular courtyard. It looked like the barrel
of a giant mortar. I held on to the rim of the door with all the
strength I had, but the grip was awkward and I could feel my
weight popping the threads of my ratty lap-strap. If the thing had
snapped, I would have been going a lot faster than Tosca when I
hit the deck. She would have been still speeding up. I would have
been going at terminal velocity. They wanted another pass to get
the shot right, but for the one and only time in my career I called
off the deal.

There was an equally grim scene waiting on the ground but
at least I wouldn't need a harness for it. To help us tell the
story of well-connected Roman decadence in faded palaces, we
had recruited a female aristocrat from the permanently historic

Vilaponte family. Though Rosetta, in common with the Colos-
seum, was no longer in possession of the full complement of her
original marble cladding, she had a beautiful daughter called
Liliana who was one of the stars of the upper-crust younger set.
Buzzing around on the pillion of Liliana's moped just behind
her perfect bottom while holding an ice-cream in each hand
spelled fun – we were trying to spell fun in large letters – but
hitting the high spots with Liliana's mother was no fun at all. The
routine was meant to be as follows: Rosetta, with her inexhaustible connections, would row us in on various high-toned Dolce
Vita-style settings, fashionable nightclubs, etc. She had the entrée,
and other denizens would fall on her neck with spontaneous
cries of greeting while we filmed over my shoulder to make me
part of the fizzing scene. The facts proved otherwise. The arrival
of Rosetta aroused no more excitement than if she had been
handing out a religious tract. She was, however, quite canny on
the financial detail. It took about an hour to set up the extra
lights outside a nightclub so that we could arrive at it by
limousine and still be visible when we climbed out. Rosetta would
invariably try to renegotiate her price after the lighting had been
done but before the camera turned. We were committed to the
shot and it was too late to fire her. Pulling similar stunts many
times, and always at the critical moment, she cost us a lot of
trouble.

We had some good stories to tell. Dado Ruspoli, by then
living in the attic of what had once been the family palazzo, was
the genuine, non-hysterical version of crumbling elegance. He
had been a favourite walk-on for Fellini. Later on, Francis Ford
Coppola used him to dress the set of *Godfather III*. Like all the
aristos, Dado spoke excellent English. He got the pronunciation of my first name right when he said things like 'Clive,
Rome is not what it was', even while the noble planes of his face
proclaimed that Rome had been what it was since the time of
Tacitus. We also got a spine-tingling interview from Mussolini's
jazz-pianist son Bruno, who revealed, for the first time in any

medium, that his father had been a fan of Fats Waller. But what held the Rome documentary together was the look of the place, which we revealed not only in some carefully chosen static shots, but in a swathe of travelling shots focused on the little car – a Lancia Lunchbox or whatever it was – that I was jokily driving. Traffic chaos was the story of Rome at that time, and we knocked ourselves out trying to tell it. My newly acquired driving skills were vital and soon proved barely adequate, but going the wrong way at the wrong speed fitted the story as long as the camera car could stay with me. If I did the wrong thing, I had to do the wrong thing again after the crew piled out of their car and set up on a tripod to catch me from in front. There was a light rigged under my dashboard to point upwards so that my facial expressions – mainly in the spectrum from fear to shame – would register on film. That kind of filming is very demanding on coverage but you have to do it. In any documentary you can always tell when the coverage has been skimped because suddenly you notice the lack of logic, and then *that* becomes the subject instead of the subject you were meant to be talking about. Take the scene where I got the Lunchbox stuck in a crowded square. It took a dozen difficult set-ups. I was getting better at helping to plan these, and at anticipating what would be required. It gave the satisfaction of being useful, but it filled up the day.

In the late afternoon and early evening, the city comes to its full life. As one who worshipped the very memory of Fellini, I asked for, and got, my scene at a cafe in the Via Veneto. If the audience had never seen *La Dolce Vita*, I would evoke it for them in voice-over. I got my scene at the Trevi Fountain. If the audience had never seen Anita Ekberg wading in it while Marcello Mastroianni looked on with suave lust, I would evoke that too. I even got a scene with the little Barberini fountain, Bernini's fountain of the bees, once a meeting point for myself and my future wife when we were first in Rome. If the audience didn't know who Bernini was, they might be encouraged to find out. For all these scenes I was in on the planning and the arranging, and I can say in general that the whole scenario proved the benefits of thinking things through in advance. But once again, as so often, the best thing wasn't planned at all. We were set up to shoot a big open-air concert in the plaza at the head of the Spanish Stairs, with the whole of fashionable Rome present including the dreaded Rosetta, who, by that time, had been fired. She threw herself in front of the camera anyway, in a rare fit of altruism. The audience kept on arriving and she kept on arriving with them. Like any fashionable audience for music, they looked as if they had been temporarily placed under arrest, but the gowns and tuxedos did the visual business, and I'm bound to say that I, too, looked the part. I was wearing a cream jacket which had been tailored for me by the famous men's outfitter Littrico in a separate sequence, during which Littrico had played up marvellously by telling me I had the same measurements as Gorbachev, for whom he had made a similar jacket the previous week. Thus several sequences tied together at the critical moment. The unexpected bonanza, however, came after the show. We were toting the gear back to the bus when I saw a familiar face at one of the tables in the cobbled street outside an expensive restaurant. It was Leonard Bernstein. Letting my crew go on ahead, I bent over his candlelit table and asked how he had liked the concert. 'It was disgusting. Absolutely disgusting. Fully in keeping with the audience.' I asked him if he would mind telling me that on camera. 'I wouldn't mind a bit.'

I raced off to catch up with the crew. Elaine, bless her, got the point instantly and we were soon back at the table, shooting from the shoulder with a little hot light held up on a stick to further illuminate the maestro's craggy face as he sat there smoking. I asked him how he had liked the concert. 'It was wonderful. Absolutely wonderful. How they love art, the Romans.' He went on to sing hosannas for the artistic taste of the Romans since Nero's first solo concert, all the while encircling my upper thighs with one arm, whose exploring hand had a mind of its own. But anything for the camera, and anyway, as he knew full well, his

affectionate embrace was happening below the frame. I thought
the world of Bernstein, whose TV series on music had been one
of the milestones of the medium. Along with Alistair Cooke,
Bernstein had been one of my models for what a television
presenter could do with a big subject. There were times, when
he conducted, say, Mahler, that his range of portentous facial
expression left the music sounding like a penny whistle at the
Apocalypse, but the man who had written the score for *On the
Town* could do no wrong in my eyes. His clear intention of
invading my trousers I took as a compliment. He showed no
signs of disappointment that I did not respond, by the way. He
was just copping a feel while it was there. And from meeting
many a prominent homosexual male I had long since learned
that from their viewpoint it was always worth a try: apparently
the rate of conversion made it well worth the effort. Perhaps
I missed a trick by never succumbing. At one time I often saw
Gore Vidal socially, and he several times assured me that my
butch facade was trembling under the pressure of ill-concealed
ambivalence. I had to tell him that much as I loved him – and I
undoubtedly did – there wasn't, from the angle of sexual desire,
even one woman in the room who didn't interest me more than
he did, including the Dowager Duchess of Dubrovnik in her
two separate wheelchairs. His vulpine smile remained undaunted.
'Talk is cheap.' But it wouldn't have been in his nature to make
a physical pass, and it was always possible that he wasn't gay
at all. Certainly the grandes dames who mobbed him seemed to
be acting on that basis. With Bernstein, however, there was never
any doubt. He was a crusader. Elaine thanked him very much as
she tore me from his embrace.

As a producer, Elaine could take charge of anything, but not
even she could control the weather, which dished us in a big way
when we made, or tried to make, *Postcard from Sydney*. Back in
the year dot, when I was making my first programmes at LWT
before I met Richard, my very first documentary had Sydney as

its subject, and I muffed it through staying loyal to a Mickey
Mouse voice-over which kept saying again what the pictures
had said already. This time I had a better plan. But it is always
important not to fall in love with the plan, no matter how good.
The lack of sunlight wasn't Elaine's fault, although she was at
her most engaging when she behaved as if it was. She danced
with anger as she cursed the sun, which resolutely failed to appear
for more than twenty minutes in two weeks. Back in London,
Richard gazed mesmerized with horror at the footage of a ferry
ride in which I stood outlined against the sky at the front rail of
the ferry as it ploughed the harbour. I looked passable for a man
fighting the onset of the fatal final calorie, but the sky looked as
if it were dying of despair. Ingmar Bergman would have thought
our exteriors too gloomy for *The Seventh Seal*. A whole day at
Bondi yielded a sequence with about twelve people in it, one of
them a beer-bellied beach inspector who said, 'Nar, ya come on
the wrong day.'

We got a few minutes of sun for a surfing sequence that we
shot at Manly. It was a rigged gag but the components were well
chosen. One of the components was an Iron Man champion
called Craig Wayne. As if sculpted from caramel marble, his
naked frame was in the crisp bloom of youth. Wearing only the
vestigial pair of trunks that the Australians call a budgie-smuggler,
he could sit on a surf ski and bend forward to touch his toes with
one hand while, with the other, he held his two-ended paddle
aloft, twirling it like a drum majorette. The other component was
myself. Clad in a neck-to-knee costume of pink and black Lycra,
I looked like an ox wrapped tightly in the flag of some unsuccess-
ful West African republic, and while sitting on the ski I could not
lean forward at all, even with the ski being steadied from behind
by the assistant cameraman. The idea, with the surf ski, is that
you sit on it and paddle. The camera dwelt briefly on Craig as he
dug in his paddle with a quick succession of darting strokes and
headed straight for New Zealand. Then the camera was pointed

at me. My idea for the gag was that I would go very slowly in comparison to Craig, but I was not ready for the possibility that I might not go anywhere.

The secret of paddling the surf ski is to compensate for each thrust of the paddle by very slightly tilting the body. After only a couple of thrusts, during which the frail craft moved forward less than half its own length, I rolled over and disappeared, leaving the ski floating upside down. To give me the small credit I've got coming, I had realized the comic possibilities before I got back to the surface, and while still puffing and blowing I was asking for all the retakes we could get of exactly the same fiasco. We had to work fast before the sun went behind the clouds again, but the rollover was well covered and I was already working out the voice-over in my head. The final result is still remembered by people who have forgotten the rest of the movie. I can say that for myself: I was getting better at realizing, on the spot, that the moment of failure is exactly the moment that you need for the story. A lot depends, however, on not doing too much with your face after you have just lost it. The really essential retake was the tight close-up in which I came up looking resigned instead of annoyed. Indeed I didn't even look resigned. I just looked impassive, as if the whole thing had been inevitable. Let the audience make the interpretation and they would reach the right conclusion: that I was a man whose dreams had been overtaken by the passing of time.

There were a lot of other good moments. For the first night of a new production of La Clemenza di Tito at the Opera House, my black-tie arrival by speedboat – stand aside, James Bond – told the story of Sydney's artistic and financial prosperity at a single stroke. But nothing could compensate for the lack of sunlight. Back in England, we put the whole thing on ice for a year and then sent out a crew to do re-shoots of the sky. Once again the sun failed to appear, so eventually I had to write the script to fit what we had, the first-ever movie about Sydney to feature empty beaches in the middle of summer. It was then, in the editing room, that I made my big error. Elaine still says that I should have strangled her for letting me commit it, but she is too kind. Richard, too, generously attempted to claim the blame. But it was entirely my own blunder, and arose out of misplaced cleverness. To tie in with our Opera House sequence, I thought it would be self-evidently absurd, and therefore cute, to say that Mozart had been born in Sydney. The fantasy failed to connect except with thousands of people who gained the impression that I was stating a fact. The worst of it was that I was going against my own principle: exaggerate by all means, but only while telling the truth. I never did it again but I shouldn't have done it then. Besides, the joke wasn't very funny, and there are never any excuses for that.

Still, the Sydney Postcard came out well for something filmed in the wrong weather, a circumstance which usually spells doom unless you can work around it. The sequences were well prepared and they connected into a plausible narrative. The Postcard format was getting a reputation for itself. It was a kind of miniature feature movie with me in the middle, doubling as pundit and clown. I was very pleased when I bumped into Ken Russell one day in Soho and he complimented me on what I was doing. 'You're making movies. You're telling stories. Keep it up.' Coming from a man who had mortgaged his house over and over just to stay in business as a director, this was high praise and I didn't forget it. The Postcards were becoming part of the television landscape and I hoped to get better at playing my part in them. The only question was how big a part that would be. It was a matter of confidence. If the story was to be under my control from point to point, then I couldn't let the director impose a visual style of his own, or there would be two narrators getting in each other's way. There had to be a unified viewpoint, even in a collaborative effort. This was a perennial problem but my naturally minimal diplomatic skills grew sharper under pressure. *Postcard from London*, an attractive prospect because we could save on travel bills, was held together by its story, not by its visual style. Our young director Dominic Brigstocke was at the start of a fruitful career and he was eager to exploit the full resources of the camera. He was naturally good at coverage. When we were filming as I walked with Peter Cook through the streets of Soho on our way to the site of his old Establishment club, we got all the shots required to make the sequence tie up. (Filming anywhere in central London you need Hollywood money to 'close the street', so if you want to keep any rubber-necking civilians out of frame you have to shoot fast and tight, which can be very tricky.) But when it came to the wide shots Dominic found it hard to resist the less humble opportunities available to his virtuoso technique. We did a sequence in Hyde Park which was meant to allow me to comment, in voice-over, on all the modern buildings that had made a hash of the skyline since I had first arrived in London more than thirty years before. Dominic wanted to do a panning shot, supposedly from my viewpoint, that swept around the skyline. I politely let him do it but I asked also for individual static shots of each building. The static shots were the ones we used in the finished film, for a simple reason: you can't comment on individual objects when the camera is panning past them, because however slowly it pans the image travels too quickly to allow even a phrase, let alone a sentence. On the whole, panning shots are to be avoided, because you can't cut into them. A panning shot controls the pace of the narrative, whereas the ideal balance is obtained when the narrative controls the pace of the cutting.

Dominic took it well. He even took it well when I told him that if I caught him using a short lens on me I would throw it into the Serpentine. (A short lens won't just make an ugly man like me look even uglier, it will distort the background, thereby reminding the audience that they are looking at an image, when you want them to be looking at reality.) Like every other young director only more so, Dominic had a prodigious knowledge of filters and focal lengths. He knew how to do it. But I knew what I wanted, and there's a difference. Later on, keeping an eye on his work, I could see him getting steadily more in control of his effects. He had learned to avoid that fatal moment when the technique takes over.

Even in the most technical of all the art forms, technique is only the servant of expression, not the instigator. At the Royal Ballet School we filmed the dancers at their morning exercises. Alessandra Ferri was there. The few minutes I spent watching her at work added up to one of the most powerful visions of the beautiful that I had ever known. Even today, the memory is still with me: and I have tried to transmit some of its intensity through the compilation, on my website, of excerpts from her performances as Juliet both at Covent Garden and La Scala. Ferri was the last great muse of Kenneth MacMillan, a man of genius. To my astonished delight, he liked the way I wrote, and wanted me to write a spoken libretto for a ballet he had in mind based on the diaries of Nijinski. The project never had a chance, but the pay-off, from my viewpoint, was that I got to spend quite a lot of time in his company. He was already sick with the disease that would slowly kill him but he generously found time to listen to my views on ballet, almost as if they might be as interesting as his. I could have handled the friendship better, and that I didn't is among my great regrets. But at least I saw something of him. The public saw less of our ballet-school sequence, because it had to be cut back to nothing in the editing room. At greater length, it would have unbalanced the picture, which had its own demands: the surest sign that it was alive.

21. PUSHING IT

So there was a second story to the travel programmes, and it was much more about me than the programmes were. The programmes were about the cities, which I was careful, in each case, to make the hero. But the story underneath was about how I wanted to push the forms we were working in towards their most concentrated possible outcome. To me this seemed a serious purpose, even if it didn't seem so to my literary friends. They were less likely to disapprove of a new format we started for BBC 2, called *The Talk Show*. The idea was that I would sit with a panel of three pundits and steer the troika through a conversation on a serious topic. Such a layout was nothing startling, but it had rarely been a success on British television, where there is a chronic shortage of intellectuals who can conduct a conversation on screen. Nearly all of them can conduct a monologue, but a conversation is a different thing. The French, Germans and Italians can all do conversation shows, and for the Americans the form is a staple, even though it usually sounds like a version of *Gladiators* fought with words for weapons. But for the British it is a regularly recurring no-no. I have to give Alan Yentob credit for thinking that I might make a fist of it. Elaine was the producer in charge and in collaboration with me and Richard she did all the casting. Alas, Yentob the Enabler was also Yentob the Destroyer. Right from the jump the show got into deep trouble because he was always on the phone demanding that every panel should have at least one woman. Elaine, herself a woman in all visible aspects, and mentally a blazing feminist, went nuts trying to tell him that there just weren't enough women to allow good casting. Fair casting yes, good casting no. There weren't enough women then and there still aren't now. The urge on the part of the controllers to satisfy the requirements of social engineering would be the ruination of serious talk shows from that day to this. In the view of those in charge, there always has to be the politically correct number of minority representatives proportionate to the size of each minority as a component of the total population. For all I know, the TV version of positive discrimination, alias affirmative action, has had beneficial effects in British society. Affirmative action certainly helped America towards a political climate in which it was conceivable that a black man could be elected President, and Britain is still a long way short of that. But I had a show to run, and just wanted the guests to be good at what they were doing. I wouldn't have cared if the guests were gay dwarves with green skin as long as they could talk. Elaine felt the same. But Yentob had an agenda, and she had to listen to him on the phone, sometimes while she was in the control room and the show was actually running.

The pressure was relentless and it jammed us up. Most of the British men were hopeless on screen anyway, with that fatal combination of diffidence and dogmatism that makes you wonder how they ever emerge alive from breakfast with their wives. We had to fly some Americans in at vast expense, on the reasonable assumption that they would be more upfront. Some of them were, but Carl Bernstein scarcely bothered to pay attention and David Mamet thought it would be cute if he said nothing at all. If it had been live television instead of a tape, I would have asked him what he thought he was doing, accepting a transatlantic plane ticket from us and then stiffing us on air: did he think he was starring in one of his own scripts about con-men? But it wasn't live television, so I couldn't face him down, and anyway I admired him too much. I admire him even today – *State and Main* is one of my favourite movies about the movies – but I can't forget my disappointment, and Elaine was out of her head with anger. Richard wrote Mamet a note that I bet he didn't keep. Strange to say, our best upfront American was a woman, the ex-model sexologist Shere Hite. She was touring the UK with one of her books so she didn't even cost us a ticket. She fought her corner well on screen and she was very glam. Off screen she was a wild soul whose company I enjoyed, because like many a male stick-in-the-mud I secretly dream of the milk-skinned strawberry blonde in the black classic who dances on the table. And Shere, although some people thought she was nuts – my agent Pat Kavanagh was among them – was very smart, with infallible radar for any incoming male-chauvinist remarks. She told me a lot of stuff that I needed to hear.

Dare I say that it didn't hurt if the females were lookers? Some of the TV critics resented that, but the truth was – is still – that with females, looks breed confidence. If you want to correct this injustice, go fix society, and tell me how you get on. (If you can work the trick, nobody will applaud louder than I: even more than Michael Frayn's 'tyranny of the fortunate', the tyranny of the attractive strikes me as an unending tragedy, a really nasty brainwave on the part of the Man Upstairs.) At the time, we went for any woman who could talk the part, and if she looked the part as well it was certainly no reason to turn her down. This aspect was crucial when it came to the only episode of the series that I later thought of as an unqualified success. It starred two male heavyweights, George Steiner and Christopher Ricks, and a female heavyweight, Annie Cohen-Solal, the biographer of Jean-Paul Sartre. Annie Cohen-Solal was a known favourite of Mitterrand and when she arrived on a plane from Paris we soon found out why. 'Heavyweight' was a misleading word. 'Angelweight' would have been closer. Though razor sharp even in her second language, she looked as if she belonged beside Anna Wintour in the front row at a couture collection, making notes on the frocks. Faced with the spectacle of her soignée silk and cashmere delicacy and the unsettling speed of her dialectical brain, Ricks and Steiner immediately went into rutting-stag mode. The nominal subject was the politics of culture but they might as well have been competing for mating rights. Their exchange of epigrammatic arguments was like a clash of antlers. Nor was there anything doe-like about the prize they were fighting for, beyond the size of her eyes. When she caught them scamping their logic she pouted with disdain before emitting an aphorism that stopped them in their tracks. But the two professors barely paused before charging each other once again. Somewhere in the middle of all this, I did my best not to beam with happiness. This was the way it was supposed to be, but hardly ever was. And not even Yentob could say that this particular panel was without a woman. But there couldn't be one and a half women. It just wasn't possible, and eventually the word came down that the show was not fulfilling the management's hopes. I myself could stand the squeeze, but I couldn't bear seeing my production staff being run ragged for what I thought was a foolish reason.

Management interference was beginning to be a general story at the BBC in that period, now known to media history as the early phase of the Birt Era. Executives at the middle level were learning Birt-speak, as speakers of Cantonese in Hong Kong learn Mandarin today. My outfit had half a floor at White City all to itself and our swish designer desks were occupied with dedicated staff who arrived early each day and left late, but our top-echelon people, often including Richard himself, spent a precious half-day each week absent at meetings where they were told how to manage. Richard loathed every minute of it and gave me scathing reports about how apparatchiks half his age, who had never made a programme in their lives, would give him instructions, couched in barely comprehensible language, on subjects he had learned about the hard way many years before. At one of these management-training sessions he was asked to form a team that would tie a thread around an egg, lower it out of the window and then discuss the group dynamics of the decisions they had made. His suggestion to just throw the egg out of the window and then go and buy a new one was not well received. He came back hopping mad, which for a man with a bad foot was a painful condition to

be in. Elaine was doing another of her angry dances about
Yentob's interference with the BBC 2 show. There was aggro at
every level.

But a fizzer on BBC 2 didn't matter so much when we had a
hit on BBC1. The weekly show was reaching a high level of development, with ratings to match. Diana, in the company of her
colonic-irrigationist, came to watch the show from the gallery one
night. She howled at all the right moments, and after the show, in
the Green Room, she was perfect, asking everyone about their jobs
and wolfing down the answers, clearly fascinated by the whole
business. Suddenly she wanted to be a television producer, a
researcher, a set designer. The divorce was on its way by then, and
it filled me with regret. What a Queen she would have made.
Having done the rounds in impeccable style, she wanted me to
join her and the irrigationist in an expedition to the nightclubs. I
would have loved to watch her dance, but I had my duties to the
troops. Her last word on the way out was that the show was like
some amazing circus. 'Really, really *amazing*.'

I'm bound to say that she had a point. For one thing, the set
was a marvel. By then the wall of monitors had grown to the size
of an entire cyclorama: a universe of images. It weighed tons,
and one day the scene-shifters tried to push it into position too
quickly and it toppled hugely forward, exploding on the floor
and filling the studio with toxic gas that took two days to clear.
But they built an identical wall in another studio and the show
was taped on time.

The guest system was further refined so that the subsidiary
guest worked for the show. If, say, Peter O'Toole was the star
guest, the subsidiary guest might be Peter Cook, whose job would
be to comment on all the video material that had appeared in the
running order up to that point. Since Cook had got to the stage
in his life when he would far rather talk about other things than
talk about himself, the spot was enjoyable for him and he gave
little trouble. His latter-day investigations into the effect of a diet
of alcohol only sparingly punctuated by food were far advanced,

and he did not always show up in suitable clothing. He might need a shave and haircut from the make-up girl while suitable clothes were collected from the wardrobe department. But when he was commenting on video material he was unbeatable. There was a video clip from German television about the making of mayonnaise. Cook used it as a springboard for a long verbal flight about German mayonnaise-making throughout history. I spent a lot of time doubled up and I wasn't mugging. After a virtuoso performance like that, we could slot in a satellite interview with Sylvester Stallone's mother and a few more fake news compilations before we fired the signal for Peter O'Toole to drift in and stretch out in his chair with his typical lazy grace. More cool than O'Toole they didn't come. It was a sumptuous change of pace and made the show look as wealthy as Byzantium in its years of glory.

O'Toole would have been a perfect guest for the BBC 2 show. He was a writer of high distinction – his autobiographies are up there with David Niven's and Dirk Bogarde's as models of the form – and he was widely cultivated in all the arts. In his dressing room he talked about the paintings of Jack B. Yeats in a way that I never forgot, and from then on I always looked out for Yeats pictures whenever I was in Dublin. (The Guinness family house in Phoenix Park is jammed with them. I probably would never have got to see them if Barry Humphries, always the most socially connected of the top performers, hadn't been with me to get me through the door, but I certainly wouldn't have understood the importance of what I was seeing if O'Toole hadn't started me on the trail.) Still in the dressing room, O'Toole put me on the spot with his raised eyebrows of wonder when he found out that I hadn't read the diaries of Schuschnigg. Why not, if I was so interested in pre-war European politics? 'Dear boy, you really haven't read them? *Really?*' The sprawling drawl was like being beaten up with a silk handkerchief. I repaired the deficiency as soon as I could. O'Toole was also learned in poetry, with a repertoire of memorized verse that he could draw upon at any time. (Years later, he quoted one of my own poems to me and it was one of the great moments of my life.) But he wouldn't have been interested in talking like that on a BBC 2 show for pundits. He had his stardom to protect, and he was right, because the world fame that had begun with *Lawrence of Arabia* had made everything else possible. My own opinion of *Lawrence of Arabia* was that it was no more spontaneous than *Dr Zhivago* on defrost. But without the global renown which O'Toole had acquired from striding dynamically around the desert, the tallest actor ever to play a short man, he would never have been at the focal point of *My Favourite Year*, which would be on my list of the ten best comedy movies ever made. In other words, he would never have made his interesting movies if he hadn't been rendered colossal by an uninteresting movie. His film career wasn't over yet and he had a lifetime's investment to protect. He was on a BBC 1 weekly show because he was a movie star with a product to push.

The same was true in almost every case. Dirk Bogarde, although he had been established for years as an important author, still thought of himself as a movie star when he took a turn as my guest. He proved his status by insisting that there was only one direction from which he could enter, because he wanted the camera on one side of his face and not the other. Through my eyes the two sides of his face looked equally distinguished but not through his. I didn't mind that he was a handful because I admired him greatly not just as someone who had come to writing late and made such a success of it, but as an actor who had been one of the few bright things about British movies from his first day. For me he wasn't just Simon Sparrow in *Doctor in the House*, he was the man who had bravely laid his career on the line to make the first film about a closet homosexual forced into the open, *Victim*, and who had used his prestige, star power and high intelligence to help Harold Pinter and Joseph Losey make *The Servant*. Bogarde was my idea of an artist and I liked him all the more for the frailty by which he counted his social connections on a par with his creative achievements and was ready to talk the higher gossip with grand ladies. Only human beings have human weaknesses. He rated himself, but then they all did. They were right to. A star is a nodal point around which everything happens. Some of them are better than others at staying sane in those circumstances but their divine right to the limelight unites them all. Even Michael Caine, who loved doing his Michael Micklethwaite act even more than the many comedians who were pleased to copy it, made sure to mention his next movie as well as the current one.

The same was true for Tom Hanks, who could give you an exact imitation of a normal human being except that he was so perfectly fluent he might have been working from a script for *Saturday Night Live*, the long-running American show on which he made regular appearances as the most accomplished of all guest hosts. His facade of normality boosted the clout that would one day enable him to translate the box-office success of his starring vehicle *Saving Private Ryan* into a monumental television production, *Band of Brothers*, in which he did not even appear, but whose stature transformed the expectations of an entire industry.

Image meant power, even for Tom Cruise. That was the only reason he was available. He came on as a satellite guest from Paris and we were lifelong friends within seconds. Since he had no monitor at his end and couldn't even see me, it spoke well for the telepathic powers conferred by his expertise in Scientology. For ten minutes his teeth lit up my wall. We were buddies. Pointing both fingers at me, he shouted, 'I feel that you and I have really formed a rapport, Clyde.'

The self-merchandising of the star guest was a law of the business, and the trick of our format was to squeeze enough original stuff into the hour to disguise the fact that its climax was an infomercial. We had got to the point where we could do that almost every time, but the ending remained a problem. It was a good idea to clinch the deal by reviving a has-been band to give another airing to its quondam hit. If it was Kid Creole and the Coconuts, the number could raise a riot. The Kid, showing remarkably few signs of wear for an ex-headliner who had played some pretty obscure clubs in recent years, had recruited a couple of new Coconuts to accompany his unexpected revival and they were entirely gorgeous. They hailed from Sweden and they hardly knew who he was, but he had rehearsed them down to the tiniest shake of the sweet hip in the tinsel microskirt. When the show was over, neither of the Coconuts wanted to go home with the Kid in the limo we had rented for him. They wanted to go home with Jeremy Irons, on the back of his motorbike. A man of principle and fidelity, Jeremy accelerated away in a fast leaning turn into Wood Lane. He was only just ahead of the Coconuts. Running side by side, they squealed, 'We love you! We love you!' in Scandinavian accents as the distance increased between them and the object of their desire. That time the ending worked, but sometimes it fizzled. There was still room for improvement.

There was still room for innovation, in fact. One format would suggest another. When you have the urge and the means to make things up, it is hard to stop before you hit the buffers. Orson Welles once called a movie studio a big train set for adults, and television could similarly feel like a plaything as long as your standard stuff was paying its way and left some budget to spare. One of the advantages of managerialism's psychotic emphasis on accountancy was that there could be no arguments if you were cost-effective: the figures were all there in the computer spreadsheets. If you kept your expenditure down while the viewing figures went up, there was an argument for funding a new venture. My introductions to the highbrow talk shows and the star interviews on the weekly show, and my voice-overs for the Postcards, had given me a taste for narrating to serious pictures that I thought I could exploit further: perhaps for a whole series, if the subject was big enough. I hadn't forgotten Alistair Cooke and Leonard Bernstein. I didn't sound as professorial as Jacob Bronowski or as aristocratic as Sir Kenneth Clark, but perhaps it would be an advantage to have a voice that could not be placed in a narrow context while I addressed a subject whose context was limitless. The minute somebody mentioned it in passing, one subject suddenly struck me as fitting the bill: it was full of historic significance, dripped with ready-made visual material, and it cried out for an informed, judicious and aphoristic commentary to hold its infinitely ramifying implications together. It was fame. Fame in the twentieth century.

I even knew something about it from the inside. For about fifteen years now my mug-shot had been all over the place and I knew for a fact that to be so recognizable had made me two different kinds of wanted man, simultaneously up there and on the run. Richard went for the idea instantly and assigned Beatrice Ballard to produce it. She was ideal for more than one reason. She, too, knew about fame from the inside. Her father, J. G. Ballard, was a famous writer and she had grown up with an icon in the house. And within her fetching form burned the soul of a staff officer, which would be a vital attribute, because to organize the research would be a taxing logistical effort. Just to secure the film footage would be a military task. Jean Twoshoes, in charge of the film-research ferrets, was about to be pushed out of an aircraft deep behind enemy lines.

Nobody flinched. Everyone went at it like a fanatic, and I still bless them all. Two assistant producers spent months working on a set of themes. Bea had all kinds of ideas about experts to consult. The Professor of Media Communications at the University of This, the Professor of Communications Media at the University of That. Endless lists were compiled and countless documents were drafted. Compilers and drafters all took it well when I insisted that the enormous beast would find its plot-line in modern history, and should have a strict chronological narration put together in voice-over, with no current face appearing except one, and even my face should show up only briefly at the top and tail of each episode. Every other face in the enormous plot-line, hundreds and hundreds of them, should be a famous face from the twentieth century, doing its famous thing while I told the story. It was simple. It was just very hard to write, and I put the complete script, running to eight hour-long episodes, through eight separate and distinct drafts before we had something we could read over the assembled footage, which took a long time to select, collect and edit. Without electronic editing, which by now had well and truly arrived, the thing would have been impossible: the reason there was no precedent for it. *Fame in the Twentieth Century* was thus entirely dependent on the state of the technology, a pre-echo of the emergence, later on, of the World Wide Web. The Web was already getting started but had not yet revealed its full potential. To say that 'it's all in the timing' is essentially meaningless. The timing is all in the engineering. When the machinery is there, you can do it, and I'm proud to say that we did it.

I have to blow my own trumpet for *Fame in the Twentieth Century* because there is nobody else left to do so. It was the television project dearest to my heart, it took more than a year out of my life, and it disappeared as if it had never existed. Nor, for copyright reasons, will it ever come back, even in the smallest part. For that very reason, I will keep short my account of its fate. Some of my part in it might have been done better. My talking-head pieces at the top and tail of each episode were shot in studio in a single day, with me sitting in front of the great, glowing word FAME in ruby neon, an idea I had got from Elvis Presley's last big special. A director, whose name I have been careful to forget – I need hardly say that his name was there in a hundred per cent title at the end of every episode, as if he had conceived the whole thing – shot the short pieces with elaborate camera movements, although the effort might have been better put into the lighting. I thought there was something wrong with it but feebly let the director do the directing. I would have done better to take Richard aside to tell him that we should think again, because I was the one with his head on the screen and the head looked more than usually like an egg. The lighting had the effect of blending the little hair I had remaining on each side of my head into the dark background, thus producing a cranium that seemed to come to a point. Some back-lighting would have helped, but there wasn't any. So the tops and tails, though they sounded, in my ears, sufficiently fluent and authoritative, looked like those moments in *Star Trek* when the weird head of the alien starship commander occupies the video screen on the bridge of the *Enterprise*. 'Surrender your ship, Captain Kirk. We, the Egg People, have you in our power.'

As for the main body of the show, I still don't think I made a mistake about the general approach – it was certainly the most careful stretch of extended writing that I ever did for television – but I might have made a crucial mistake politically. Bea, though she served my conception of the format with her full commitment, never abandoned her conviction that we should have talked to experts on screen. It might have gone over better upstairs, which was where our inexorable problem lay. The management just never got behind the show, even though it had cost them a lot of money. The price for copyright footage kept on going up all the time as the agencies who controlled it got a better idea of the goldmine they were sitting on, but somehow we contrived to buy the rights on the basis that all the material could be screened four times. The American PBS network, who put in a million dollars, screened the whole thing the full four times to their sparse audience. The Australians, who put in another million, screened it twice. But the BBC, who paid the bulk of its enormous cost, screened it exactly once, during the week, and without even a repeat at the weekends. On its weeknight it was given suicide scheduling against ITV's *Inspector Morse*, the biggest ratings hit of the day – my own family never missed an episode – but we still peaked at seven million viewers and averaged about five million for the whole run. Such figures would be a sensation today. Nevertheless the series was regarded as a failure.

I'm afraid it was pre-judged as a failure, simply because of its format. Alan Yentob was a dedicated enemy of the presenter-led documentary. Ever since the deserved success of a programme he had produced about the Ford Cortina, it had become BBC orthodoxy that a documentary on any subject should have no central face, but simply narrate itself, with a voice-over recited by an actor, preferably from a script written by the producer. There was something to be said for this approach, but the cost of making it a dogma was that the outgoing generation of over-qualified writer-presenters was the last to practise the form, and a new generation was not recruited. No more would Robert Kee, who really knew something about Ireland, head up a series that would tell you about Ireland. Some producer who knew not much more about Ireland than what he read in the *Guardian* would tell you about Ireland. There would be no new John Betjeman until Jonathan Meades came along half a lifetime later. Eventually it was discovered that for some subjects a narrator in vision was indispensable, especially if the subject was not as inherently telegenic as a Ford Cortina. Indeed Alan Yentob himself, in a later incarnation as head of BBC Arts, rediscovered the necessity at the turn of the millennium, and in the absence of other candidates was forced to appoint himself in the role of anchor man for the arts series *Image*. In his post as Head of Arts, Alan Yentob had searched high and low and found that only Alan Yentob could handle the task. Having hired himself at a suitable salary, he did some excellent programmes – the one about the Soane Museum was especially fine – but I often wondered, while watching him in action, if he ever thought back to the days when his decisions had made life difficult for those of us who were doing the same thing.

Still, there is no point complaining. The series on fame got made, and quite a lot of people saw it. (As Richard never failed to remind me when I showed too much concern with the ratings, a million people was a city, five million people was a country, and there was no other form of writing I could practise that would ever come near reaching that many people so directly, with their attention on nothing else.) There was even a book of the series, written by me with all the care I could summon. It got one very laudatory review, from Neil Kinnock of all people, but it didn't sell very well in the UK, although eventually it was put into paperback as my one and only Penguin. In America it hardly sold at all, which made me sorry for my publisher, Harry Evans at Random House. Harry Evans and Tina Brown, the most radiant celebrity couple in New York, threw a launch party for the book at their house in Sutton Place. All of fashionable New York was there to hear a modest speech from me. Modesty is always a mistake in America. I should have said that it was the greatest book in the world and that anybody who didn't read it would get warts. But the book wouldn't have taken off no matter how I promoted it, because it was essentially a book of opinions about modern history, and my qualifications for having such opinions were not clear. In America, opinions are accepted only from licensed opinion-makers. Looking back, I can now see that the fame book was one of the precursors for a heftier work that I would write in the next decade, *Cultural Amnesia*; and that the central thesis of the series, about the connection between celebrity and politics, was simply ahead of its time. But to say that you are ahead of your time is just a consoling way of saying you have failed. The worst aspect of *Fame in the Twentieth Century*'s gradual but terminal dive towards death, however, was that there was never any question of its resurrection. If I didn't own the rights to the footage, then the thing was gone. More than a year and a half of work had vanished. I resolved never to be in such a situation again if I could help it.

22. BACK TO BASICS

It felt, far and away, like the biggest setback of my career, but I was the only one who noticed. It's the only bearable thing about having a flop in show business. By definition, most people don't see it. Even in the office, life went on. The weekly show kept getting more assured, and the End of the Year show was now a recognized part of the festive season. Everyone who didn't go out for the evening – in effect, that meant anyone who wasn't too young to understand it – tuned in to watch our annual fantasy. Though the bulk of the show was mainly news footage talked in and out with a script by me and Bostock, there were guests at the end. We played the beauty card ruthlessly. Fake awards were handed out, and there was always a glamour girl to read the names and open the envelopes. Jerry Hall, Elle McPherson, Louise Lombard: they all took a turn. There were production numbers. Tom Jones presented his pelvis while belting out 'It's Not Unusual' in that raging baritone he could have used to sing the title role in *Don Giovanni*. It was a butch moment, but standing right there beside him was Kiri te Kanawa, all aflutter to be on screen with the rock star. Kylie Minogue bounced up and down in a delirious fit of song and dance. I didn't have to do much acting to convey the impression that I loved them all. Each was my favourite. I liked Jerry for her gameness, her general determination to be not just a stunningly statuesque blonde in a couture frock. With her catwalk stardom coming to an end, she was determined to have a professional life apart from being Mrs Jagger, and appearing on our show was part of her break-out plan.

I was surprised when, during a supper in Soho with Mick Jagger and his admirable parents, he seemed scornful of Jerry's extramural activities. When I asked him, foolishly, if he thought she had done well in my show – never ask a question if you might not like the answer – he said, 'Didn't watch it, Clive.' For a while I thought less of him for that, but later on I heard that ructions were taking place. So all I had been hearing was noises off at the edge of a battle.

Unless you are actually closely acquainted with a star of Mick Jagger's magnitude – and I wasn't – a casual meeting will tell you nothing. Most likely it will tell you even less. The truth is that someone as famous as Mick Jagger is living his life well if he even continues in one piece. Even when considering how big the Stones still are now, it is hard to credit how very big they were then. History wasn't allowed to happen unless they were there. In Prague after the Velvet Revolution, I chanced to be backstage when the Stones gave the first rock concert that the audience had heard in many years. Most of them had the words by heart and they sang along. 'Icon GEDNO saddest FACTION . . .' It was the sound of their freedom, once stolen, now restored. Mick Jagger was the bearer of the torch. The audience didn't know that their heroes, several of whom had no idea of which city they were in, were already in the limo and on the way to the airport before the last of the applause had died. The Stones had a whole world to look after. Jerry was married to a tribune of Planet Earth, so she did pretty well too. She was a bonus for the show, sweet and sassy, although of course not a show-business pro like Kylie.

In our house, Kylie was a great favourite, especially with my younger daughter, who had grown up with the Kylie hits pumped into her head through earphones. If it wasn't Abba it was Kylie. Nobody who hasn't met Kylie can quite realize how little she is. She could dance on your hand, but the astonishing thing is how good her dancing is. She rehearsed the routine for our show at the Pineapple Studios in Covent Garden and I went down there to help her block out the moves and rehearse her lines. She

worked like a cattle dog. On the day, she had the whole thing
pat and looked terrific in every shot. We taped the post-midnight
production numbers in the afternoon so as to leave time for
editing. With Kylie we didn't need a single retake except when
she had to stand beside Elle McPherson. Elle, you probably
won't need telling, is very tall. But already you have guessed the
problem. It was hard to get them into the same shot.

My literary friends smiled tolerantly about my dance number
with Kylie, but my nose-to-neck badinage with Elle was not forgiven. Nobody could expect his reputation as a poet and literary
critic to survive intact when he appeared on screen in a clinch
with a young woman who looked as if she had arrived by shell-
shaped elevator in the penthouse of Vulcan. Things were, if
possible, made even worse when Louise Lombard took her turn
as the young lady who opened the envelopes. She was not only a
lyric poem to look at, she was genuinely funny. Later on she built
another television career in America because the British scene
didn't know how to use her. I simply loved having her around
and I still think we should have brought her back on a regular
basis, but it was thought better to ring the changes in what was
meant to be a subsidiary role. (Actually the thing to do, when
someone has a hit in a subsidiary role, is to keep them on and
make the role bigger, which is exactly what happened ten years
later with Martin Sheen in *The West Wing*: but the lesson is
always being lost because the plans stretch too far ahead.) Within
the framework we had set for ourselves, I always had a say in the
casting; and I had powers of veto, so I have to take the blame for
the only real mistake we made. It didn't show, because it wasn't
a case of casting the wrong person, it was a case of not casting
the right one. I had seen Catherine Zeta-Jones in *The Darling
Buds of May* and I made the classic mistake of thinking that the
performance I saw on screen was the only one she could do. So
we didn't book her. What an error.

But generally the End of the Year show was getting to the
point where we couldn't improve it, so already I was getting

restless, and starting to wonder when we might shut it down. In five years you can make an impression but still get out clean. In ten years, you're stuck, and it takes another ten years to shake the memory. We weren't going to do any better than when we brought on Pavarotti as our after-midnight main man. This time we had to fly him in from Italy on a private jet, and when he showed up at the studio he turned out to be even bigger than last time. The expression 'on his last legs' was not inappropriate, because the weight of his upper works had finally wrought irreversible damage to his knees. By that time, when he sang the role of Cavaradossi in *Tosca*, he had to sit down for the firing squad. This development was unfortunate because we had a big white set with a grand staircase we wanted him to walk down when he made his entrance. His management team didn't even need to see the studio floor-plan before they announced that their star wouldn't be walking down anything. He would be walking on from the side. We readjusted the scheme.

We were always ready to rejig the layout for the star, even when the requirements seemed irrational. Diana Ross, when she was our star guest, had a contract that said she wouldn't even walk diagonally without a week's notice. She was as difficult as could be but I didn't blame her. She was coming out of a culture that had spent three hundred years being screwed by Whitey and she was sensible in wanting to take control. And also, she was who she was. I thought that the 1966 *Ready Steady Go!* Tamla Special, hosted by Dusty Springfield, was the greatest single TV music show ever screened, and now one of its brightest stars, Diana Ross, was living and breathing right there beside me: the fabulous face was singing her fabulous songs, or at any rate miming to playback. I was knocked out, along with the public.

Jason Donovan was equally difficult but with perhaps a touch less reason to believe that the results would be worth it from our angle. The year that he appeared, we had a cyclorama of a rather subtle tint somewhere between aubergine and egg-plant, if those aren't the same thing. Jason Donovan turned up in his

standard fetchingly casual attire, the trousers of which proved to
be coloured somewhere between aubergine and egg-plant. By a
million to one coincidence, they exactly matched the cyclorama.
The result, to the camera, was that he spent a whole hour of
our first rehearsal period minus his legs. Wearing his regulation stitch-on cheerful smile, the rest of him floated around the
studio thirty inches above his shoes, which uncannily matched
his progress as he swerved about mouthing the pious banalities
of his chosen song. It looked like a horror movie, and Elaine,
who was in charge that year, moved from the control room out
into the studio to make direct contact with the apparition. With
her powers of charm cranked up to the max, she asked him
whether he would consider changing his pants. He wouldn't
change his pants. They were his lucky pants, containing the secret
of his mojo. It was in these very pants, he explained, that he had
first sung to an adoring public and realized that he had a duty to
their love. Elaine smiled nicely, marched back to the control
room, and did her dance of anger. The dance was of small radius
– she merely placed her elfin weight alternately on each foot
while tossing her head and muttering things like 'Really, is it
worth it?' through gritted teeth – but to anyone familiar with it,
this was the full-scale version. Then she went out there again and
told the superstar that there was no option: the pants would have
to be changed. Jason thought about it for a bit and declared that
he would not change the pants. It was a question of integrity. It
was a question of his art. So we changed the cyclorama. It took
half an hour but there were other things we could do while it was
happening, such as slitting our wrists.

Beside that kind of artistically determined display of uncom-
promising values, Pavarotti's demands were slight, and fully in
accord with the unalterable physical facts. He was a pussy-cat
in rehearsal, and it wasn't his fault that we ran out of time.
Production numbers need a complicated camera plot and if just
one camera blows a valve then the whole thing slows to a crawl.
The clock dictated that we would get only one go at taping the

complete ending, which was meant to be climaxed by me and the world's most famous tenor framed in a close two-shot as we led the singing of 'Auld Lang Syne'. You might think that a close two-shot with Pavarotti would need to be in Cinerama but actually it looked quite good. There was a potential problem, however, with the words. 'Clivay, what is the words of this song?' He already knew the melody but not the lyrics. I told him it would be no sweat. The words, I explained, were written in huge letters on a giant song sheet which would be lowered from the gallery at the right moment, and he just had to sing what he saw. With the clock ticking like a bomb, we launched into the production number, which went like a dream until the backing track surged into the melody, the song sheet came winching down, and Luciano was faced with the first stanza. He managed the first three lines all right, but when he saw the final three words of the fourth line 'For the sake of auld lang syne' the whole town was suddenly underwater. He sang it as he saw it, which in this case, when you think about it, is the last thing anyone should do. The word 'ah-ooled' came out more or less all right, but the rest of it was an out-take from *La Bohème*. However weird it sounded, though, our duet looked superb, and I treasure it as one of my showbiz golden moments. A duet with the most famous singer of all time: tell me if it isn't among your dreams too. The confetti rained down, balloons were released, the great man opened his arms to embrace me as a Kodiak bear in black tie might approach its lunch, and I was in heaven. When we played the tape in real time after midnight, with more confetti and more balloons to augment what was already on the tape, the studio audience erupted, no doubt wondering where the beloved man was. He was already back in Italy, where the tax-gatherers and a phalanx of vengeful women were sharpening their knives for the moment when the magnificent beast would finally fall.

Heaven. I suppose it wasn't a metaphor. I loved doing that kind of television and I think it showed. But at the BBC it was getting increasingly difficult to do, because the paperwork and the pie charts were turning themselves into the main event. Birtism had its rationale. Even Richard admitted that. 'Something', he said, 'had to be done to sort this place out.' And Birt was prescient about the Web, for which he laid the foundations of a BBC presence that dominates the field today. But at the operational level the bureaucracy had become Kafkaesque. Nevertheless we were determined to persist. With the skilled advice of Norman North, we approached the management with our ideas for the next stage of our rolling contract. With the proviso that the End of the Year show should now be retired, our ideas consisted mainly of providing more of what we knew how to accomplish in the formats we had devised, with less administrative hassle in carrying out the work. Really we were saying that they could leave it to us and they would get a guaranteed return, with savings all round even though my own price had gone up. The efficiency we could offer would offset my fees, which, I should hasten to say, were minuscule compared with what happens today, although I would undoubtedly be doing a lot better than a taxi-driver. By a miracle, Alan Yentob was located, and persuaded by Will Wyatt, my oldest friend among the executives – he had risen to be the highest-placed operational officer in BBC television before you got to the level where programmes were never mentioned except in a language that only a Martian intelligence officer could decode – to attend a breakfast where negotiation could occur. The negotiation went well and even Yentob pronounced himself satisfied with the prospects. He had to leave early for a meeting with Gustav Mahler or somebody but he wished us well, and I am sure he was sincere. (One of the many good things about him is that he is too rude to lie.) What happened next, however, was nothing. The paperwork was all prepared, but nobody in the continuously reorganized management seemed to have the power to sign it. Not even Will Wyatt, who was keen for the deal, could prevail upon the bean-counters to get their fingers out. For months, the nothing that had happened before was succeeded by the nothing that happened next. In desperation we tried to contact Yentob, hoping that he might translate his spoken approval into a written executive order. Nobody could find him. As always, rumours of his location abounded. He was on an ice floe in the Red Sea, in conversation with the Dalai Lama. He was in the Aleutians with Lord Lucan. Finally the day came when we could take no more. We had about fifty staff members milling about, talking about their mortgages. Just at that moment, by the kind of wild coincidence that looks like a plan only in retrospect, Richard and I were lunching in Mayfair with Jonathan Powell, who had powers of decision at ITV. Under the combined influence of Valpolicella and existential angst, we spilled our story and Jonathan made a suggestion. Suppose we made the same proposal to him, how would it be framed? We said that we could not only offer the same set of formats, we would undertake to organize their manufacture, through our own production company which we would set up for the purpose. So all he would have to do would be to pay the bill. Jonathan said that he had a cut-off point coming up because of the timing of the financial year, but if he could see all that in writing on his desk by the following Monday, he would sign it. Norman North spent the weekend rewriting the papers, they were delivered by courier, and the deal was done.

The news got out pronto throughout the industry, because an independent production company with just one on-screen asset was still quite rare. In fact David Frost's Paradine Productions was almost the only instance, and even he ran other horses if he could. Some of the independent outfits were already important. Cinema Verity, the organization put together by the prodigiously gifted Verity Lambert, had been a pioneer, but now there were Tiger Aspect, Hat Trick, Talkback and others. Most of the others were grouped around John Lloyd, a creative demiurge whose every idea turned into an industry. All of these enterprises, however, had a whole range of on-screen personnel. Ours had just me. We didn't even have a name for the company. The moment that set the symbolic seal to our unusual move was a phone call I received in Cambridge. It was Alan Yentob. He was calling from the deck of Charles Saatchi's yacht in the Mediterranean. He sounded genuinely disappointed when he said, 'Clive, this is one of the worst moments of my professional career. How did we lose you?' But the bit that floored me was when he said, 'Why didn't you phone me?' Never one for the right reply at the right time, for once I had the gumption to state the awkward truth. 'Alan, we couldn't find you.'

So the switch was made. I should say at this point, to stave off accusations of fickleness, that I am a believer in sticking with an institution even through its days of uncertainty. But a media organization is not like a royal family or a marriage. Wittgenstein said a game consists of the rules by which it is played. A media organization consists of the qualities it can bring about and protect. Its formal charter is a mere document if the things produced don't live up to it. The BBC had a great tradition but it was going through a time when it was hard for someone like me to do his best work under its aegis. (The word 'aegis' repays study: it means a shield, not a set of shackles.) The opposition offered better opportunities for creative work, so I switched sides. Morecambe and Wise notoriously made a huge mistake when they transferred from the BBC to ITV, but they did it for the money, and fatally neglected the likelihood that their new employer would not have the production expertise to protect their work. But I wasn't after the money, I was after the oxygen, and anyway our production skills belonged to us, not to the corporation. There is no need to accuse oneself of treason in such circumstances. One hasn't deserted the King in his time of trouble. It is the duty of a cavalier, if the institution he serves should falter, to take his stand in the last ditch and die in a muddy shirt. But if a broadcasting company has become uninhabitable, then to transfer one's efforts to a rival is logical, and if one does well in the new home it can only serve to remind the old one that it needs to get its act back together.

Over the course of twenty years I went from one side to the other as it suited my work, not my whim. The organizations, whatever they thought of themselves, were no better than what they could do. Though I believe that the BBC's right to a licence fee, far from being a political imposition, is a political freedom that should be defended with all our hearts, not even the BBC deserves unquestioning loyalty from its creative personnel if it contrives to frustrate their efforts. I was loyal to both sides of television because I thought that they added up to the one valuable thing. In the whole period, whenever I was asked to make a speech to the Royal Television Society, I stressed the essential unity of the binary system, and I did the same when I wrote articles about the state of British television, a topic perennially fascinating to the press. Taking the task seriously, I kept the manuscripts of my ex cathedra pronouncements and eventually collected them into a volume called *The Dreaming Swimmer*, undoubtedly the thinnest of my essay collections, but with a solid subject, in my view. (The reason that I no longer write such pieces is that I am out of touch with British television, because rather than suffer through the brain-curdling fatuities of *Celebrity Big Brother* I much prefer to sit up all night watching boxed sets of American television such as *The West Wing*, *The Sopranos*, *Entourage*, *30 Rock* and *The Wire*. Only a moron wouldn't.) The subject was the parallel structure of an industry, whose components drew part of their energy from the freedom to move between them.

I followed the same principle in the print media, and never lost a night's sleep when I jumped ship. When Faber and Faber were, in my opinion, slow to see the possibilities of what I could do best, I went to Jonathan Cape, who did see the possibilities, and twenty years later, when Cape showed signs of wanting me only for what suited them, I went to Picador, who were ready to see the possibilities in what might suit me. I was loyal to all of them. But first and foremost I was loyal to an ideal. It was the same with the *Observer*, which, after I left it, several times tried to ask me back. But if I thought the paper was being badly led, I never answered the call, and when I was asked to help with an *Observer* museum they had in mind, I told them that museums were for obsolete institutions. Really the media organizations aren't institutions at all, in the strict sense. They are facilities, and when they start laying claim to a perennial mystique it is usually a sign that they are in decay. So move to another, or start your own.

23. COMPANY STORE

To start your own media facility, however, you need a business brain. Luckily I had one, in the form of Richard Drewett. On my own, I could barely organize my own lunch. But Richard could have organized D-Day. It was a talent, and a talent will always express itself to the full if it can. Out in Sydney, where Richard was acting as my manager while I did some stage appearances, we sat beside the swimming pool of the Regent Hotel and worked on a name for our company. After two days and a stack of lists, I was the one who got struck by lightning. Richard was mad about classic watches. He had a collection of them, and would occasionally give me one to mark a significant occasion, even though he knew I never collected anything, was not interested in the value of objects, and would inevitably lose the gift or leave it lying neglected. (The only reason I have a drawer full of his gift watches is that I also neglect to throw anything out.) On every trip in any direction, Richard collected high-quality things, which he called 'stuff'. In the duty-free shops he sought out the best stuff with the most favourable discounts. He had a collection of cameras. He had a collection of antique model cars that he added to in every city in the world. Richard never missed a bargain. He was systematic, for example, about keeping track of his air miles. I never did and still don't. After a quarter of a century of flying everywhere, I probably could have piled up enough air miles for a free trip to the Moon. To the despair and wonder of my frugal family, I just couldn't be bothered. It's a bad character flaw and I'm sorry for it. I continually buy a new cheap watch because I abandon the old one when the battery runs out or when the wrist band rots through. You might ask why I don't just reach into my drawer of Richard Drewett Presentation Classics, but they all need winding. My carelessness about what I strapped around my wrist was a particular puzzle to Richard, who wanted his watch to say 'Cartier' at the very least, even if he had to wind it every five minutes. 'Do you realize the workmanship that goes into a thing like this?' He was winding his latest treasure beside the swimming pool when suddenly the perfect name hit me. Watchmaker. It was a pun. We would make people watch. And it was a simile. We would be meticulous craftsmen. It was neat and sweet. It was perfect. Richard said, 'That's it.'

So we built a company called Watchmaker. It was a huge job of organization and thank God it wasn't up to me. Richard and I were equal senior partners but he did the heavy lifting, starting with the working capital, which came from the Chrysalis corporation, by means of a management buy-out deal, timed to reach fruition in five years: a deal which I still don't understand today even in its smallest part. The simplest interpretation I can manage is that Chrysalis would share in the production fees we received from the television companies and when the lustrum expired near the end of the millennium, Chrysalis would reward us by buying the company back from us. You understand? Neither do I. But Richard, a very practical man, had it all taped. He was so practical that he realized we would need a junior partner as a programmes executive. From the several candidates we had in mind, we chose Elaine Bedell primarily because she had the fire to face us down whether separately or together. She started off by demanding a salary and a share fifty per cent bigger than the highest figure we had conceived of. There was no way of paying it without giving up some of our own whack, but we did it anyway.

After that, the fun started. Luckily I missed most of it. I just went to the office each day and tried to be grateful as it was steadily transformed from an empty space into a thriving community with all the right filing cabinets. Our first, temporary, office was a large suite of rooms in a building somewhere in the Ladbroke Grove area. The building was so anonymous that I can't even remember where it was, and seldom could remember at the time. I had to be delivered to it by car from my flat in the Barbican: from one dead zone to another. I still marvel at the patience of a bunch of people who could devote such meticulous labour to moving all their stuff into a place that they would soon have to move out of, but before we could switch to a permanent office on a whole floor of the Chrysalis building we had had to make our first programmes, just to stay in business. In those short five years of Watchmaker's existence there was a whole string of Postcard programmes made practically back to back, and that tempo was at its height in the very beginning of the company, so that I was filming when I wasn't flying, and flying when I wasn't filming.

The Bombay Postcard was typical of the tight new approach. We poured the effort into preparation so that not one precious hour on location was wasted. Mumbai, still called Bombay in those days (it is still called Bombay now by everyone in the city who doesn't care about nationalist posturing, which effectively means everyone), hit me right between the eyes from the moment we moved into the Taj Mahal Hotel and I realized that most actual Indians had the same chance of seeing its lavish interior as they had of being invited to a White House ball. The story of the city was poverty, all right. The problem was not how to tell it, but how to tell anything else. Poverty got into everything. Anything that wasn't soaked in poverty had a view of poverty just outside the window. In streets that were already shanty towns, there were shanty towns in the gutters. All you had to do was point the camera. It was pointed by John Bowring, a well-fed Australian cameraman/director who was surprisingly light on his feet. He could do a smooth travelling shot while running backwards downstairs. When we filmed in the Pacific area we always used him because, based in Australia, he was less expensive on flight costs. Also he was exceptionally efficient, so the savings were doubled. And he was cheerful, which really helped. He had seen everything the Far East had to offer in terms of human suffering, but in Bombay even he sometimes surfaced from the eyepiece and said 'Christ almighty' after seeing something in the frame that passed all imagining for sheer misery. Yet that wasn't the whole story, even then. There was a new energy getting set to burst, rather like the bombs which terrorists were planting as their contribution towards solving the insoluble. If there was going to be an answer, prosperity was it, and prosperity was visibly getting started. Some of it took a ridiculous form, laying the place wide open for a standard City of Contrasts commentary. (In television documentaries, the phrase 'city of contrasts', along with 'land of contrasts', comes just behind 'meeting the challenge' and 'time was running out' as a sign that you won't be hearing anything remarkable.) If only to keep faith with the poor, I would try to do better than that.

The fine ladies of the social elite, all in their saris, gathered in a function room at the Hilton to check out Pierre Cardin's collection especially designed for India. Draped on loosely stalking imported models, none of his designs looked even remotely as good as the saris in the audience. Pierre Cardin himself, a carefully restored listed building in a suit, made an appearance at the end of the show, prancing on with the massed models and reaching down from the catwalk to make contact with a tiny percentage of the population of India, which he congratulated on its taste. I thought his own taste was exceeded for elegance by the merest fishwife, who could be filmed at the sea's edge as she came swerving though the uproar and the filth, her gracile figure infinitely poetic in an emerald sari as she balanced a basket of cuttlefish on her finely chiselled head. John Bowring caught her on a long lens against the gathering dusk and I already knew it would be the last shot of the finished movie, the shot over which I would narrate my conclusions. The beauty among the squalor was the key to the film's texture.

Other signs of incipient prosperity were a lot more fun than the irrelevant Frenchified frocks, which I knew I was going to call, in voice-over, the exact equivalent of coals to Newcastle. The burgeoning of a new Bombay could be seen at its most outrageous in Bollywood. Not yet world-famous but soon to be so, already the Bollywood system was generating half a dozen films a week and we went out to the main open-air set to include me in one of them. (This inclusion principle, by the way, had been pioneered long before by George Plimpton, and I lay no claim to its invention, although Plimpton, who had a solid literary background, seldom gave his television narrative the depth of his journalism: an opportunity which I thought was there to be taken.) In a musical drama telling the standard story of an attack by pirates on the stronghold of the runaway princess, I played a man with a moustache, a sword and pointed hat. The film was about as ludicrous as I was, but it was vital. The whole business was teeming with life. And the set itself was fascinating. It was a castle made of lath, plaster and cardboard, the whole thing painted silver. It must have cost fourpence and it looked like . . . well, I can't say it looked like a million dollars, even to the camera. It looked like a million rupees, which was only a few hundred quid, but all kinds of stuff was going on in its courtyards and on its battlements, and going on all the time. Everybody had a real job, even if it was only carrying props about. You would see a dozen blokes go tottering by carrying the components of a plaster pavilion. Miming their hearts out to booming dance tracks, some of the female stars were working on three different movies simultaneously. There were whole chorus lines of sinuous soubrettes with bare midriffs, the fake jewels plugged into their navels glittering like a sexy galaxy. The sense of purposeful occupation was a big contrast to what was happening in the streets of the city, which was nearly nothing, multiplied by millions and stirred into chaos. If a taxi broke down, a thousand people would gather to watch the driver failing to fix it. All of them found the camera even more fascinating than the taxi, so there was no choice except to make rubber-necking a theme of the movie. John Bowring was uncannily good at picking faces out of the crowd. When his eye was glued to the eyepiece, he had the precious gift of being able to scan with the other eye and spot opportunities. Very few cameramen can do that.

We filmed at a school for pavement children. Most of them, with no home except a traffic roundabout or a piece of tin in the gutter, had been employed collecting and sorting rubbish before they had been rounded up by the cops and forcibly enrolled at the school. Where they might go next, nobody could say, but it didn't look hopeful. Outside the school there were hundreds more urchins trying to get in: these didn't need to be rounded up, because they had been lured by rumours of a free sandwich every day. Filming inside the school playground late one morning, I spotted, among the shouting crowd of dust-balls at the gate, a particular face, and asked John to get a shot of him. I knew already that the question of what would happen to him would be at the core of the movie. I didn't yet know that it would also be at the core of a novel, but I figured it out before we left the city, and I wrote the first chapter on the plane home.

The urge to write *The Silver Castle* was my first big clue that the Postcard format, much as I treasured it, would eventually not be sufficient to make me feel that I was covering a subject. Some subjects need a deeper texture than film to ponder, and poverty is one of them, because the camera always glamorizes it no matter how honestly you shoot. For one thing, a picture doesn't stink, so that when you get a close-up of tots playing in a puddle of raw sewage, their paddling pool will just look shiny, without wrenching your guts. And anyway, I was telling a story about my real, non-media self: a story which would have been an indulgence on film. The hopeless little boy at the gate could have been me. If I had been born in Bombay, minus the advantages I had inherited without effort in democratic and prosperous Australia, I would have had no chance. As it turned out, the novel had no chance either. I still don't quite see why. Perhaps there were just too many novels about India written by real Indians. I thought

The Silver Castle by far my best stretch of fictional writing. As usual, most publications handed it for review to their resident wag, on the principle that a television face who had produced a book was asking for the same treatment as a dog doing new tricks, and that the wag, suitably inspired by contempt, would produce 'lively copy' as he dipped into his own well of comic inspiration. (My main reason for hating such treatment wasn't the injury to my self-esteem, but that I was always revolted by the idea of being enrolled, even inadvertently, in a conspiracy to bore the public.) But the book got some very good reviews in Britain and Australia, even from some of the older reviewers who were still wedded to the belief that media prominence had got in the way of my true vocation. Anthony Thwaite, a senior poet of real stature, wrote a review for the *Telegraph* that answered all my prayers. But reviews don't sell a book, although they can certainly help to bury one. Later on I was told that if I had held the book back until Bollywood became an international news story ten years later I might have had a hit. But no complaints, and the book did well enough, after it got to paperback, to pay for itself, if no more. It just refused to take off towards any level beyond respectability, and in America it died the death even with the logo of Random House on its spine. The *New York Times* review killed it at birth.

With thousands of books a week to choose from, Michiko Kakutani, tenured star book reviewer for the *New York Times*, could choose one book a week to review and decide its fate. She chose *The Silver Castle*, a book which I had thought to be seriously concerned with the effects of Indian poverty. She, however, by the application of her critical powers, was able to detect that I had been insufficiently concerned with the effects of Indian poverty. Bombay, she explained, is full of poor people. Michiko has been kind to other books I have written since, so I must be prudent in what I say, and my American publishers would have a fit at the very idea of my bringing her authority into question. But really, this prostration before a guru is one of the most unsettling things about America. Especially in the field of culture, gurus acquire an absurd degree of authority. They become immortal legends without having lived in the first place. In the benighted heyday of old Broadway, the *New York Times* theatre reviewer, a worthy plodder called Brooks Atkinson, could kill a play in a single night. More recently, the ineffable Michiko can kill a book. She is better qualified than Atkinson ever was, but the great German man of letters Marcel Reich-Ranicki was right when he said that a critic, though he might write a death certificate, should never have the power to write a death sentence.

I had bigger trouble with *The Silver Castle* than that, however. I had handed Jonathan Cape what I thought was a striking novel about India, but for some reason they couldn't supply it with a striking design. One design after another came up looking no more interesting than a panoramic photograph of Swindon. Tom Maschler was seldom on the scene any more – while retaining an advisory role, he had cashed in his pile of chips and retired to a villa in France – but on a trip back to London he agreed that the proposed final design for the book looked like nothing, and he joined me at the computer while we patched something together from material on the Web. But I regarded the company's lack of concern as the writing on the wall, and when the new chief executive suggested that my next book of essays, provisionally entitled *Even As We Speak*, might have to wait for an extra year, I took it as a sign that I was being put up with. Peter Straus, the chief executive at my paperback publishers, Picador, had been saying for several years that he would like, if he could, to publish me 'vertically' (it meant that he would do the hardback as well as the paperback) and after a quick conversation with Pat Kavanagh I fired the signal to jump ship. My pangs of compunction lasted exactly one and a half minutes. When they take you for granted it's time to go.

All this happened in London, where I seldom was. Mainly I was in mid-air, or what felt like it even if I was on the ground. In Mexico City there was more poverty, but it was tidier. Mexico

City has more people in it than the whole of Australia and most of them are a lot less well off than the people who govern them. This imbalance has obtained since the time of the Aztecs, and even today, with the vaunted 'permanent revolution' solidly installed and universal justice theoretically secured for all time, the centre of the city, dominated by a cathedral steadily sinking into the earth, is still the place to hang out if you want to see what a power structure can do to a population when it gets out of hand. In the normal course of events, however, the poor people are out at the periphery. The periphery was bigger than anything we could hope to film without a fleet of helicopters. In the centre, things looked more picturesque than desperate. The begging groups who had trekked in from the hinterland put on a little circus at the traffic island, so that when you tossed some money to a couple of kids in clown costumes you could congratulate yourself you were rewarding enterprise. The rich, in fact, evoked as much pity as the poor. We filmed a wedding party for one of the unluckily privileged children of a wealthy banker at his hacienda. Masquerading as an old-style landowner in real life, in his fantasy life he masqueraded further as a cowboy, complete with tight trousers, jangling spurs and a sombrero that could have been worn simultaneously by all three of the Three Amigos. He gave us a self-satisfied interview that might have been designed to incite the next revolution. A whole phalanx of such off-putting plutocrats played collective host to us at a rodeo in an arena in the heart of the city. Horsemen in big sombreros raced towards our camera and came to a stop. At least they stopped in the right spot – I still had memories of Willie Nelson – but as with almost all horse-based activities anywhere in the world that are accompanied with many a cry of 'Hey, Hey!' in whatever language, there was an irreducible boredom to it all. We had planned some extra life for the scene by getting me trained to whirl a lariat. Naturally I was dressed as a cowboy in an absurdly big sombrero. It was hard to get the effect of an absurdly big hat when everybody else's hat was absurdly big already, but my tight outfit helped. As with the other numerous facetious outfits I wore on location in the course of twenty years, the publicity stills of my Mexican cowboy incarnation are still out there in the database somewhere, patiently waiting to decorate my obituary. Before we get to the stirring scene when I twirled the lariat at the rodeo, let me digress for a moment on the tedium of being photographed.

Being photographed for publicity stills is something that should not happen to normal human beings if they can avoid it. Perhaps optimistically, I never ceased to regard myself as one of those, but I couldn't dodge the chore. It's in the nature of the business. If you dress up in the movie, the publicity stills show what you look like dressed up. Usually, in any medium, I learned to cope with the chores by making a performance out of them: when pushing a book on radio, for example, it takes less out of you, and makes more sense, to be prepared even if your interviewer isn't. If he hasn't read it, don't tell him he's a dunce, tell him that your book would be the most exciting thriller since *Thunderball* if it wasn't marred by an excessive number of sex scenes. But there was no redeeming a publicity-stills photo session. I could have wept with boredom as I posed endlessly in this hat and that hat. I wore white suits for the sun, wetsuits for the surf, black boots for the boondocks, high heels for the nightclubs. Invariably the photographer kept on shooting until I twinkled. In real life I seldom twinkle, but when a photographer was giving me the benefit of his bedside wit I would finally twinkle to shorten the agony. 'Smile, Clive. It might never happen. Come on, give us a smile.' A tiny, dull gleam of weathered teeth would appear, and that was the shot they used. Gradually, over the course of decades, an archive accumulated, featuring a man whose mirth was irrepressible, a fountain of merriment at the fall of civilization. Always the shot I hated most was the one that got into print.

Strangely enough, being photographed for the literary papers and magazines was even worse. Every publication always wanted its very own portrait photograph of me, even though it could scarcely be much different from the portrait I sat for the previous week. You might think that nothing apart from my unfortunate physical appearance could make a literary portrait shot look weird, but you would be wrong. A short lens can make Hugh Grant look like a conger eel poking its head out of a hole in the coral. And once again, the photographer will want you to twinkle, even if the picture is meant to decorate an article about your book about the Gulag. (Editors call it 'a wry smile'. Have you ever wanted to extend your acquaintance with anyone who smiles wryly?) On being told that you would sooner die in a pool of your own vomit, the photographer, conceding that you might look more impressive being thoughtful, suggests that you will look even more thoughtful if you cup your chin in your hand, preferably with one or more fingers extended upwards. Since nobody ever does this in real life even to scratch a pimple beneath the eye, the fingers-to-the-face portrait looks as artificial as can be, but that's exactly why the photographers want it: it looks like a photograph. So they keep on at you until they get it. American female photographers are the worst. They all want to be Annie Liebowitz, and they will assure you that with your fingers to your face you look more thoughtful than their favourite philosopher, Deepak Chopra. Timidly you give in, just once, and from the several hundred individual frames that have been secured in the course of an entire hour – another chunk of your life gone – the one that the editor will use is the one where you have your fingers to your face. I have thrown in this apparent digression mainly to suggest the way in which, over the course of years, the little, incidental irritations can mount up to sap your will for pursuing a larger object. The larger object might be a more attractive prospect than, say, coal-mining, but the irritations are like the drip of water on your helmet. Eventually you will tear it off and crawl screaming back down the tunnel. But Mexico awaits, and the hushed arena in which the gringo will twirl his lariat.

Guess what, I twirled my lariat and it went nowhere. The scene was a dud, plus a funny hat. But at least, in voice over, I could contrast my lack of skill with the undoubted expertise of our chosen young bullfighter. Called something like Pedro Cojones, he was a truly gorgeous young man who would have looked good in overalls, but in his tightly fitting *traje de luces*, the suit of lights, he was so beautiful he looked sacred. We shot the build-up to his big day and as part of his preparation he managed to seduce an Australian jounalist who was trailing us around. Married with children, and famously faithful to her husband, she was a byword for strict ethics, but she wasn't going to miss out on Pedro. Not this time. Just this once. No doubt buoyed up by his exotic conquest – the endless supply of local beauties scarcely counted in his estimation – Pedro, on the appointed day, killed one bull after another without even bending his sword. It went straight in, every time. Hemingway was fond of saying that you should not condemn bullfighting until you see it. I saw it and I condemned it immediately. Indeed I was rather glad of the transmission rule which dictated that we would not be able to show the Moment of Truth, which looked to me like the Moment of Butchery whatever way you sliced it. But Pedro sure looked good when he swung the cape, and there was no denying that the legato linking of the different passes, the *faena*, had a kind of poetry. This macho thing had something to it: just not enough. As the basis for a view of life, it had the incurable drawback of adding more cruelty to a world that was already choking on it.

The exaltation of machismo took a more palatable form when I interviewed the writer Carlos Fuentes in the library of his house. In Mexico City the architecture that really counts is within doors. The old public buildings aren't bad, but inside a modern house you see a different kind of creativity, less monumental but much more human. The library of Carlos Fuentes was a masterpiece. So was his face. Carlos looks the way a writer should look but so few writers do. There are always a few good-looking writers on the scene. My friend Ian Hamilton could brood so darkly it was unfair, and the merest smile from the poet Mick Imlah – dead too soon, alas – would make women lean together to console each other for the pain in their breasts. But most writers look like the wreck of the Hesperus. Carlos, however, was up there with Benicio del Toro, or Antonio Banderas without the pout. For me, though, the centre of fascination lay in his books. There was shelf upon shelf of Aguillar editions, their spines gold-stamped on maroon morocco. I lusted after them. They were a reminder of what I should be doing.

In Mexico City I did quite a lot of it, but only with difficulty, because there was very little downtime. The *New Yorker* had asked me to review a new book by Daniel Goldhagen called *Hitler's Willing Executioners*. The book advanced the idea that all Germans, whether Nazis or not, had been out to kill Jews. Though it might conceivably have done something to counteract the perilous delusion that only the Nazis had been in on the conspiracy, I thought Goldhagen's thesis was even more perilous in the other direction, because the last tactic you should use in condemning racism is to indulge in a new racism of your own. I thought that this diligent young academic's brainwave blurred the point of the whole tragedy, and I was eager to rebut it, but my argument needed a lot of backing up and of course I didn't have my own library with me, so I had to rely on my memory when I wrote the piece. Tina liked what she saw when I faxed it through to the *New Yorker* but she wanted more of it, so that she could uprate it from a book review to a 'Critic at Large' piece for the middle of the magazine. That requirement altered the proportions of every paragraph, so I had to write it again.

It was a bit of a wrench to be working on such a serious piece of writing late at night and then heading out in the early morning for a day on the pleasure canals where punt-loads of citizens were poled about among the overhanging trees, singing the while and downing the soda pop. By then the mariachi trios, omnipresent in the city, had become our running gag, popping up all the time like a triple-threat version of Kato in the Inspector Clouseau movies, but with less musical interest. Every trio had only two songs, and both of them were versions of 'Guantanamera', one of those international ditties favoured by tourist parties and holiday makers who can't sing but won't be stopped from trying. They want to hear 'Guantanamera' from a mariachi trio, so that they can join in. They want to hear the song delivered at high volume from beneath big sombreros while guitars are hammered in unison, six rows of unkempt teeth are bared and skin-tight velvet trousers pop at the seams. In our pleasure-garden sequence there was no need to bring in a mariachi trio from the city in order to cap the gag. There were mariachi trios lurking in the shrubbery and hiding in single file behind trees. Stealth is part of every mariachi trio's plan because the element of surprise is thought to be crucial, in order to maximize your delight. The essential purpose of a mariachi trio is to show up suddenly wherever you are and whatever you are doing – burying your uncle, for instance – and start singing 'Guantanamera'. In my punt, suitably staffed with extras hired for a few pesos and a free tortilla, we got the shot when our chosen mariachi trio leapt aboard and burst into 'Guantanamera'. Then we got the same shot from the bank of the canal. 'Guantanamera', they howled. Then we got the same shot from the other bank. 'Guantanamera', they howled again. I stayed alert, but all the time I couldn't stop thinking about Hitler, who had the power to stop this kind of thing with a written order. There would have been three closely spaced pistol shots and that would have been it.

24. FIRST TANGO

Back in my London library, I checked all the references in my Goldhagen piece, which I entitled 'Hitler's Unwitting Exculpator', and sent it off. Then began the notorious process of *New Yorker* fact-checking, by which one of the magazine's vast graduate research team rings up the Professor of Political Science at the University of Heidelberg in the middle of the night to establish incontrovertibly that Germany is in Europe. But I try not to inveigh against the fact-checkers because often enough they save you from a howler. It's the magazine's style police, the ones who wreck your rhythm for the sake of a comma, who drive me nuts. This time Tina had them under the gun and the text was finalized within a week. When the piece came out, it generated a big postbag, most of it in approval. There were even family members of Holocaust victims who approved: they agreed that to say everybody was guilty was just another way of saying that nobody was. But the note of approval that moved me most was verbal. It came from Ian McEwan, who said, '*That* is what you should be doing.' It moved me to anxiety, because I knew he was right. The time was coming when I would have to get back to bedrock. I still believed that my work in television was giving me a wider scope, but here was a reminder that it would take concentration to go deep, and there was only so much of life left.

By then, Watchmaker was installed in its permanent home on two whole floors of the Chrysalis building, not far from Ladbroke Grove station and a million miles from anywhere you would like to be. Inside our teeming complex I had my own little office with a door I could close and a z-bed inside on which I could stretch out for an hour's sleep every day after lunch, thereby turning every day's work into two. I needed the extra time because the work-rate kept on going up. Since I was still the only asset, the fifty or so toilers outside my door were all dependent on my health, so I suppose it was no surprise that they catered to my every whim, including a cup of tea every fifteen minutes. (When we were writing together, Bostock drank twice as much tea as I did: nobody knew at the time that it was a form of caffeine addiction. We thought we were high on our own inspiration.) It would have been nice to have been spoiled by such attentiveness but there wasn't time. Apart from our office management squad, the key factor in holding the whole enterprise together was Richard's secretary, Wendy Gay, an orchidaceous bombshell who dressed like a film star from the early 1950s, with high-piled spun gold hair, cinched waist, stiff petticoats and peekaboo shoes. At first acquaintance, the unwary tended to belittle her until she quietly corrected their spelling. She wrote short stories about the death of Jayne Mansfield but she was so full of smiling life that it was almost a joke. The best kind of joke, however: we were always glad to see her in the morning as she bopped around getting things done. In the evening she was still doing that. She made a point of telling me, when she thought I was being a sad sack, that life was very brief. Since she had seen scarcely thirty years of life herself, this was quite a perception.

There was another reminder of life's brevity in Buenos Aires, where we almost got our director killed. All my other cameramen/directors won't mind my saying that Robert Payton was the most accomplished of their breed I ever worked with, because only he had something they hadn't: a spare silver camera box full of vintage wines. Rob had a gift for not lowering his standard of living when he was on the road. Emperor of the air miles, king of the upgraded ticket, he rivalled even Richard in collecting high-quality stuff. Unusually for a sybarite, he was also very quick on the uptake, so it was a rare lapse when he set up the camera on a tripod to film the gauchos taking delivery of their new horses. Out on the pampas, the gauchos form a camp once a year so that the older men can stun the youngsters with their skill at breaking in the *postros*, the next generation of their flying steeds. As noted earlier, horse-related activities are almost invariably tedious, but when a grizzled old gaucho on board an insane young horse comes thundering towards you it can be quite exciting. Too exciting, in this case. Ideally Rob should have had the camera on his shoulder, so that he could move with it. But he had his eye glued to a camera that wasn't going anywhere. The old man on board the horse was waving his hat and shouting an imprecation which, we were told later on, was the dialect version of 'This horse is out of control. Get out of there or die.' Valiantly filming until the last moment, Rob finally took off and left the camera to its fate. The *postro* went straight through it, pausing only to turn around and start kicking it to bits while the experienced old gaucho left the saddle, hat in hand, described a high parabola and dived head first into the crowd of his cheering colleagues.

Apart from his courage, technical acumen and tireless cunning in search of the *petit bonheur*, Rob had the precious, ego-free gift of trusting me when I thought I was on to something. When the gauchos sat down at a trestle table to eat, they were served with plates of meat straight from the fire. Their only eating utensil was the knife each of them carried at his waist. Each gaucho would hold a hunk of meat in one hand, stick the end of it in his mouth, and cut off a chewable piece close to his teeth with an upward swipe of the knife. The knife would go very close to his nose. I asked for one specific shot after another of different gauchos doing this. I had already spotted that one of the gauchos had the end of his nose prominently wrapped in sticking plaster, perhaps because of a boil. Rob got the shot without my even asking because he had already guessed that I would climax the sequence in voice-over by saying that this method of dining was a test of manhood.

Things threatened to be less interesting back in town. The

way our hotel in the high-tab Recoleta district fleeced us would have been a story in itself, had we been able to tell it. Phone calls home were out of the question because of the mark-up, and the laundry service was so expensive that we had to do all our washing in a laundrette. But the hotel managers were offering us their bargain showbiz deal – the full whack was set at the spending levels of an Arab prince – and we couldn't rat them out. Nor was there any filming my discovery of Henschel's bookshop. Henschel has gone out of business by now but at the time he still tended his books personally. The bookshop was in a big room a flight up from one of the cross-streets leading off the downtown end of the Avenida Corrientes, and of all the bookshops in the world that I have ever haunted it was my top favourite. A lot of German Jewish refugees had come to Buenos Aires and later on a lot of Nazi refugees came there as well, so the stock was an enticing mixture for any student of European cultural disaster in the twentieth century. In the next few years I spent thousands of pounds in there and the results fill the shelves before me as I write this. But my discovery of the place would have made a dull sequence. There was another scene available, however, that filmed like a dream. It was the tango.

How a dance so complicated, refined and beautiful had come to being in Argentina is a question that still puzzles scholars. Little else about Argentina is notable for those qualities. As Juan Perón and his dreadful wife proved, they couldn't even do populism without turning it into fascism – 'We shirtless ones!' Evita would cry to the peasants, rattling her jewellery at them – and the adventure in the Malvinas had proved that a whole junta of generals, otherwise quite efficient at things like electric torture, had been too dumb to realize that they were picking on a dragon. As previously noted, no country with an ample supply of meat on the hoof has much idea of how to cook it, but the way the most famous meat eatery in Buenos Aires presented its product left any restaurant in Nairobi looking like Maxim's. We filmed a sequence where I lunched alone, from a mixed grill called an *asada grande*. Every cut and kind of beef in Argentina had been heaped on the plate after being incinerated with napalm. Though Buenos Aires fancied itself as the most European city in Latin America, the resemblances were notional in all respects, and yet out of all the uproar of pretension, inflation and macho posturing had come this poem of a dance.

On an afternoon recce at one of the daylight ballrooms I took one look at the dancing couples and had my big idea. We had already filmed me having elementary lessons so that I could chug about the floor in the required graceless manner while the locals provided a stunning contrast, but the question remained of how to shoot the story on the night. Here in the afternoon, with the windows full of sunlight and no romantic atmosphere whatsoever, the best of the couples were creating poetry. I could see that the Argentinian tango was nothing like the Hollywood version, in which rigid poses are dramatically struck while a rose is passed with stunning brutality from one set of teeth to another. The real thing was more like an ideal conversation. Like the local version of the Spanish language, which features a smooth, sumptuous, almost Russian 'zh' sound for the double 'l', every step was a smooth glide, one step sliding without a break into the next, the progress of one partner providing a silent commentary to the progress of the other. I watched one young man, about my height, performing a series of smoothly connected steps that sent his lovely partner through a whole linked sequence of attitudes you could have stopped with a still camera at any time and you would have had a picture to hang on your wall. She looked like a heavenly visitation and it was partly because of what he was doing. I knew I couldn't do that, but suddenly I wanted something more illustrative than just cutting from him being brilliant to me being awful. Then I noticed that he looked, from the waist down at least, roughly the same as me. He even had the same shade of dark blue suit.

Rob got the idea as soon as I explained it. On the night, in a tango salon full of carefully cast extras, we shot plenty of coverage

of me lurching through the elegant milieu with a champion
female in my arms. Though I was theoretically leading her, she
was actually doing most of the steering, by squeezing me in the
right places. She was so commanding that she could probably
have made me do cartwheels, but the tango isn't an athletic
feat, it's a visible meditation. I could, however, with her subtle
guidance, manage just well enough to get along. Having secured
the master shot, our next task was to do a close-up which
gradually travelled down my body as I danced. Then we shot the
good guy's legs as he did a dazzlingly intricate set of *giros*, turning
on the spot with much flashing of the spare foot while my
partner's pretty shoes whirled around him through the frame.
This was timed so that it could be inserted between the shot
travelling down my body and another shot travelling in the other
direction. When the footage got back to the editing room, it
would be possible to turn my lower body into a genius before
panning back up to reality, at which point I could announce in
voice-over that it was all a dream. I knew on the spot that it
would all work exactly as planned. I hadn't learned much yet
about dancing the tango, but I had learned something about
making movies. Fifteen years before, I would have had no clue
how to achieve that sequence, even if I had been capable of
thinking it up.

These were the little triumphs that I took away from the
programmes I was making, and I still like to think that the results
were worth the effort. Even the most acute critics rarely noticed
how the work was done, because they themselves had not been
through the slog. Like any other form of art, it had to be done
first of all for its own sake. I didn't mind that. The ability to
plough a lonely furrow without much thought of immediate
applause is one of my strengths, if I have any. There could be no
question, though, that I was feeling the squeeze. As the programmes got nearer to where I thought they ought to go, the
urge to have done with them and do something else crept further
into my mind: it's the weakness that goes with the strength, a

restlessness born of the very ambition that gets things made in the first place. (The supreme case of that itch was Leonardo da Vinci, but he was a truly terrible tango dancer.) At least the weekly show still had a glaring gap: we still had no reliable way of ending it. Doing a final dance with the star guest was all right if the guest was Dannii Minogue or Victoria Wood, but if it was, say, Sir Richard Attenborough, then the effect could be less disarming.

Out of nowhere, our problem was solved. We had a stringer in New York whose life was spent collecting awful things for us off the cable channels: biker astrologists, transvestite psychics, body-building sexologists, stuff like that. He lived in a cold-water flat somewhere on the Upper West Side dodging cockroaches the size of rats while he survived on pizza. One night he was watching a cable channel unbelievably called Channel 69. Exercising their rights under the First Amendment, anyone at all could pay ten dollars and go on Channel 69 to do a number, because in America everyone is entitled to self-expression: it's in the Constitution. Our stringer was halfway though a five-cheese pizza with extra cheese when he was suddenly face to face with an Hispanic woman in a green feather boa singing the Lionel Ritchie hit 'Hello' while she pounded away at a Yamaha portable piano. He had never seen anything like her in his life and for a while he thought there might be something wrong with the pizza, but when he recovered his mind he sent me a video by courier. The video had the artist's name handwritten on the label. It was Margarita Pracatan.

I took one look at her in action and realized that it was payday. Against the evidence of his senses, I persuaded Richard that Margarita was a yodelling bonanza. The musician in Richard rebelled against the notion but the showman in him recognized that she had the screen presence of an avalanche. There was a new season of ten programmes coming up and we had a hole to fill. I suggested that we fly her in for a couple of days, shoot ten numbers, and fly her out again. If it didn't work, it would cost us no more than an economy-class return ticket and a cheap hotel bill. On that basis, he agreed, and that's what we did.

After she arrived at Heathrow, and managed to hustle her boa through customs without having it quarantined, we didn't see much of the actual Margarita, because she went straight from jet-lag to the taping session and then back to the airport. But we tacked her first number, 'Hello', on to the end of our first programme, and she was an immediate sensation. Twirling her boa, shaking her spangles, hammering away at the helpless Yamaha, filling the screen to the very edge with her hair extensions, in every sense she was bigger than I was, and by the end of the first season I was a guest on my own show. I didn't begrudge that at all. Enjoying the accomplishments of others is one of my few virtues and I regard my happiness for Margarita's success as the clearest proof.

To jump forward a bit, the enjoyment was put to a harsher test the following year. It was my mistake. I suggested that we do it right this time: fly her in for the whole season and back her up with a band. We had the excellent Harry Stoneham and his quintet as a resident orchestra and the musical aspect went quite well. Margarita had no real idea of standard musical rhythm but she had a brio – not say a *rubato* and a *basso profundo* – that was all her own, and anyway Harry, who had seen it all, could have provided the musical accompaniment for a banshee. The difficulties arose from the awkward fact that Margarita was high maintenance. She was even more exuberant when she wasn't singing than when she was. 'Darleeng!' she would cry to a policeman. 'I LARV YOU!' Like many Cubans she sat down to dinner at midnight and was still dancing on the table at dawn. We had to provide one of our young men to look after her and she was using them up at the rate of one a week. The connection was purely Platonic but the guys had to eat amphetamines to stay with her. Just to use up some of her energy we sent her out on a theatrical tour. The audiences loved her, especially when she climbed down among them and sat on their laps. But there was a downside. She was making a lot of money and she did not always spend it wisely from our angle. She spent some of it on singing lessons: the last thing we wanted. But you couldn't blame her. Despite the contrary evidence supplied by her songs in English, she could sing quite accurately in Spanish (things went wrong in English only because she would forget which word came next) and understandably she wanted to improve her gift, as all true artists do. The audience was puzzled, however, when she launched into a string of Vikki Carr hits in the original lingo. With Margarita in our lives, we could never relax – a frequent result when you finally meet your dream girl.

But the weekly show was now clearly in its most fully developed form. Though Bostock and I still had an indecent amount of fun writing it, there were no new techniques left to discover. (In the next generation, the brilliant Harry Hill would take the business of interacting with snatched footage to a whole new level, but the electronics he uses now weren't available then even for a cruise missile.) The same should have been harder to say about the Postcards. After all, they had a different subject every time. Yet my own part in them was becoming predictable to me, if not to the audience. Quite often, in any form of creativity, you hit the point where you are walking in your sleep. So it proved with *Postcard from Berlin*. I pulled all my now standard tricks, including driving the bad car, dressing up for the bad party and eating in the bad restaurant. But the subject was so rich that the whole thing pulled itself together as if pre-ordained. A lot of this was due to a new producer, Martin Cunning.

He's a media tycoon now and it's no surprise, but he himself would have been surprised had he been told his future when he first came to us. So broke that he was sleeping under a bridge, he was so young that his long trousers looked like an affectation. He had a lop-sided smile that went halfway around his head, and his Scottish accent was so thick that I couldn't understand a word. Richard and Elaine, however, both spotted him, correctly, as a fountain of ideas, which he advanced with daunting certitude and defended with bitter scorn. Generously, however, he paid attention to what I wanted to do in Berlin. This time I wanted to get the history in, because the history was everything. The Wall was down and some of the old Weimar Berlin had come back, but the Nazis were still a terrible memory. In the East of the city, though the skyline was thick with cranes, the old buildings still bore, all the way to the rooftops, the grey tidemark of the dreary empire that had retreated to the east before it boiled away. Somehow we had to get that in. It would mean doing a lot of narration while I drove the car.

The car was a Trabant from the communist era and it was perfect casting. We didn't have to rig it to emit smoke, go backwards at the wrong moment and burst into flames. It did all that anyway. Up and down the Unter den Linden I drove, popping and banging through the Brandenburg Gate time after time. Goebbels had once ordered the Nazi torchlight parade to do the same thing while he improved the lighting. He was there ahead of us. So, of course, was Hitler. One of the best things we did in Berlin was to realize that the bunker where he spent his last days was a key location. There was nothing left to look at except a low bump in the wasteland, but the very fact that it looked like nothing made it mean everything. We got a long shot of me standing there in my blue suit on the apparently meaning-less heap of dirt. But I knew what my voice-over was going to be. Finally it had come to this.

Hitler had never loved Berlin and I didn't either. It was history I was in love with, and here was the place to talk about it, at its focal point. The great buildings are mainly a long way out of town, in the Mark Brandenburg, and most of the city was architectural blah: shop windows in the West, the old stone-faced apartment buildings in the East, block after block. But if I had been a young student again, and just starting off in Europe, I would have started there rather than in London or Paris. I would have had a room in Prenzlauerberg and sat at a table outside one of the cafes writing poems to the Russian waitresses. The story of the city in its dreadful modern times would have become mine. I tried to make it mine even though it was too late. The attempt to understand twentieth-century politics – by now I was writing about almost nothing else – had become one of my preoccupations, joining the urge to write poetry at the centre of my mental life. For a writer, comprehension is as close to being politically effective as he can ever get, or ever should. In the few years since the Wall came down, a seismic shift in the world's political history had taken place, and I had played no part in it except, I hoped, to understand it.

The Velvet Revolution in Czechoslovakia had partly been made possible by the ability of the leaders to communicate by computer. Harold Pinter had bought a computer for Vaclav Havel. The new President was lastingly grateful to Pinter and took care to be gentle every time he had to tell his fellow playwright, during one of Pinter's visits to liberated Prague, to go easy on his tirades about the ruthlessness of the Americans when everybody listening to him was still getting over the ruthlessness of the Russians. But Pinter, though his geopolitical picture was essentially a prop doorway through which he could make entrances in profile, had his heart in the right place, and giving Havel a computer was exactly the right thing to do. I bought a computer for Rita Klimova. Though she died of leukaemia not long after the victory, she had been a vital figure in her country's recovery of its freedoms. But all I had done was write a cheque.

Later on I wrote a few more cheques for the Viborg, the outfit, headed by Olga Havel, that devoted itself to the endless task of looking after some of the thousands of wrecked people left behind by a regime so dedicated to pollution that the children's milk was full of acid rain. Olga had already suffered enough but she volunteered to suffer some more because she thought it was her duty. With the aid of my good friend Diana Phipps, who had now returned to her homeland in her original role as Countess Sternberg, Olga coped nobly with the heartbreaking task of bringing a measure of redress to a river of human ruin. Very feminine and graceful in appearance, she had an iron soul and could be quite tough with fools and bores. I was dining with her once at a restaurant beside the river. The steak was a challenge – unlike in Argentina, it had probably never been very good even while it was alive – and she caught me picking my teeth with a fingernail. She handed me a toothpick. I liked her for that. But financing a computer and a couple of oxygen machines for blue babies was as close as I ever physically got to being effective in the biggest set of European events in the late twentieth century. Mentally, however, I was right in the middle of it, and never more so than in Berlin. This, I finally realized, was why I had been collecting and reading all those old books that had been scattered across the world.

What I loved about young Martin was that he could go with my ideas even when he could not foresee how they would add up until we got the footage home. He could read my heart, if not my mind. It was easy for him to let me have my head when one of the Trabi's regular nervous breakdowns happened at a set of traffic lights in the West as night fell on a long day's work. A sports car full of party girls slowed down to heckle me and I thought of a sequence on the spot. We enrolled the girls, rigged more lights, and went on shooting for an hour so it would appear that the car full of raving lovelies stopped beside me, told me to follow them to a party and then, when the lights changed and I put my foot down to roar off after them, the Trabi went backwards before conking out. A baby spotlight clipped under the dashboard lit up my face to show me doing my patent resigned-loser look. It was an expensive hour but the results would obviously be worth the graft.

It was far less obvious that the outcome would be worth it when I asked for a whole afternoon of filming in the Ploetzensee prison, where the conspirators of 20 July 1944 were executed after the failure of their plot against Hitler's life. Once again, like Hitler's bunker, the location looked like nothing. But I knew what had happened there. I knew that the sluice in the middle of the stone floor was where the blood had gone after victims were guillotined, and that the rail high up at one end of the room was where the hooks had been from which the July conspirators had been hanged to strangle slowly in nooses of thin wire. Martin got the point, and okayed the extended static shots which would give me the space to tell the story when we got home. I was already writing the commentary in my head, though, while we were filming in the execution chamber. I never wrote anything more carefully in my life. The brightest of the conspirators had known that they would probably fail. But they went ahead anyway, because they thought it was a ceremony. I respected that ceremony. To understand, and to express, why their practical failure was a spiritual triumph – that would be my contribution. Increasingly I was becoming aware that such understanding was all I was good for. But I never belittled the privilege of being able to express it in a mass medium. I thought it was one of the things television should do, and precisely because the audience had not read all the books. Ideally, I thought, an entertainment programme of any kind should bring the human world in, not shut it out: and history was the supreme example of the human world.

This conviction, however, was on a collision course with the oncoming celebrity culture, which would have no concern with the past, and exist only in the present. But I was slow to accept that. Like a hedgehog on the highway, bathed in the lights of an oncoming truck, I persisted in believing there might be room for both of us. The Postcard programmes meant a lot to me. Readers today might wonder why. Later on the format became a staple, with every known comedian sent off to be astonished by a City of Contrasts. But it was less usual then, and I thought it my best chance to say something serious in a entertaining way. I still have critics who suppose that I can have no reason for doing that except to show off. But I never struck myself as an egotist: more as someone with a sense of duty who might fail to fulfil it if his concentration lapsed. Although there again, I suppose, only an egotist would think that. Quicker to plead guilty.

25. IN THIS VALLEY OF DYING STARS

Most of the stars of *Postcard from Berlin* had been a long time dead. Our leading lady was Marlene Dietrich, represented by her gravestone, and her voice over the closing titles as she sang '*In den Ruinen von Berlin*'. In Los Angeles most of our stars were alive, although some of them were teetering on the brink. The movie pullulated with famous faces but that fact in itself was enough to remind me that it was a step sideways, if not downwards, because I wanted by then to treat harder subjects more closely. Avowedly to treat a shallow one, though that was a theme in itself, had no significance except in the broader context of what a free society might aspire to if only it could get over its obsessions with celebrity and spoon its brains back into its empty head. One day I would have to write about that, but in Los Angeles the pace was too hot to think. The best thing I did there was ask for a tour of the domestic architecture, with selected shots of all the demented houses, so that I could compose a syncopated scene-setting paragraph which I still count among my plums in writing for film. ('The neo-colonial baronial pagoda . . .' etc.) The rest of the movie, however, was famous faces, and some of them looked strained.

Charity events were the best place to catch them out of school. Richard Dreyfuss made himself available as long as he could plug his charity. I had only a few seconds to convince him that I admired his work – I was telling the truth, which always helps –and he was quick and funny, but you could tell that all kinds of uproar were going on in his head, perhaps because he had never got over the fact that it was not far enough from the ground. There are plenty of short men who can make any tall man feel awkward just by the confidence they radiate, but Richard Dreyfuss seemed to have no such assurance left. I had never seen a pair of elevator shoes quite like his. In most cases, men who wear elevator shoes must get used to standing on their toes. The front of the shoe looks quite normal and it's only when you spot what's going on at the back that you realize something's up, as it were. But Richard Dreyfuss had a whole thick platform under each foot, like the Mikado. Why? Who knows. You see how perfectly, wonderfully, he can incarnate a sensitive, self-critical human being in a minor movie like *Stake-Out*, and you assume that a man like that would be equally in command of every other aspect of his life. But then you discover that in real life he clumps around on a pair of kabuki shoes. You don't stare, though. In Hollywood, nobody notices. If Larry Longstaff, erstwhile romantic leading man of the 1950s, turns up at a party with most of his head replaced by a piece of machinery, people will tell him he's looking good. People will slap him on the back and say, 'Same old Larry,' even though the only part of the old Larry still in existence is his left eyeball.

In Hollywood, the intention is always taken for the deed. If your capped teeth look like the assembled tombstones of a graveyard in the snow, they will still be universally regarded as your own teeth, and not as a piece of engineering. The veteran television star Milton Berle smiled into our camera, his head from a vanished era, his mouth from beyond tomorrow. For anyone in my generation, Kirk Douglas would have looked like our greatest catch, but my generation was passing, and Kirk was well aware that his fame had passed to his son Michael. To get to Michael, we would have needed a congressional order. Kirk, however, was available, at the kind of charity event where they passed out caviar on a cardboard plate. His face was a challenge to credibility. I should say straight away that this encounter took place years before he had a stroke, after which he coped very bravely with impaired speech, a condition that would

undoubtedly reduce me to tears of self-pity. But at this charity
event, where everyone including me was dressed for the Wild
West, Kirk was still in a condition where everything that had
happened to his face recently had been a matter of choice. Once,
Kirk's face had been recognizable even if extreme. I think Barry
Humphries was the first to say that the dimple in Kirk's chin had
originally been his navel, but in fact he had looked like that even
before his first facelift. The first facelift, however, was now far in
the past. Fifty-seven varieties of facelift had happened since,
including that drastic intervention by which the flapping wattle
below the jaw is not only removed, but the line under the jaw is
lifted to conform with the line of the jawbone, so that in profile
the victim looks as if his throat has been torn out by a wolf.
Around his eyes, all the wrinkles had been removed, reducing the
whole area to a glassy surface, from which the eyeballs popped
like penguin's eggs from sheet ice. The missing wrinkles had been
bunched together and added to the edge of his face as a crêpe
ruff. All of this is less fun to say than it sounds, but I have to
record it because Kirk Douglas was a hero of mine for his realistic
approach to show business. The author of an unusually sane
autobiography, he was the man who had made the great analysis
of fame, an analysis which can be paraphrased more or less like
this: 'Fame doesn't change the way you behave, it changes the
way other people behave towards you.' It's true. That is indeed
fame's most savage effect. Unless you keep your family close, you
will hardly ever hear a trustworthy word from anyone. Kirk left
out, though, the further fact that when a famous person tries to
stay that way too long, all the changed behaviour of others will
eventually change his behaviour as well. If the famous person is
smart enough, he will try to take his name out of the sky at the
right time. But Kirk wanted to go on being Kirk: hence the facial
roadworks. At least the hair on top of his head looked like his
own, even if some of it had not started its life on that part of his
body. With other male stars, the hairpiece was widely in use.

Most of the hairpieces were so improbable that they defied

you not to burst out laughing. But some of them were convincing, and we decided that, rather than going for the obvious gag and kitting me out with a stupid wig, we should go through the process of having an upmarket version custom-made for me by the celebrated hair stylist José Eber. In his white silk suit, high-heeled boots and cowboy hat with feathers, José was better company than the plastic surgeon we had met the previous day. The plastic surgeon had shown me, on his computer, how my profile could be improved by taking a piece off the end of my nose and adding it to my chin. He also suggested that I should have my eyes lifted. This was good dialogue but he spoiled it by saying that he wanted to get into comedy and could I give him some tips. José was more confident in his mission. With many a sweeping gesture, he explained that I would need four copies of the piece: one for the day, one for the open car, one for the pool and one in the garage for repairs. 'The one for the car you wear anywhere there is wind there. If there is a party you don't want the piece flying off your head and ending up in the avocado dip there.' He gestured with his scissors to indicate a flying rug. This he did while he was cutting the raw piece as it sat in situ on my bare skull. He was a master. Steadily the thing looked more normal. José had earned an Academy Award for his work on the back of Tom Cruise's head in *Rain Man* and he was giving me the works. The results were stunning. Suddenly I saw the point. I had lost twenty years. I would also have lost twenty thousand dollars if José had built me the whole kit of pieces, but he was giving us one for free just to be in the movie.

To try the effect of José's masterpiece of a piece on someone who had known me in days gone by, we enlisted the services of Dudley Moore, who at that stage of his life was spending more time running his Santa Monica restaurant than in the movie studios. His time as a Hollywood headliner was over and he wasn't taking it well: too many pills and too many of the wrong women, all of them twice as tall as he was and most of them with half his intelligence. But somewhere in the depths of his racial memory he was still Dudley, and he took a visit by a crew from the old country as a chance to step back into his original persona as the sharp British wit while momentarily abandoning his Californian quest for spiritual fulfilment assisted by chemicals and a six-foot blonde sitting on his face. I explained the number to him and as an old revue hand he saw immediately where the sketch was going. I would walk in, complete with piece, and take up my position at the bar. In his role as proprietor, he would walk into shot, start a conversation and gradually become fixated on what was taking place on top of my head. He had his line ready first time. 'Bought, or rented?' We did a single shot on him and he added, 'I know it isn't yours, because the last time we met you had the same hairstyle as Telly Savalas. It's a great job, though. I can't see the join.' In the editing room we had to trim the scene back for time, but there was enough left to show him in all his elfin charm, the Cuddly Dudley of old, brimming with talent and quick as light, still sparkling even as he drove the extra mile on the road to destruction. He was still a star.

Except for Chuck Pick of Pick's Parking, the star faces were the story in Los Angeles. I remembered Chuck Pick from the night I saw him shouting hysterical orders to his team of drivers while they parked the vehicles of the arriving guests at a gala dinner for the visiting Queen in 1983. When the Postcard programme came up I said we had to get Chuck. When they saw Chuck in action, my crew realized why I had insisted. He and his team of Top Gun car-parkers were parking the cars at a party thrown by Cubby Broccoli. In the front drive of the house, Chuck jumped around shrieking to his drivers, telling them which car was to be parked where, screaming, 'Go, go, go!' and 'Yeah, man, *park* that car!' Ryan O'Neal and Farrah Fawcett, still together in those days, stepped out of a Bentley and were greeted by Chuck as personal friends. It looked like a surprise to them but it was great on film. Chuck carried on like a celebrity but he well knew that the movie stars outranked him, even though very few of them would know how to park a car under pressure.

The stars outranked everyone in the world. Continually in search of one star after another, I linked the narrative by driving around in one of the first examples of the Mercedes 500 drophead coupe. It was expensive to hire and we were lucky I didn't ding it. In Nashville I had driven a borrowed brand-new Chevrolet pick-up truck whose owner had been assured that it would be returned to him in one piece. It was, but the rear end was a different shape, because during a night shoot in the woods I had backed it into the steel stanchion of a letter box. We had some high-grade assets lined up in Nashville and the film should have clicked. Chet Atkins gave me a guitar lesson, Tammy Wynette gave me personal advice on the creative consolations of heartbreak and Mark Knopfler composed the melody for a lyric I had written. The song was performed at the Grand Old Opry by an up-and-coming female singer. Resplendent in a pastel-blue cowboy suit with silver trim, Porter Wagoner, acting as MC, said, 'Pretty girl, pretty song.' My bliss was complete, but the film was a flop in the British ratings, because only a small part of the British television audience cared anything at all about American country music. Here was a harsh reminder that the presenter depends on the subject, and that the best setting for my kind of documentary should be full of stars; real ones, internationally famous; faces you had seen on television or, even better, at the movies.

My own activities were thus abetting the celebrity culture of which I had become suspicious: an anomaly that had begun to nag. But that was the way it was, and in that respect Hollywood was the location without equal. In Hollywood the famous faces know how to lead their strange lives. The strangeness was their answer to a violently artificial condition, by which people became symbols of themselves. In their wigs and facelifts and elevator shoes, they understood each other even if nobody else did. Kirstie Alley was a delight to talk to but she believed in Scientology. Perhaps it was her protection against the kind of reporters who had no means of talking about her talent but were always ready to talk about her increasing weight. Shirley MacLaine, who had been given both the beauty and the talent when her brother Warren Beatty had been given only the beauty, was as smart as a whip but she believed that flying saucers made the journey across the universe specifically to land in her garden. What they all really believed in, because they had to, was the indispensable efficacy of the special air they breathed, the modified atmosphere of their stellar context. Deprived of that, they went out like lights.

26. WHAT BECOMES OF THE BROKEN-HEARTED?

It was what Diana died of. She should have been in show business, where there is a protocol for survival after your life has been eaten hollow by dreams come true. But she was on her own. I was working late in my London apartment when I got the news, and for several days afterwards I couldn't stop crying. Such an outburst of grief had never happened to me before in my life. I spent a couple of days at the office but I was useless. Behind the closed door of my cubicle I lay on my little z-bed and sobbed. Outside the door, Wendy Gay fended off callers from every media organization in Britain and Australia, all wanting my opinion. My opinion of what? The wrath of God? I went to ground in Cambridge and still couldn't stop crying. My family, stricken too but still upright, were very nice to their cot case. My wife, whose tenderness was a lesson in generosity, was good at cutting the incoming phone calls short. Finally a call came through from Tina Brown at the *New Yorker*. I owed her too much to give her the freeze, so I took the call. She wanted me to write a memoir of Diana. I said I couldn't. Tina, always the master psychologist, asked me what else I would be doing in the next few days. I took the point, got a car to the office and wrote a piece called 'Requiem'. It was a kind of poem, its every paragraph starting with the word 'No'. I was still crying while I worked on it but it was something to do.

During this time, there had been a national emotional outpouring which reached its focal point of expression as a field of flowers in London. Later it became fashionable to claim that one had never joined in, but I can claim no such thing, although I still believe that the Royal Family should not have been dragooned into a populist gesture by the very newspapers which had done so much to make Diana's life a lethal fantasy. Charles looked concussed but anyone with any sense realized that his anguish was without limit. The truth was that nobody really knew what they were doing because nobody was ready for it. This will be the hardest thing to explain to the next generation. Nobody knew that she would die. Only from the fake wisdom of hindsight can her life be seen as leading up to that event. Her own expectations, like anybody else's, were quite otherwise. She had a future in front of her, and all kinds of qualities to make it fruitful. Perhaps she would have found, in time – time which we all need – a peaceful balance into which her corroding neuroses might have melted away. And now her future had been cancelled. One among millions, I coped with a sense of loss whose intensity defied explanation. A psychologist might have said that I was weeping the tears that I had never wept for my own family tragedy, the death of my father when I was young. But that same psychologist would have done better to say that I had seen my mother's life ruined in a single moment, and never since had I been able to tolerate the spectacle of a vital young woman being stopped by misfortune from achieving what she might have done. Either way, the psychologist wasn't available, and all I had, apart from the kindness of my wife and children, was my own resources. They seemed to me to have broken down completely. But I got my article written, so perhaps they had not.

Some commentators said that what I had written was embarrassing, but when the piece came out in a special issue of the magazine it got the biggest postbag I ever received for anything. There were hundreds of letters, all saying that they felt the same, and I knew that there were countless more people who would never read a magazine with so many words in it and so few pictures, but who had likewise been surprised by the same grief. This solidarity of response among people from all walks of life, and from everywhere in the world, is the thing I remember best. Of the funeral in the Abbey I remember only fleeting impressions. I thought that the way Tony Blair read the lesson, with an ornately bogus display of pious emphasis, was enough to prove that he was an actor to the core of his nature. I thought that Elton John did a good job of singing a bad song. I thought the Earl Spencer's speech bordered on sedition but was well spoken. But mainly I thought nothing. I just sat there, in my seat on the aisle, halfway along the central block at the left-hand end. Then, as the ceremony wound to a close, this thing happened that I knew I would remember until my own turn came to die. Down the aisle towards me came the Guardsmen carrying the coffin on their shoulders. I thought they would go right past me on the way to the front door. But just across from me on the left, a side aisle had been left between the rows of seats. The side aisle led to a little door in the stone wall. Right beside me, the Guardsmen turned into the side aisle and carried the coffin through the door, with only a few inches between the coffin lid and the roof of the corridor they had entered. The soft crunch of their spit-polished boots on the flagstones became a whispered conversation of lingering echoes as she went away into the dark.

It was said that when people wept at Diana's death they were weeping for their own mortality. If they did, why should they not have done? To treat your life as if it will last is an illusion. If chance doesn't stop you early, decrepitude will get you later on. Even when I was young I could hear the clock tick. Now, with my sixtieth year coming up, I could hear it boom. I was pledged to work out my time at Watchmaker, but as the formats, one by one, got to where there was no more I could do that was new, I had begun to look beyond, and sometimes with longing. I made the first promise to my wife that some day soon I would get out of television. She looked sceptical, but I meant it. There were still, however, several things I had to do first. The company had to be built up beyond one asset, if only to keep faith with our backers. Jonathan Ross, whose gifts I admired, had just hit the wall with his own production company, which had made all the classic mistakes that start with getting the office furniture designed by a friend instead of just buying it off the peg. Jonathan had his suits designed too, apparently by a team of satirical tailors. He put a lot of emphasis on personal appearance, almost as if he had no talent. But it all cost a lot of money, and at that stage he had blown his budget. We tried to offer him a home with us. He liked the look of our office. When Wendy Gay went bopping by he must have thought that he had dreamed her up. Several times we took him out to dinner but the deal was never sealed. Eventually it became clear that he was enjoying our company at dinner far more than the idea of being beholden to anyone except himself. He must have been right, because later on he became a

BBC star of such magnitude that they paid him more money every two months than I ever earned in my entire television career. I bear no grudge, but sometimes it does make me wish that I, too, had been born with a speech impediment. All I had was an Australian accent.

Collaring extra assets was proving less easy than it sounded. As a friend of Nigella Lawson, I had watched her getting nowhere with book shows and often wondered why she wasn't being given the formats that would make her a star. But neither Richard nor Elaine thought that Nigella had a chance: too posh a voice, the network would never go for it. The poshness was exactly what I loved, and I thought the public would love it too, but I was outvoted. I have to admit I didn't realize that one of the conditions for her finally reaching stellar status was that she would have to have a frying pan in her hand. Trying to promote Nigella without the frying pan was like recommending Gabriella Sabatini without the tennis racket. But as Nigella, with me in the passenger seat, scooted around Shepherd's Bush at the wheel of her rattletrap Mercedes 190 sports car – it was a pit, like her handbag – I knew she would make it somehow. It just wouldn't be with Watchmaker.

We had better luck with Jeremy Clarkson. Richard and Elaine thought of him first but I took one look at him on air and knew that he couldn't miss. He was too big, too burly and he was full of bluster, but he could write it and say it. He was that rarest thing in England, the articulate bloke. I thought he was tremendous and I was very proud that he made his first couple of series under our logo. I liked him a lot. He eventually decided that he didn't like me one bit, apparently because he thought that I had made some remark that insulted his family. I can't imagine doing any such thing to anybody, but you can't expect everybody to love you. He went on to become, in the next decade, almost the biggest television star on earth, partly because, like Nigella and her frying pan, he had got himself identified with a universal activity. Cars are an object of fascination in every country, and especially in any country that doesn't have any. There are Clarkson fans in the upper regions of Nepal. Thus it was that the Watchmaker office became the launching pad for a globe-girdling career that left mine looking the size of a game of marbles: a clear case of television as a new kind of British Empire. I didn't resent his success at all and I still watch his programmes with a professional admiration for how he can pack so much into a paragraph, although few of his opinions are congruent with my own, and for his central premise I have an ineradicable objection. I think that to encourage ordinary citizens to drive fast cars on ordinary roads is the exact equivalent of handing real guns to schoolboys, and that's that. But it's a free country, and young petrol-heads who watch him in Libya probably say the same.

Nor would I have had any comeback if somebody had accused me of doing more than my fair share to encourage the ambitions of the boy racers. When the rights to broadcast the F1 carnival were switched from BBC to ITV, the network wanted a big studio programme to mark the event, and my well-known amateur affiliation to the sport got me the job of host. I would rather that the cup had passed from me, because I knew there would be trouble: but it was too fat a contract for Watchmaker to turn down. At the command of Bernie Ecclestone, all the drivers were in the studio. All except one. Michael Schumacher underlined his status as top dog by refusing to turn up in person. He appeared only as a satellite image on the back wall. When I spun around in my swivel chair and interviewed this banana-faced apparition, I thought I could hear, behind me, the first soft explosions of a rich crop of raspberries blown by the other drivers. For the ruthless exploitation of supremacy, Schumacher left even Ayrton Senna nowhere. Right up until the moment when he was killed at Imola, Senna had behaved as if the road ahead belonged exclusively to him. Schumi felt the same, in a German accent. He was just quieter about it, and more polite. I often wonder if the camaraderie of all the other drivers was not based on their common annoyance of Schumi's supercilious cool. Perhaps he played the same role as Zeppo Marx, who was disliked by the other Marx Brothers because he was good with money.

Along with the thrill and the glamour, money mattered to the drivers, and you couldn't blame them. The better they did, the more cash they had to lay out for protection against an intrusive world. A world champion needed a castle with high walls. Damon Hill's castle was still in Ireland when we did a special about him. We filmed him at home with his family and he impressed me straight away with his sensitivity and sanity. Somehow he would make it all balance up: the artificially illuminated public life, and the domestic peace that made it bearable. That he was brave went without question, but not even a man as brave as he was could afford a gamble that might weaken his base. When he left Williams he could have gone to McLaren but he would have been paid only to win. Another team, with a slower car, would pay him a guaranteed wedge, win or lose. He had a choice to make.

He was still making it when we went with him to watch him race in Hungary. After the race he had to make a quick trip to Bulgaria for the sponsor. I was his passenger when he drove to the airport, with only half an hour to get there. It was a challenge and time was running out. While I sat there holding on to my seatbelt like a lifeline as he followed the leaning police escort motorcyclists into the turns, he started giving me the low-down on the politics. How he could drive that fast and still speak rationally was a mystery to me. We were doing a hundred miles an hour nearly all the time but I suppose for him it was half speed. On the private jet he told me more. It all sounded a bit like the politics of television: do this now so you can do that later, guard your base, build up a bank so you can quit while you're ahead. The main difference was the velocity. I liked Damon very much, perhaps partly because he could focus on what he was doing without falling prey to a circumscription of his interests. (He asked me whether Carlos Saura's film *Carmen* was as good as he had heard, and I was glad to be able to tell him that it most certainly was.) In his world of machinery, he himself had not become a machine. The finished movie drew an audience far exceeding the total number of petrol-heads. I was pleased about that because I felt that we had captured at least something of a human personality. I never saw him angry even once, not even with his own team when they cost him a win by muffing a pit-stop. Later on, though, when he moved his castle to England, one of the tabloids published an aerial map of the layout that might as well have had arrows on it telling the thieves and kidnappers where they could get in. He got angry then.

As the millennium year approached, heralded by dire warnings of mass computer malfunction and imminent heat-death, the old British Empire was lowering the flag in its last few outposts. Our *Postcard from Hong Kong* felt like part of the ceremony. The day of the handover was not far off and Chris Patten, the last governor, had a lot to deal with, including the irritating task of shooing the blowflies of the tabloid press away from his beautiful daughters; but he found time to deal with us. An hour in his company was enough to tell you that Britain was in trouble if it couldn't find a way of making a man like that Prime Minister. After a tennis match in which I had to do little pretending in order to lose miserably, we settled down on the veranda to film one of the best interviews I ever did. Eloquence, historical sweep, charm, wit: he had it all. He also had a family of clever women with a collective talent for keeping him down to earth, a condition with which I was familiar. Together, the Pattens had turned the official residence into the best kind of country house, much more a literary salon than a hunting lodge. In the evening, justifiably celebrated names came in for drinks after dinner and spread themselves around in the cushioned couches as if this was a second home. Jung Chang was one of them. I thought that her *Wild Swans* was one of the great political books of modern times and told her so. She didn't mind hearing it, but she was possibly less impressed with my opinion that China, with any luck, would change Hong Kong less than Hong Kong would change China. Patten, however, flatteringly thought that I might be right. He wanted to know why Hong Kong mattered to me so much and I told him the reason: that my father was buried there.

I went out to Sai Wan Bay to visit my father's grave, as I always did when I was in Hong Kong. He had given his life in the fight against the totalitarians and soon they would be here again. But nothing shook my confidence that this time it would be different. The Chinese leaders on the mainland had an unchanging system but they were now living in a changed world, where PR mattered even to them. In that way, and in my time, the development of global communications had altered the flow of history. In the main part of the movie I did all the standard things to bring out the city's always teeming, shouting, hyperactively productive character. I argued with the mad woman driver of a sampan, I got lost in the underground labyrinth of a suburb-sized nightclub in Kowloon, I visited the gold-plated house of the nutty plutocrat and his doting wife. The doting wife gave us a ten-minute piece to camera on how to prepare shark's fin soup ('First you boil the fin for two days . . .') which was probably the single most boring stretch of film in the world until Baz Luhrmann directed the closing scenes of *Australia*. In a restaurant on the Peak, the exquisite actress Maggie Cheung showed me how to spit out chicken bones in a polite manner. (Don't believe her air of gloom in *In the Mood for Love*: the real-life Maggie is a spiritual descendant of Carole Lombard.) But I didn't bother to face the camera to ask the mandatory question about meeting the challenge as time ran out in the city of contrasts. I didn't ask: will all this come to an end? Somehow I knew it wouldn't. The mainlanders, if they wanted to, could do to Hong Kong what they did to Tibet. But they wouldn't want to. Instead of changing it, they would see the advantage in letting it alone. I said that last line on the deck of a junk as the sun went down towards the sea. It was setting on my screen career. Not yet, but soon, I would have said all I had to say as a presenter of television documentaries. It was just too expensive a form in which to be pressed for time. I ached to express my opinions as chapters instead of paragraphs.

But I worked harder than ever on the paragraphs. *Postcard from New York* ended with the most tightly written paragraphs I ever wrote for television, and they did much more than illustrate the pictures, just as the pictures did much more than illustrate them. The final scene wasn't planned. It emerged during the packed two-week shooting schedule, and came as the kind of light-touch surprise that always made the heavy lifting seem worthwhile. We had a good cast of characters: the cute lady cop with the gun, the stick-thin socialite, the aromatherapist who wrapped me in seaweed while talking balls about crystals, the crazy gerontocrat party girl whose apartment walls were covered with two-shots of her embracing every celebrity she had ever trapped.

Most bizarrely of all, Ivana Trump gave us an audience in her gold-plated apartment in Trump Tower. For one terrible moment, when we walked in, I thought I had been returned to Hong Kong through some kind of space warp. But then things got worse. Already in position on a velvet couch, Ivana, suited and coiffed as an air hostess with dreams of greatness, was looking at her watch. Incorrectly supposing that there was nothing off-putting about her air of superior knowledge, she came forth readily enough with a supply of polished banalities – the only true privilege of wealth, apparently, was to express one's taste – but seemed insulted at the very idea that we should take more of her precious afternoon by shooting coverage. We wanted some shots of her walking into the room so that I could narrate a short introduction, but she demurred. I told her that Katharine Hepburn hadn't minded walking six times around her own garden but it cut no ice. So in the finished picture Ivana appeared suddenly in the sitting position, with a one-line introduction in which I was able to suggest that she had magical powers of teleportation. I would also have liked to suggest that she was a nitwit, but there was no time. And anyway, she gave the film some of the star lustre which it was otherwise a bit short of. It had some names more worthy of note, but they were less recognizable than Ivana, whose face, at the time, was familiar to flax-gatherers in Zimbabwe.

The writer Richard Price, whose low-life novels and screenplays were especially distinguished for their compulsively quotable dialogue, gave us an interview in a Bleecker Street cafe, correctly advising us that Downtown was the area that mattered now. But Downtown did not, in those days, have a hotel remotely like the Royalton on 44th Street. Festering down there near the Village, the Chelsea Hotel had its memories of badly behaved poets and musicians dead from drugs, but there was nothing to film except the proprietor's bad shave. The Royalton was something else: a nodal point of contemporary glamour to which all of New York's trendies came in the evening to have a drink, just so they could say that they had been there. We were staying there at my suggestion, which I made as soon as I heard that it had been renovated throughout according to the designs of none other than our old friend Philippe Starck, he whose concept of the reinterpreted three-legged chair had left such a lasting memory of Paris imprinted on my brain. At the Royalton he had been given a big budget to go mad with, and he had excelled himself. He had reinterpreted the concept of the elevator so that you couldn't find the buttons, and when you were inside it you couldn't see. The lighting levels, throughout the hotel, were set according to his specifications, so that the place could be navigated with any degree of assurance only by a bat. On my first evening there, I groped my way out of my room, located the elevator by touch, got into it and had travelled several floors downward in the direction of the reinterpreted lobby – it looked like a bar, whereas the bar looked like a funeral parlour – before I realized that I was not alone. There was a dark, mysterious figure in there with me. It whispered, 'Hello, Clive.' I was scared to death. They know where I live! When the door finally opened on the slightly less dark lobby, I recognized Pete Townshend. He said, 'If you ever get used to this place, it means you've gone crazy.'

He was right. The room furniture was especially memorable evidence of Starck's genius for the irrelevant. There were pointlessly low armchairs, needlessly high tables. There was a circular bath about a foot deep suitable for bathing a chihuahua. From the walls, shining horn-like objects in brushed aluminium protruded, for no apparent purpose except to be bumped into in the half-light by occupants searching in vain for the reinterpreted air-conditioning control unit, which turned on the television that looked like a mini-bar. (The mini-bar looked like a toilet.) Anywhere in mid-town, you could tell which people were staying at the Royalton by their plaster casts and eyepatches. Knowing that I could do a good voice-over about my room, I suggested to Beatrice Ballard that we should set up the camera and get some shots. Our cameraman, who she subsequently married, had one of the new Steadicams among his kit, and they both suggested that we should get a slow, virtuoso 360-degree panning shot of the room, to illustrate my viewpoint as I stood in the middle of it, gazing in wonder. Knowing that it would be even harder to cut into such a shot than to narrate over it, I asked for some individual static shots as well. Later on, back in the editing room, the usual rule applied: the static shots were the ones we used, and a few fragments of the Steadicam shot were all that survived. So in twenty years I had learned that much. Watch out for the technical improvements. Do they bring new limitations?

But the best thing I had learned was to grab the chance when the gods present it to you. One day early in the shoot, we were filming one of those long walking shots on a crowded sidewalk. The camera was halfway up a building somewhere, filming me on a long lens while I negotiated a couple of blocks in the lunchtime crush. When walking through a crowd, the secret of staying visible in the centre of the screen is to keep your eyes on the camera position, even if it is a mile away. If you can see the camera, it can see you. The process becomes automatic over the years, and you need fewer and fewer retakes, but it is always very boring, and I was asleep on my feet until I saw a roller-blader racing towards me among the buses and taxis. The traffic lights changed and he had to pause in his flight for a while, so he danced, swerving about in tight figures of eight, sometimes going forwards, sometimes backwards, with no moment of hesitation. With a shock of spiked blond hair and an outfit consisting mainly of shorts and a T-shirt, he was the all-American version of a solo act from Cirque du Soleil. He was a Cab Dancer. He danced with cabs the way Kevin Costner danced with wolves. Remembering what I had missed that night in Chicago, I shouted, 'Get him!' but the lights had changed and he was already gone.

Nothing, though, could get away from Bea. It took her a week to track him down but she found him. By then I had the sequence planned in detail. We would film him in Times Square late at night, and so get two scenes at once: him and the magic lights. You would think that there would be enough light in Times Square to shoot without any more, but it never worked out like that. The film camera, far more specific than the video camera that would soon take over the trade, needed buckets of light aimed at the chosen spot, which in this case was the few square yards at the traffic lights where the Cab Dancer would come to a halt and do his routine before taking off again. With the cops in attendance to check the abundance of paper that you have to have in New York before you can film a sparrow on a windowsill, it took our gaffers an hour to rig the lights. The Cab Dancer practised his routine in the right position while flaps on the lights were adjusted and focal lengths were checked on the camera. It took another hour. Then the Cab Dancer was despatched upstream to his starting point so that he could come back down with the traffic and stop when the lights turned red. They stayed green and he kept going. Back he went again and this time they changed too early. Why was I suddenly thinking of Willie Nelson? It took another hour before things went right. He came to a halt at the same time as the traffic, did his number and took off again. Then we had to film the dance routine several times on various lenses. The whole deal took from just before midnight until just after three in the morning. Back at Watchmaker, I sat at the Avid machine right beside the editor for two days while we put that scene together. (In olden times, before the electronics came to save us, we would have been in there for a month.) I shaped and trimmed my paragraph over and over until everything fitted. What I wrote had nothing to do with roller-blading but every-thing to do with American energy, the urge and freedom to excel, the spirit of the city. It was the last scene in the main body of the movie. On the tail of it we tacked the panoramic night-time footage that would form the end-title sequence as *Rhapsody in Blue* took over from my voice and ended the picture. The results looked like a miracle of spontaneity.

After the show was transmitted, the television critics were unusually kind, but only on the understanding that the subject matter had done all the work and we had just been lucky enough to have a camera with us that we could point at it. I met one of them socially and she said, 'I loved the way you spotted that skater going past and just grabbed him.' It's an ideal of art: make it look as if it just happened. But it was a bit harder than it looked and it took me twenty years to get ready. I knew that I would never do anything better on screen than those few minutes. Two kinds of writing had joined at a single apogee. The written words were as good as I could do, and the unwritten words, the pictures, were as good as I could arrange.

28. LATE FINAL EXTRAS

The complete film was popular but not wildly so, mainly because it was short of stars. If Robert De Niro had been in it, there might have been more impact. At the time, De Niro was already active in his transformation of the TriBeCa district, but we couldn't get to him, because he didn't want to be got to until the work was more advanced. Other stars of comparable magnitude were less elusive. As the time approached for Watchmaker's backers to buy us out, we went on increasing the company's income by supplying the broadcasters with star interviews filmed on location. Earlier on there had been a *Postcard from Cairo* that was essentially a star interview because Omar Sharif was the only face in the picture that anyone would have tuned in to see. I spent the rest of the movie doing my Indiana James number, striding around among the pyramids in my brown fedora. At one point, for a fantasy sequence, I was kitted up as Lawrence of Arabia in the full set of flowing robes, only my eyes showing as I gazed hawk-like towards destiny. I was meant to climb into the saddle of a racing camel and head off to the horizon. The camel looked to me like a hairy version of an Italian helicopter so I requested that its saddle be taken off and parked on the desert for a low shot of me climbing aboard. Then a local stunt-man in the same outfit did the actual riding.

It was not a brave moment but it fitted my mood, because Cairo held few thrills for me. Some of the mosques were magnificent but everything else was a bazaar, including the City of the Dead, which the security police didn't want to let us into until the pile of money we were offering them reached a sufficient

height. I liked to be in places where I could read the books. Our
driver was a natural teacher so I made a good start at speaking
Arabic – I can still say *yalla bina*, which means 'let's go' – but I
never got far with learning to read. That was a mistake. I should
have pushed on with it, because in the next decade I would have
been able to read the fatwas as soon as they were issued, instead
of waiting for the translation. But the assertive future, for the
Arab nations, had not yet arrived. High society in Cairo was
one big inferiority complex about the enticements of the West.
The city's leading hostess, reigning supreme over her daughter's
wedding party, moved in an aura of vulgarity that left Ivana
Trump looking like Diane de Poitiers. The US was pouring at
least as much money into Egypt as it did into Israel and most of
it was pouring out again through the necks of champagne bottles.
Behind closed doors, where people who claimed to despise
alcohol behaved as if they had invented it, the whole culture was
as tediously dedicated to hedonism as Playboy Mansion West
without the hamburgers. And all the men were exponents of this
terrible dance, in which they held their hands high above their
heads, snapped their fingers occasionally to no discernible beat,
shifted their hips about an inch without moving their feet and
pursed their lips in profound thoughtfulness while the women
expired with admiration. The tuneless revelry was so dire that
you grew old just watching. At last I figured out why the Sphinx
looked like that: it had been to a party in Cairo. Omar Sharif,
born and raised in Alexandria, did a polite job of pretending that
Cairo was the city of his dreams. We interviewed him in a
houseboat restaurant on the Nile and his radiant dentition was
an assurance that he was having as much fun as if he were in
Monaco. But he was acting, and I knew that the secret of his
show of happiness was that he had a date to play bridge in
Geneva the next day. There he was, though, up on our screen,
his eyes gleaming like fresh dates: Dr Zhivago in person. Fame
had trumped the background yet again.

     The same thing happened in a Postcard we did about the

Paris catwalks. Almost two decades after having fronted the first television special ever made on the subject, there I was again, trying to flog myself into the same enthusiasm for the frocks. But the only reason the network wanted the show was because Naomi Campbell would be the central attraction. She was intensely celebrated at the time, partly because of her erratic behaviour. After long negotiations with her phalanx of representatives, a deal was struck: I would meet her at Orly Airport when she flew in after her latest holiday in Morocco and keep close company with her as she went through the two-week season of preparing for, and participating in, the fashion shows in which she would be by far the most stellar model to strut her stuff. She arrived at the airport, I presented her with a tree-sized bunch of flowers while the camera watched, and I accompanied her to her limousine, into which she stepped with lithe grace. The door slammed behind her while I still had one foot in the air. She disappeared for a week. We camped outside the building that contained her new apartment, two floors up. Periodically her latest personal assistant emerged to reveal, by instalments, that her boss was up there with her new friend, the fledgling diva Kate Moss, and that the two of them were engaged in scientific research, to establish how a termite mound of white powder could be reduced to the dimensions of a crushed aspirin. Days went by. Not even the dress designers, who were increasingly frantic to get the two British stars to the fitting rooms, could insert their envoys through the door. Our movie was going down the drain. Finally I hit on the idea of altering the title. We could call the thing *Waiting for Naomi* and I could do a voice-over based on her absence.

As it happened, Naomi eventually did make herself manifest, and we were able to contemplate the possibility of gracing the second half of the movie with her actual physical presence. Her original written commitment to give us unlimited personal access, however, turned out to have been a hallucination on our part. Her representatives assured us that if such a document had ever been signed, she had not been present at the signing. Since she had not been present at the writing of her own novel, this contention sounded quite plausible, but it did leave the way open for a third configuration of the title, *Litigation with Naomi*. I personally vetoed that course of action and I was glad I did. She had enough trouble in her life and I didn't want to be remembered as having added to it. We just trailed her abjectly around as she went through the motions at one show after another. The motions, of course, looked wonderful: at the challenging task of walking fifty yards in both directions, there was no one to beat her. But the schmutter worn by her and all the other models was pale stuff compared to what I had once seen. I hailed from the days when Yves Saint Laurent used to arrive at the venue in the boot of a car and had to be held upright at the end of the show while the audience went berserk with gratitude at the beauty he had created. Now I was supposed to be moved by the prospect of John Galliano trying to make the girls look as freaky as himself. It was more thrilling to point the camera at Anna Wintour's dark glasses so that I could speculate about what was going on behind them. If it wasn't boredom, why did her mouth look so bitter?

Our movie was on its way to being a complete bust, but luckily for us, if unluckily for Naomi, at her last show one of the other models accidentally stepped on the hem of her best dress and tore the thing in half. Naomi thought it had happened accidentally on purpose. Suddenly she was once again the girl who had been picked on once too often in the school playground. She collapsed in tears against the wall of a corridor. I interviewed her there, and, perhaps because I genuinely sympathized with her plight, she poured out her heart. What she was saying between sobs amounted to a protest that it was all too much. The attention was too much. Her life was too much. The sequence would save the movie but I felt like a thief. If I could have left her alone, I would have. But I stayed on the case and got my scene with the damsel in distress. It was against my nature, though, and if my nature had altered to the point where I could do what went against it, perhaps the time was approaching when I should pack it in and try to get back to square one. The finished movie was amusing in spots but the high-priced ambience went for nothing. Either the frocks looked like rags, or my eye was jaded.

It was getting to the point where it was easier to leave out the background and just go for the fame. The networks were going steadily colder on the Postcards because they wanted famous faces instead. This had already been true when we filmed Polanski and Katharine Hepburn and it became truer still when Jane Fonda became available, which happened because nothing else except that kind of publicity would make anyone go to see her latest movie. It was called *Old Gringo* and she was starring opposite some revolution in Mexico. For any star – Robert Redford was the most prominent example – a sudden urge, against all advice, to set up the film that furthers the cause of the poor people of Mexico is a sure sign that a rich actor has lost his marbles. Jane Fonda was no exception but she was terribly nice about it. I was suspicious of her Hanoi Jane track record but the first few minutes in her company told me where her political enthusiasms came from: she had a generous nature. She was a dream, in fact: smart, funny and without pretensions. Instead of a gated stronghold in Bel Air she had an ordinary frame house in Santa Monica and didn't at all mind walking with me barefoot along the beach a few times while we got the coverage. I had already figured out why one egomaniac after another had fallen for her: she gave them the humility they lacked. She was full of affection and there would always be some cold-hearted male monster to suck it up. Posing with me for production stills, she embraced me from behind with one leg wrapped around my waist. Eyebrows were raised at home but you could tell she would have done the same for Ronald Reagan.

I talked to Reagan, too. The flight to Los Angeles was becoming familiar and always at the end of it there were these world-famous figures ready to pretend that they were giving their all. Actually Reagan held relatively little back. He was no longer in office but was still addressed, in the American manner, as Mr President. His autobiography had just come out; he had no idea what was in it; and he told me a few things that weren't there in its pages. I interviewed him in one of the bungalow suites of the Beverly Hills Hotel. Nobody yet knew that he had Alzheimer's disease. It was assumed that he had merely become forgetful. When I brought up the subject of Nicaragua, he forgot the name 'Somoza' and started referring to 'that guy down there'. Helpfully I mouthed the name 'Somoza' and he must have thought I was saying 'move over', because he moved over. Always a tractable actor, he was touchingly ready to take direction. In fact he had a daunting eagerness to please generally. He wasn't stupid, though. The only trade union leader ever to have become President of the United States, he knew all the angles, and would have protected himself against a hostile question. Not believing in the adversarial technique, I didn't ask him any. The touchiest subject on my list revolved around the question of the post-war Hollywood days when he had crusaded against communists in the film industry. If I had asked him 'Were you a stoolie for the FBI?' he would have just smiled nicely while the bodyguards moved in to carry me away. But I had a better question. 'Just how serious was the communist menace in Hollywood?' He was out of the starting gate in a rush, with plenty of stories that told you more than anything in his book. 'There were these men in black cars, and they would pass out money in brown, you know, envelopes . . .'

The audience would be able to deduce that here was a man whose imaginative frame of reference was made up from flickering fragments of old movies, mainly ones that he had been in. Even his plainest statements had to be decorated with special effects to hold the audience: a trick I know well. Had he been like that with Gorbachev in Reykjavik? But the charm was real. Where he might have been as truculent about requests for coverage as Ivana Trump, he was as eager to cooperate as if it was his first time on a film set. The main interview done and dusted, we walked together down the concrete footpath that led through the carefully landscaped shrubbery to the bungalow. Over this walk would go my introductory paragraph, so it needed to be quite long. We had to do the walk a few extra times because he was talking to me with such fervour that he tended to wander off the concrete and disappear among the palmettos. The finished show got big ratings and I suppose that if it turns up again on the history channels one day it will serve as a historical document. It didn't go deep, but television interviews rarely do. They give an impression. This one gave an impression of a kind man devoid of guile. If he had been devoid of brains as well, the deficiency would have shown up on screen. It didn't, but nothing can stop a legend. The orthodox opinion remains that Ronald Reagan was some kind of right-wing ogre limited in his depredations only by his stupidity. The facts say otherwise. When Reagan came to office, only two of the USA's client states in Latin America were democracies. When he left office, only two of them weren't. But the facts can say all they like and a myth will remain what it was. All I could do was help to prove that he was a human being. It did something to offset my bad memories of a social occasion in London when I had met Nancy Reagan and made the usual mistake of trying to say something unexpected so as to capture a celebrity's attention. 'Go on,' I said, 'admit that sometimes it's fun.' Considering that her husband had only just been released from hospital after somebody shot him, it was kind of her to glide past me with a smile.

Our backers bought us out between one star interview and another. It was the only really big money I ever made in show business and by today's standards it seems like nothing, but I was able, for the first time, to feel that my family's future was secure no matter what follies I might commit next, including the folly of walking away from the fountain that had gushed the cash. But I couldn't do that yet. In order to convince our backers that they had not bought a pig in a poke, we felt honour bound to go on building up the company for another year. (Later on, one of the backers asked me, 'Why on earth didn't you people bugger off

straight away?') Outside the door of Richard's office, in which
he, I and Elaine sat sipping champagne and congratulating ourselves on our hard-won affluence, the Watchmaker headquarters
stretched away into the distance, went up a flight of stairs and
stretched back again in the other direction, the whole expanse
buzzing with dedicated people whose futures were still in our
hands. They deserved a decent interval in which to make their
plans. They were all out there: Wendy Gay, Jean Twoshoes, the
whole crew. I owed them a lot, and for once in my life I saw my
duty at the time instead of after. I had never been very good at
remembering birthdays, sending cards, choosing gifts, and doing
the little things that matter. It's a missing piece of my mentality.
But this was a big thing: too big for even me to overlook.

29. DRIVEN MEN

Back we went to Los Angeles to meet Mel Gibson. If I had tabs on myself as an Australian empire-builder, here was an example of what the species really looked like after a full meal of energy pills. This movie wasn't just a star interview with a top and a tail, it was a complete two-week shoot showing every aspect of the star's activity as he ran his production office and went about the complex business of being a Global Brand. In cruel fact, the reason for his being available was that one of the production office's latest efforts, *Conspiracy Theory*, starring the Brand as the rebellious victim of a CIA plot, needed all the help it could get. I had seen the movie before its release and I knew it to be a stiff, which meant I had to tread carefully when talking to the Brand, who had a tendency to treat anything less than complete approval as an armed attack. To that extent, the system had sucked him in, but in most respects he had a right to think of himself as a pillar of integrity in an industry otherwise devoted to the main chance. The movies he made in the *Lethal Weapon* franchise – big hair, dumb plot, bang bang, let's go – raked in hundreds of millions of dollars for the parent studio, but he had parlayed his star power into a string of genuinely interesting projects. Even *Braveheart* wasn't just your average bloodbath. In its plot it was yet another example of Mel's continuing counter-attack against Perfidious Albion, but it was beautifully directed, and he had directed it. (Note the naturalness with which the key characters speak French and Latin as well as English, and ask yourself whether any other director, even in France, has ever brought out the full sumptuous beauty of Sophie Marceau.) Mel knew everything about making movies and he was determined to push his vision to the limit. The vision was uncomfortable but, I think, considerable. If there is such a thing as a necessary contribution to be made from a right-wing viewpoint, it is to take account of the facts of human cruelty. Mel would go on to do so in *The Passion of the Christ*; and his almost unwatchably violent *Apocalypto* is, in my view, an important work of art. Every minute of it scares me witless, but it is meant to. A man who can conceive a thing like that has a direct mental connection to a primeval state. (The reason why he likes to have his actors speaking foreign languages, or no language at all, could well be that he wants to remove the consolatory filters of speech that lie between us and the primal scream.) Mel has always heard the Devil's voice within himself. In his younger days he tried to drown it with drink, but it can swim. Later on he learned to live with it, but only at the price of a rigorous discipline.

As to the accusations of anti-Semitism, Mel didn't look very anti-Semitic to me when we both sat down to dinner with Joel Silver. A producer of great commercial acumen, Joel Silver is responsible for movies like *Die Hard*, in which Bruce Willis implausibly maintains his pout while slaughtering terrorists by the bus-load. But while he revels in such vulgarity, Joel Silver is a man of exquisite personal taste. He lives in Frank Lloyd Wright houses which he restores at his own expense. Even amid the frenzied hokum of *Die Hard*, the quick of eye will note that the treasure in the vault of the Sumitomo Corporation includes a set of pastels by Degas. Joel Silver does low-life on top dollar. Rich, influential, cosmopolitan and domineering, he is a Jewish mogul out of the worst nightmares of Hamas. But it was clear that Mel respected him. The Brand made his anti-Semitic remarks when he fell off the wagon. The poison is deep in his memory, where he would like to keep it bottled up. Most likely he got it from his father, who really was an anti-Semite: a Holocaust-denier of the classic demented stamp. Mel heard it all when he was a child and clearly it got into him. But the grown-up Mel

Gibson doesn't believe any of it. He can't, however, attack his own mental inheritance in public, because he honours his father, as I do mine. So he is torn. The tensions in his mind are fierce, but they make him what he is. Though he smiles with winning charm, there is nothing easy about him, and I think our film showed that.

Helping to show it was the contrast between him and his friend George Clooney, who was just then emerging as a fully accredited film star after a long apprenticeship in the television series *ER*, where he was worshipped by every female member of my family in the most abject manner: one and all, they would sit back with their knees up and coo like pigeons. In our Mel movie, we had a scene where I toured the back lot in a golf cart with Mel at the wheel. George Clooney, in his downtime from an *ER* episode, was discovered shooting hoops. He shot a last hoop, fronted up to the golf cart and got into a dialogue with me and the Brand. None of it was scripted but Clooney was hilarious. Above all, he was relaxed. You could tell that he would do everything with the same casual grace. He had the advantage of his heritage. Mel had come up from nowhere, slogging all the way and learning from his mistakes. Clooney had never made any. Raised in a showbiz household, he knew, from the start, the rules and the limitations. Just by being what he was, he stole our movie from Mel in two minutes. When I got him alone for a few seconds I asked him if he would be my guest one day and he said, 'Sure. Count on it.'

I left mainstream television before I could call in the marker, but I didn't forget that easy moment. Nothing else seemed to be easy any more. Putting the screws on the network, we got the finance for one more Postcard. The subject was Havana and the network hated the idea because it was obviously destined to be another of those historical background things they were getting so nervous about. (Market research, on which the younger executives had come to rely, was supplying more and more evidence that nobody in the desirable demographic had the slightest interest in any historical period earlier than the previous Tuesday.) If they hadn't needed our weekly show to fill slots, they would never have coughed up. So I was dragging a piano from the start. Cuba looked good to the camera because not even Castro, in four decades of trying, had been able to make it look bad. I had long before formed the opinion that if the Cuban revolution had happened in a European climate it would never have lasted beyond the first winter.

During the course of Castro's rule the total number of people who left the island by any means of transport they could find had amounted to at least half the population of Israel, and they had all taken off because they couldn't stand the regime's brainless dedication to a command economy that was able to command nothing except the approximately equal distribution of grinding poverty. Without the sunlight and the sparkling water, everyone would have gone. But since the best things in life were free, there was some apparent happiness to be filmed, and we dutifully filmed it. Our best interview was with Che Guevara's daughter, who spoke well on behalf of the health system, in which she worked as a doctor. She deserved respect, and nobody, certainly not I, would have wanted to tell her that her father, who she revered, had a habit of assessing the guilt of any suspected traitors by shooting them through the head to see which way they fell.

We were staying at the old Hotel Nacional, where the waiter who once had a love affair with Ava Gardner was still available to bring you a mojito and reluctantly reveal his secret, as he had done to every visiting journalist and film crew for forty years. The Tropicana cabaret was still in business, giving the same show that I had first seen decades before. The beautiful girl was still up there in the floodlit trees singing that lovelorn song about her crying need to be kissed. She was a different girl but she was wearing the same feathered costume. Everything was still roughly the same, but even more roughly because it was all decaying. I did my best to be fair, though. In the market square where the second-hand books were on sale, I scored, as always, every

Aguillar edition I could find – not all of the morocco bindings had been ruined by the humidity – but I was careful also to buy the booklets that featured Castro's speeches and interviews. They were very good for my Spanish because they used the same phrases over and over, so I could easily improve my knowledge of the syntax and the grammar by underlining the various ways in which the clichés were held together. But in another square nearby, the moment of truth arrived. Sitting at a table outside a cafe, I was reading Castro's *Nothing Can Hold Back the March of History* (a bad choice of title from a man who had managed, all by himself, to do exactly that) when a fourteen-year-old girl in pink hot pants and a sea-green halter top approached me and offered herself to me for twenty dollars. The crew was filming something else just around the corner. After telling her to take a seat, I dived around the corner, brought back the crew and asked her to go back to where she had been when she had first seen me, approach me again and ask me the same question.

She did it, and she got fifty dollars for it without even having to lie down. A uniformed female member of Cuba's ubiquitous neighbourhood watch spotted the transaction and came sprinting over to give the poor kid a wigging, but she wasn't arrested. There was a good reason for that. It was all official. Just for the tourist dollars, Cuba had made prostitution legal again. Back in the day – when the revolution of the bearded ones was the revolution of all of us, all over the world, who had beards too – Castro had come to power with the promise that there would never again be any slot machines or their female equivalent. But the peso, theoretically at parity with the dollar, was now almost worthless, and finally the real money talks.

Karl Marx, wrong about so much, had been right about that. Merely to be alive can be beautiful in Cuba, even when everything you eat is rationed. In the food queues, the people smiled for our camera while they waited for the pat of butter that would have to last them a week. On any airline that serves food, you get two pats of butter with a bread roll and you can ask for more if you run out. It costs you nothing except the effort of pressing a button. In Cuba, a single pat of butter will cost you an hour of waiting. How many hours are there in a life? I knew that most of our audience would blame the American embargo, although really the fault was all with Castro's ideological arrogance. As the awful old joke goes, 'What would happen if the Sahara went communist? Nothing, for the first ten years, and then there would be a shortage of sand.' The effect of an economy of shortages is to use up, by making them wait, the energy that the people might otherwise devote to protest. Thus the revolution stifles all rebellion. If the Americans hadn't been so dumb, they would have bombed Havana with a million pairs of trainer shoes, and the revolution would have been washed away. The young people dreamed of nothing except imported trainer shoes. Such was the power and persistence of the dream that the government eventually felt obliged to respond, and came forth with an official all-Cuban sneaker which had apparently been designed to the requirements of Khrushchev's mother. Some of our crew were wearing new Reeboks and the Cuban kids eyed them as if they were made of gold. They were: they were made of the unattainable. Yet it could have all been so easily attained. The reasonable standard of living that even the unemployed take for granted in the decadent capitalist West had been stopped cold in the warm air of Cuba by nothing but an idea. It was the wrong idea but the sun shone on it anyway. We filmed the sun sinking behind me as I walked along the Malecón for our final shot. From the sea wall, boys in shorts somersaulted into the waves to impress the girls. I thought we had done well. From some angles, even the revolution had done well. At least its children would be safer there from knives and guns than they would have been in Brixton, because in Cuba all the weapons belong to the government.

But as we put the movie together in the editing room, I knew it would be the last. I had too much to say about these things by now, and in an hour of television there was too little space, even with the pictures doing half the talking. And there were no stars, so the network executives – all of them born long after Che and Fidel came down from the Sierra Maestre – could offer us no firm idea of when they would schedule it. The studio show was what they cared about, and they cared in the wrong way.

They liked it when we booked Tony Curtis, because Tony Curtis was famous in America, and therefore in the whole world. The British media's abject enthralment to everything American had by then become so total that its victims didn't even realize they were in its grip. But that's a subject for another book. Let's stay with the stars. Somewhere beneath a hairpiece of improbable luxuriance, Tony Curtis arrived at our studio in a state of nervous breakdown and he wouldn't come out of his dressing room when it was time for him to go on. Out in the studio, there were people in the audience who had adored him since he had starred in *The Black Shield of Falworth*, and that might have been the trouble. He was feeling his age. He was feeling it in the dark. He had turned the lights off, disabled the switch, and anyone who came in could detect his presence only by his breathing. One after the other, in ascending order of authority, the whole hierarchy went in to try and winkle him out: researcher, assistant producer, producer, executive producer. He wouldn't speak to any of them. Finally I was sent in and said what he really wanted to hear. 'Some people say that you were the key element in three of the greatest movies ever made: *Some Like It Hot*, *Sweet Smell of Success* and *The Boston Strangler*. But I think there's a fourth: *Insignificance.* Your performance in that one left me overwhelmed with helpless awe.' Somewhere in the corner of the dark, a familiar Bronx accent whispered: 'You forgot *Spartacus*.' And out he came. Equalling Peter Sellers's trick of suddenly turning into a normal human being under the lights, he gave me a brilliantly funny interview, but it was all pretty unsettling. If fame had done that to him, what was it doing to me? Mine was on an infinitely smaller scale, of course. I clutched that fact to me for comfort.

And anyway, some of the famous guests seemed perfectly sane. Goldie Hawn was a model of politeness. We had such a bubbling time on air that we talked over each other at one point, and a joke got lost. Later on she came to say goodbye, put her hand over her mouth in mock horror and said, 'I trod on your *line!*' And Alice Cooper, whose whole schtick was to carry on like a psychopath, couldn't have been more sardonically witty or down to earth. My spot with him was one of the neatest things I ever did on air. Every crack the host made, the guest capped: which is just how it ought to be. (The American talk shows work in the opposite direction.) The layout of the set was at its dizzy height by then: a panoply of images and colour, like a book of hours. But it occurred to me that the inspired Alice would have been just as dazzling with nothing in the background at all. I had recently seen the very first successful webcast. The image, only about as big as a postage stamp, stuttered and fluttered, but it didn't take Nostradamus to predict that the computer screen would one day be able to transmit the only thing about face-to-face television that really counted. In the studio we were surrounded by thousands of tons of concrete and millions of pounds' worth of machinery. I had begun to wonder if any of all that hoo-hah was any longer necessary. There could be another way.

The network executives still liked it, although a good deal less, when we booked Freddie Starr, who was at least a draw, mainly because everyone in the country hoped that the famous headline FREDDIE STARR ATE MY HAMSTER would one day be topped by something like FREDDIE STARR SETS FIRE TO WINDSOR CASTLE AFTER BEING CAUGHT IN BED WITH ANNE. I should say, going in, that Freddie Starr is a lavishly accomplished performer. He can sing, dance, do magic and write whole sketches on the spot, playing every character with no pause for transition. While his elfin features are filling the screen with knowing innocence, he can fire, out of the corner of his mouth, a scatological joke so perfectly constructed in its shock value that it is worth a whole hour from most of our laboriously offensive stand-up comedians. But he is harder to handle on air than a runaway train. There was no way of knowing what he would do next. For a few minutes he would sit there being reasonably normal, and then suddenly he was out of his chair and marching in circles, pretending to have messed his pants. Then he was goose-stepping around in his Nazi routine. Then he was in the audience, sitting on an old lady's lap. And he was just warming up. When he got into his sex-crazed werewolf phase he was ready to rock. The ratio of what we shot and what we could transmit was about four to one. The editors had to work half the night. The worst thing from my angle was that I would have been enjoying the mayhem much more in the previous decade. I, like Freddie, had been in the kitchen too long. But whereas his brains were merely scrambled, mine were turning into an overcooked omelette.

The network executives didn't like it all when I lobbied to book Deborah Bull, prima ballerina at Covent Garden. I had admired *Dancing Away*, her book about becoming a ballerina, and I had more than admired her BBC2 series about dancing, especially the episode devoted to the tango, in which I had participated. Ever since I returned from Buenos Aires I had been learning to dance the tango – sometimes I flew back there just to get some lessons – and Deborah's documentary had been the first time that I had gone public with my passion. The results could have been worse, and Deborah couldn't have been better. Telegenic, knowledgeable and highly articulate, she was the dance presenter that the BBC bigwigs had been looking for since forever and would have built up into a screen superstar if they had had any sense. I thought Deborah was the goods in all respects and I knew her well enough to be sure that she would give us an incandescent interview. But the network executives thought that a ballerina was too elitist for the general public. They wanted me to interview Geri Halliwell. My previous interview with the emerging Spice Girls had been a big hit and they wanted more of the same. Worse, my own colleagues agreed with them. Richard, by that stage, was paying the same kind of attention to the ratings that he had once discouraged in me. When I asked him what was up he told me the dreadful truth. From the network's viewpoint, the show was only just holding on. I realized how tough things were getting when all my producers, speaking as one, advanced the idea that I should interview the Duchess of York. Ever since I had first seen her dishing up food in the hospitality marquee of the McLaren F1 team, I had always thought her a cheerful soul. But I had no interest in interviewing her on screen. Yet I now found myself having long lunches with her social secretaries, who assured me that what was really, really *amazing* about the Duchess was that she worked jolly, jolly *hard*. I was asleep already. What would it be like when I had to ask her questions? Luckily she had more important things to do and the idea went away, but it had been a rude shock to find Richard so intent on persuading me to do the very kind of thing that we had set up our own outfit in order to avoid.

30. TRUMPETS AT SUNSET

The same was true for many of our early hopes. One of them had been to get control of the product, but here we were, after years of work, and the control was back in the hands of the controllers. We had made our fortunes, but the programmes we made didn't belong to us. For the next generation of independent producers, it would be a sine qua non to retain their rights in the sell-on, but we had arrived too early in the game. I was too tired for the next fight. Even more daunting, Richard seemed tired too. That was a real worry, because all the time I had known him his nervous energy had been as inexhaustible as his judgement was sound. If I may be permitted for a moment to compare the lesser with the greater, we had always worked together like Yves Saint Laurent and Pierre Bergé. Saint Laurent was the nutty creative one and Bergé was the practical brain. Theirs had been a productive relationship right up until the time when Saint Laurent, bombed out of his skull on multiple medication, finally wigged out for keeps. But if the practical brain shows the same kind of impulsiveness even for a week, the thing is over. It had seemed like a good idea to revive the End of the Year show format for the end of the millennium. I had my doubts, because I was still meeting people who told me they always watched the End of the Year show even though we had last done it five years before. If we did it again even once, I would be back in the same frame, perhaps for another decade. But the occasion sounded too good to miss, and the thing was scheduled. Six months ahead, the deal was sealed, the studio was booked for the show, and then Richard said he wanted to replace Bostock.

Richard said that we had got stuck in a groove and I needed a fresh mind to bounce off. I didn't believe that for a moment but I had at last run full-tilt into a problem that had been inherent in our command set-up from the beginning. We had no mechanism for disagreeing with each other at a fundamental level. We had always done everything by mutual agreement: there had never been a time when we hadn't been able to settle on a plan even if it was preceded by a quarrel. But this time I thought his proposal was so wrong that I couldn't see his point at all. And there was the flaw. My only effective course of action would have been to walk out, and I couldn't walk out on my own company. So I caved in, to my lasting shame. Bostock was pissed off, and I don't blame him. I blame myself. I should have pulled the plug, no matter what the cost. A true egomaniac would have done so. But my own ego, though more than sufficiently robust, is tempered, I like to think, by an underlying sense of the reasonable. The trouble with a sense of the reasonable, however, is that it has, built into it, a dangerous readiness to believe that the opposing voice might have something to it. Perhaps the fresh mind would energize me.

The fresh mind turned out to be two fresh minds, answering to the names of Andrew Collins and Stuart Maconie. When they arrived in my cubicle they were very nice about not noticing that I lived like a prisoner. They were already well known as a tightly scripted radio double act, and I found out why in the first five minutes. Each of them had verbal talent spraying out of his ears. But I'm bound to say that they seemed very young. Barely adding up to my own age, they could tell I was missing Bostock but they did all they could to help. They were smart and full of up-to-date ideas. My problem, however, was that I myself was no more up to date than Queen Victoria, and was thus very soon tipped head-first into a permanent state of being puzzled. I couldn't stump them with the Bayeux Tapestry, but when they talked about the Beastie Boys I was clueless. For all their impressive range of reference, however, they knew a lot more about movies and music than they did about history, which, in a show concerning a whole millennium, had to be the main subject. Carolyn Longton was one of our best producers – she had put together the Mexico City shoot, which was a tough one – but she won't mind my saying that history wasn't her thing. She said it herself. 'We didn't do history at school.' The British school system, by that stage, was giving As at A-level to young people who had to consult a database before they found out that World War I came before World War II. In just such events, of course, lay the show's insoluble problem, and I might not have been able to crack it even if Bostock had been at my elbow. When the story got to the twentieth century, there was just too much stuff that I couldn't be funny about. When people made jokes about Hitler and Stalin, I seldom laughed, so why, if I made jokes about Hitler and Stalin, would anybody else laugh? They would hear the sense of strain, and humour is always a shared relaxation.

While the gargantuan preparations for the End of the Millennium show were still in the works, I flew briefly back to Los Angeles with Richard for our last star interview special. Barbra Streisand was still the number-one female showbiz name on earth at the time, and therefore impossible to approach. We had been after her for fifteen years at least. She became momentarily available only because she had a stiff album to push. Recorded in company with her marginally gifted husband, the album was dead at birth, but the opportunity to interview her had attracted production teams from every major broadcasting outlet in the world. Theoretically she would give them half an hour each, but in practice each interview took at least an hour because she insisted on rearranging the lighting, choosing the lenses, checking on the pollen count, etc. That was her right, but it meant we had to wait. The crew ahead of us ran out of budget and had to fly home to Munich, so we got bumped up by a couple of hours, but we were still running a day late when we finally got through the door to do our set-up. Five hours after our scheduled starting time, she finally arrived on set and launched herself into the task of changing the layout in every detail. I was busting for a pee, but now that she was at last physically present it would have been foolish of me to leave, so I held it in.

When we got talking, things went smoothly enough. I genuinely admired the way she had turned Hollywood around for women, making the studios dance to her tune instead of the other way about. On being told repeatedly that her success in revolutionizing the film industry was almost as impressive as her creative genius, she gave several signs that she was taking my pitiless interrogation quite well. Three-quarters of the way into our allotted time frame, however, I had to put my hand up and ask permission for a toilet break. Nothing like that had happened to her in years. She was stunned. Our camera kept rolling, so somewhere in the archives there must be a few feet of film of Barbra Streisand looking as if she had seen the Devil rise out of the earth and expose his flaming member while announcing his intention of overthrowing the government of the United States by force. I went off to pee and made one of my early discoveries that my waterworks were no longer what they were. I had always found it hard to urinate when I was under pressure but this was ridiculous. It was like tapping a rubber plant. I expected her to be gone by the time I got back to the set but she was still there. What Tom Cruise would have called our rapport, however, had disappeared. She responded with only mild enthusiasm to my final few questions about how she coped with her excess of inspiration. Then she rose to leave and it was all over.

The whole thing was over. In the end, nobody beats the grind. Richard said it first. 'I could never go through that again.' I felt the same. At the airport, he didn't even buy a watch. At first I took it as a sign of his annoyance, but there was something listless about him, and on the plane home, for the first time in our lives together, I saw him fall asleep.

Back we went to the millennium show, waiting for us in the office like some many-headed, tendril-bedecked monster from a John Carpenter horror movie, or a frog in a pond. As the chief author of the script I did my best to convince myself that it was hilarious, but I would go home to my family and spread no more cheer than a bomb-disposal expert granted two days' leave for nervous exhaustion. Finally the main show was taped over a period of two days, with a further day reserved for editing before it was transmitted. Richard, for the first time in his career as an executive producer, didn't turn up for the edit. He had gone sick. I had been worried about his health for some time. His hands had always trembled but I thought it was nervous energy. Lately, though, I had been hearing his knife and fork rattle when he ate. And now, on the vital day, he wasn't there. The kids had to do the edit themselves and they made their first mistake only two minutes into the show. They neglected to weld a laugh over a cut. When the laugh stopped abruptly, it suggested that every laugh in the show would be artificial. I had extracted every one of the hundreds of laughs in the show from a live studio audience, but the audience at home would assume it was a laugh track. Glumly, as another thousand years came to an end, I watched the show go out. It wasn't all that bad, but if it couldn't be better than any of its predecessors, why had we done it? My only consolation was that a few million fewer people than usual would be watching with me.

As the time approached when I would at last be free of my weekly schedule in the Watchmaker office, I got sick of wondering when the executives would screen the Havana postcard and I rang up the most senior factotum who would take my call. He sounded about twelve years old. Resisting the urge to ask, 'Is your father in?' I asked why the show, which they had paid for, had not been on the air. He cleared his throat and said that there was a problem. 'What problem?' The answer told me all I would ever need to know. 'We've done some market research and not enough people know about the Cuban revolution. We thought we might wait for a big news story and then peg the screening to that.' And what big news story would that be? 'We thought that we might wait for Castro to die.' I told him that I would see if I could arrange to die in the same week, so that they would have two pegs. But I got the impression that he thought there would still be only one.

I was still shaking my head when Wendy Gay told me that Richard wouldn't be coming in at all for a while. She looked stricken, obviously knowing something that I didn't. Elaine Bedell, always a blunt speaker, told me straight out. 'Richard's sick. Really sick. He might not be coming back.' I made the call and he said there was nothing to worry about. But he also said that it was time for me to go home. I packed a few books in a box, said my goodbyes and left. In the cupboards of my office there was a row of blue suits and on the shelves and on my desk were the drafts of all the scripts I had ever written. I planned to come back and get all that stuff one day but I never did.

EPILOGUE: THE RETURN OF THE METROPOLITAN CRITIC

So I did a fade. In my telling of it, I may have overdone the neatness. The milestones in life are seldom so squarely cut. Well before the end, before it had become fully clear that the network, driven by its hunger for the youthful demographic, wanted the celebrity culture and no other kind, Richard had put feelers out to the BBC. But Alan Yentob, even if he had wanted me back, was in no position to pay the tab for my whole organization. He had just got through forking out the down-payment for a couple of newly emergent front-men and the total bill had left him traumatized. (One of these fledglings cost the Beeb millions until it was at last realized that he had nothing to offer except a built-in grin, and the other, although he can at least put his own sentences together, expects us to be astonished when he *doesn't* swear.) For me, Yentob was the executive who had had the boldness to buy in the magnificent German series *Heimat* and screen the whole thing on BBC2. If a man as clever as that made a decision that was not in my interest, I could have no quarrel.

Besides, I didn't really want to continue. The will was gone: not so much because I had ceased to enjoy the limelight, but because I wanted to be alone again with my writing. Most of the essays in my collection *Even As We Speak* were written during the transition period when I was getting ready to leave mainstream television, but the book came out after I had made the jump, and its publication marked, in my own mind at least, the moment when my erstwhile persona, the Metropolitan Critic, made his comeback. I didn't expect the reviewers to say the same. I expected them to review my book as if it had been written by Bruce Forsyth. But in the event the response was gratifying, even though the fact that I had definitely kicked the crystal bucket was slow to sink in. I had no beef about that, and still haven't. Most of the television faces hang in there if they can. I am always careful not to speak against the ones who go on forever. Terry Wogan will be worth the money if he broadcasts from an iron lung. There are plenty of presenters who agree with the press that there is no life beyond television. Most of them end up trying to convince themselves that their new spot on a cable channel, with nobody watching, is even more exciting than their old spot on a mainstream channel, when everybody watched, but there are always a few that look as if they are only fulfilling their destiny when they grow old and die on the big-time air, still twinkling as they go.

I wouldn't have been one of them. I had other things I was longing to do, and I would have cared little if they came with no celebrity factor attached. After too many years of pestering the stars while they glowed and faded, it had become all too apparent to me that celebrity, unless it was based on real achievement, would always decay at the same rate as time marched. I made that the major theme of my next book of essays, *The Meaning of Recognition*. That book, too, got a thoughtful press, whose general effect helped to eliminate the impression that I might be mourning for my lost prominence. In the tabloids, it was not long before the nametag 'TV Clive' was transferred from me to Clive Anderson, who had started his career as my warm-up man but was now the go-to guy for any show that needed fronting by a flip lip. So I was relatively safe from the attentions of the gossip writers. For as long as the press is free, there will always be the concept that a private life is an offence against the public's right to know; and the turnover merchants will thrive as a consequence. They wouldn't enjoy being turned over themselves – a fact which tells you all you need to know about the putative legitimacy of their trade – but there is no point complaining. All I can say is that I don't envy them their job. The lucky ones get sick of their work; the unlucky ones come to regard it as normal; and it is hard to know which fate is worse. But now they were busy chasing faces they could see on the screen, and my face had gone missing.

The profile-writers, however, were still on the case. Television executives don't place much value on the press profiles of a star, but for publishers such attention counts for a lot, and the more 'thoughtful' the profile the better. Alas, the thoughtful press profile is the one I hate most, because I am just no good at sitting still to be summed up. After moving from the Barbican to a loft across the river, and lining the loft with books as a soldier might stack sandbags to heighten the rim of his foxhole, I had dreams of being left alone, but it still hasn't worked out that way. The profile-writers still get in. I sincerely wish I could make their job easier, but I can't. They still want to know what I am really out to achieve, and they tend to get impatient when they find out that I don't know. The best of them are highly intelligent, but the sum total of their attentions was already driving me to distraction as the next thousand years got started. I wouldn't be seeing many of those years in person, so any time wasted hit me hard. I can't complain, however, about the general tone of the press I have been getting in recent years. Even those Australian journalists who once accused the expatriates of treason are nowadays likely to concede that we flew the flag. For those of us who took off so long ago to find out what the moon was made of, the most dangerous part of the flight used to be the re-entry. You had to get the angle exactly right, or there would be flames in the sky. The press liked nothing better than a mismanaged homecoming. Now, however, there is a welcome waiting. I cherish my share of the approbation. Besides, what the press says never matters as much as what the common people think. Whenever I am in Sydney in these last, less hectic years, I sit down to write at one of the open-air tables of Rossini's cafe on Circular Quay. Kindly

saying that they are sorry to interrupt, passers-by thank me for
my books or my television programmes. If I didn't enjoy being
interrupted, I would sit somewhere else. Once a performer, always
a performer. But the writing still gets done.

One of the penalties of living out your allotted span is that
some of the people whose existence you relied on will cash in
their chips. 'At my age, of course,' Anthony Powell once told me,
'they start dropping orf like flies.' During the later part of the
time span covered by this book, Kingsley Amis died. He could be
tough company, especially towards the end, but I always revered
him. Terry Kilmartin, of whom I thought the world, died too.
When I spoke at his memorial service, I tried to tell the story of
what a privilege and an education it has been to have him as an
editor. Peter Cook I knew less well but I had never doubted that
he was a formative influence on all of us who aspired to putting
a commentary into comedy. My wife and I were skiing at Aspen
when we got the news. At a restaurant high up on Ajax, Barry
Humphries suddenly appeared, clad in the splendid ski-suit that
kept him warm as he rode up and down the mountain in the
chair-lift. He must have skied about ten yards on the whole trip,
and was perfectly ready to make a joke of it. But for once he
looked bereft. He said, 'Peter Cook died.' I didn't know what to
say. Barry, by a heroic act of will, had saved himself from the
menace that nailed his friend. But Peter would never have gone
on drinking unless he wanted to get it over. The same applied to
Dudley Moore: he chose other means, but to embrace extinction
was his aim. I know the impulse well, but nobody succumbs to it
unless they feel that their work is done.

Bad news travels fast among those in the same business. Not
long after the computers surprised us all by ringing in the new
millennium on time instead of announcing a re-run of the Battle
of Hastings, I was at some literary festival or other. I met Al
Alvarez in the bar of my hotel and he said, 'Ian Hamilton is very
sick.' Always a picture of health even when his latest physical
adventure had left him busted up, Al loathed the idea of illness

taking a friend, and so did I. Ian had cancer and he died soon after. He had been the key man at the start of my literary career and I felt cut off from my beginnings. It made going on with the end-game feel all the stranger. More recently, that feeling was redoubled when Pat Kavanagh died, from a brain tumour that struck at only a moment's notice. Her memorial service was a gathering of all the people whose lives she had enriched, and I won't pretend to have grieved more than they did, and still do: but I had always been grateful for the work and thought she put into helping give shape to my literary career. To dedicate my book of essays *The Revolt of the Pendulum* to her memory was the best tribute I could think of, when my only consolation was that she had not, at least, been cut down young; even though she was always young, at any age, just as she was always beautiful.

Ian went too early, but at least he had lived a life. Lorna Sage, who had adored him as so many women did, also went too early. The woman with the most enchanting name in the literary world had a way of flattering the male writers in her life with her admiration, but few of us realized soon enough that she had the power to write rings around us. When, just before her death, her autobiographical memoir *Bad Blood* was published, it left all of us wondering whether we would ever do anything as good. Had she lived to write a few more books like it, her position as the dominant female voice of a generation might have been assured. But she got far enough to make her voice count.

Terence Donovan frightened me by choosing to die. I had always thought I understood him, and then he proved that I had never understood him at all. The cockney photographers had always impressed me with their boldness. Unlike the invading Australians, for whom the British class structure was no obstacle because they had never seen such a thing when they were young, the cockneys had to fight their way up. They did it with good cheer. David Bailey, with whom I collaborated both in print and on film, could deal out withering sardonic punishment for any loose word, but his company was a constant delight; and

Donovan was a belly laugh every minute. I had thought that such a funny man must be full of joy. His dreadful suicide was a bad blow but at least it was a mystery.

When Sarah Raphael went, it was no mystery at all. Chance, which I knew all about, had simply reminded us that it is our only ruler. But why choose her, when she was still in the opening stages of a career that might have changed the modern history of her art? She caught a cold; the cold turned to something worse, and then to something worse still, and she was gone. The shock was terrible. Ustinov, Pavarotti, Pinter, Ayrton Senna, Olga Havel, Dirk Bogarde, Katharine Hepburn, Alan Coren, Kenneth Mac-Millan: they have all gone, but they went in the fullness of their achievement. Sarah was only at the beginning of hers. The loss blew like a freezing wind into hundreds of lives. For her funeral, the chapel was an atoll in a sea of people. I was one of them, and when I saw the faces of her parents I found it hard to keep my feet. For her father, an adept of the classical languages, it must have been as if the concept of tragic irony had been redefined for him by jealous gods. Only a month had gone by since I had made my exit from television and I had not yet begun to construct my website, but the day would come when I would ask his permission to include, in the site's gallery section, a pavilion devoted to his daughter's work. At several meetings to discuss the project, we became even closer friends. The friendship had begun through mutual wonder at his daughter's gift, and it grew through mutual grief at her death: but my share of the grief, thank God, could only be a tiny fraction of his.

Perhaps it would be better to leave God out of it, because His casual violence, if He exists, can have no excuse. Better always to blame chance, which is without a mind. When chance takes the older and fulfilled, it can seem wise and even benevolent, but when it takes the young and the barely begun, its arbitrary vandalism stands revealed. Wendy Gay sent me her first short stories to look at. I was, I really was, going to get back to her and tell her that they were full of promise; but I was short of time.

Not, however, as short of time as she was. She was out cycling and she was killed by a lorry. The driver said that she didn't see him. It could be said that he should have seen her, but such arguments are just whistling in the dark. To know just how dark the dark is, you have to lose a daughter. I rang her parents and said the most useless of all things. 'I only wish I had something useful to say.' They were nice about it, but I would have done better to say nothing. The truth was that I felt guilty. When the young die, I always feel guilty, because I have been granted a long life. So was my mother, and when she at last died, after having lain in the nursing home for several years, I tried to be thankful that she had lived to see her son achieve at least some of the things that her husband might have done if his life had not been cut short. But the story of her passing will be told at its proper length in the first chapter of my next, and presumably final, volume. The end of her life marked a new beginning for mine; the last of my new beginnings.

Nor is this the place to tell how I wrote *Cultural Amnesia*, published my collected poems, went back on stage, re-launched my song-writing career as Pete Atkin's lyricist, found a new position as a broadcaster on BBC Radio 4 and built the first few levels of my multimedia website – which might prove to be my most characteristic means of expression, if only because, having made a start with it, I have no real idea of where it might end. All I need to say now, in closing, is that I would have been far less well equipped for any of this if I had not done twenty years of television first. At the time it might have looked like a false trail. In our family we have an expression about the trail to Kublis. The expression can be used about any of us but is most commonly used about me. At Davos, near the bottom of the mountain, it was possible, at the end of the day's skiing, to take the trail back to town, or else, by mistake, to take the trail to Kublis, a little town much further down the valley. The trail led for miles over fields that were cow pastures in the summer. When the snow was thin the cow pats would be near the surface. The effect of skiing over a cow pat is to stop the ski while the skier goes on, often to fall face down in the cow pat after next. The complete trip could take a couple of hours and the trip back up the valley by train took another half hour on top of that, so the victim would arrive late for dinner and be greeted by universal mockery. All of us took the trail to Kublis once but I was the only one who took it twice. On the second trip the snow was particularly thin, which made the cow pats easier to spot in the moonlight but also provided a surface consisting mainly of grass and dirt. I was sobbing with fatigue when I arrived in Kublis and only just caught the very last train. Having missed dinner altogether, I was not regaled with the full chorus of derision until breakfast. Many a time during my years in television I heard, from one or other member of my family and often from all of them at once, the expression, 'He went to Kublis.' But I still think that it was the most instructive way to reach Davos. How else would I have learned so much about cow pats, or acquired the all-important skills to ski on dirt?

I might have forgotten to say that I had a lot of fun in mainstream television. But I would have been glad to be in it even if the whole thing had been a sweat, because the long-term pay-off was a sum of practical experience that has served me well. Much of the fun was provided by the personality of Richard Drewett. At his funeral service in 2008, the chapel was packed with quondam ferrets. Some of them had arrived in limousines: they were the new hierarchs. All of us who spoke drew on the fund of running gags that he had brought into being and made part of the texture of our working lives. Right to the end, even as he wasted away to nothing, his merriment was always there. When he was being lifted onto the trolley that would take him into the last hospital room he would have to see, he whispered, 'Any chance of an upgrade?' This book has been, in its largest part, the story of the career he gave me in television. He was convinced, and helped to convince me whenever I wavered, that it was worth doing in itself; but he could not have foreseen that it would be crucial in what happened to me next. From the practical matters of putting a studio show together, I learned more about the structure of writing, and of the necessity to make every word count; and from the films we made when we travelled, I learned more about the world. The films were only little things. Making documentaries about Hugh Hefner and Naomi Campbell didn't turn me into, say, Bill Forsyth. But they did turn me into a more informed critic, who could appreciate a miracle like *Local Hero* not only on the level of its bewitching lyricism, which everyone enjoys, but on the level of its construction, which not everyone can see. And from all our films, and from all our other programmes, and from all the other experience that my measure of fame had made possible, I brought home a stock of memories that made me a much more cogent writer in general.

Sometimes the memories lasted in my mind only as particular images, in the way that our dreams are assembled from fragments. But the images are sharp, and all the sharper when they are reduced to trinkets. In that regard, everyone is a dreaming swimmer. As time runs out, we might remember the precise mentality of a treasured friend in the winding of a watch, and the death of a princess as a single earring that was found in the crumpled dashboard of a crashed Mercedes. In my last essays, my last poems, my last anything, these granules of recollection will provide the substance. I might never live to write my novel about the Pacific War: the book to which, in my mind, I have already given its title, *The River in the Sky*. But one tiny part of it is already written, even if not yet written down. Once, in Japan, on the shore of the Bay of Toba, I watched the sun rise over the pearl farms, and saw the still, pale water turn to silver fire. There was no camera there to catch it, but I was there. I would not be able to do the things I do now, and might do next, if I had not done those other things first. It was sheer luck, of course, that I lived long enough to start again. I have always been a lucky man. Try to forgive me if I pay myself the compliment that I was wise enough to know it.

picador.com

blog
videos
interviews
extracts